Volume 1

Building Control by Legislation:
The UK Experience

THE THEORY AND PRACTICE OF BUILDING CONTROL

edited by

J. H. GARNHAM WRIGHT, Garnham Wright Associates

and

R. DERRICOTT, West Midlands County Council

Titles in series

volume 1

BUILDING CONTROL BY LEGISLATION: THE UK EXPERIENCE

J. H. Garnham Wright

Volume 1

Building Control by Legislation: The UK Experience

by

J. H. GARNHAM WRIGHT

Garnham Wright Associates

Illustrations by Penelope Garnham Pope

A Wiley–Interscience Publication

JOHN WILEY & SONS

Chichester · New York · Brisbane · Toronto · Singapore

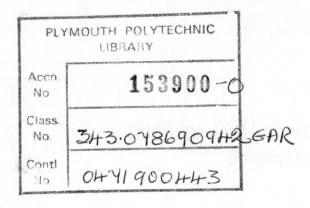
Library of Congress Cataloguing in Publication Data

Garnham Wright, J. H.
   The theory and practice of building control.
   BUILDING CONTROL BY LEGISLATION:
   THE UK EXPERIENCE
   (The Theory and practice of building control)
   "A Wiley–Interscience publication."

   1. Building Laws—Great Britain. I. Title. II. Series.
KD1140.G37   1983   343.41'07869   82–21762
ISBN 0 471 90044 3   344.1037869

British Library Cataloguing in Publication Data

Garnham Wright, J. H.
   The theory and practice of building control.
   —(The theory and practice of building control)
   1. Building laws—Great Britain
   I. Title   II. Series
   344.103'7869   KD1140

   ISBN 0 471 90044 3

Photo-Graphics, Honiton, Devon.
Printed by Page Bros (Norwich) Ltd.

*to my partners; and former colleagues
of the RIBA Building Control Committee*

Contents

Preface

Most books about building control are commentaries on the building regulations, intended to explain what the legal provisions mean. They are illustrated with diagrams and constructional drawings, and kept like manuals in technical libraries alongside the statutory instruments that they transcribe into more normal prose, though at greater length than the originals. They are popular as guides, and the practice of referring to them has long since become commonplace, even though strictly speaking they have never enjoyed any legal authenticity as interpretations of the law's requirements.

The Housing and Building Control Bill, whose passage through Parliament coincides with the writing of this preface, may help to put an end to the confusion about the status of these supportive essays. It will acknowledge the strange necessity for the official pronouncements of the law to be recast into a language whose meaning is more readily understood. The new Act is likely to allow other documents to be used 'for the purpose of providing practical guidance with respect to the requirements…of the building regulations', and in this regard it follows the provision of the Health and Safety at Work Act of 1974, which permitted regulations to be framed 'by reference to a document published by or on behalf of the Secretary of State'.

In both cases the objective is to enable the regulations, on account of their complexities of legal language, to be supplemented (though not supplanted) by other statements in plainer English which also make use of graphic illustrations of a type not normally admitted into mandatory instruments.

The adoption of such an aim as a policy of the central government seems like an admission that the law-makers cannot be expected to express their legal requirements with the kind of lucidity suited to their users. It also bears out the truth of the claim made in the consultative document preceding the Act: that the building control system in use in the UK is 'more cumbersome and bureaucratic than it need be', even though it manages to ensure that buildings are reasonably safe.

The new Act also seeks to reform enforcement procedures, by allowing private inspectors to certify that building work complies with the regulations and by providing for approved organisations to adopt 'self-certification'—all in the same declared interest of reducing the complexities of control to achieve more simplicity and economy in operation. But it is an endemic hazard for the would-be reformer of legislatory systems that good intentions may only pave the way to a greater labyrinth.

This is evident from the continuing proliferation of the controlling instruments, which now affects not only the enabling Acts, but also the building regulations made under their authority. Until 1961 there had been only the one enabling Act affecting England and Wales; now with the new Act there will be four. Since 1961 there has been only one set of national building regulations, but with the legislation now proposed there need be no limit to the number of documents that the Secretary of State could adopt for that same purpose. The day of the surrogate regulation may be at hand, when the incentive for producing explanatory memoranda will be the powerful attraction of having them officially adopted as authorized versions of the measures they seek to clarify.

The art of controlling building is difficult, especially in regard to keeping the service efficient and up-to-date. The tacit acceptance of a belief that commentaries should be so necessary as to be mandated is an indication of the problem. Building control at once enjoys the benefits and suffers the penalties of traditional habits. Its established canon is a formidable collection of primary laws and secondary by-laws and regulations, which grows by the accretion of amendments and supplementary ordinances until the system is too encumbered to function smoothly, while the administering bureaucracy becomes powerfully entrenched. Methods of assessing dangers and providing protection for the public, adopted long ago, become outmoded, but remain in use almost as treasured requirements, long after the original conditions that made them necessary have gone. Alongside them are contemporary provisions couched in the more scientific terms informed by industrial research. The conglomerate framework of control becomes a service that is no longer properly suited to the industry it is intended to restrain, nor to the public it seeks to protect. Such is the influence of tradition that the form and content of the building regulations seem almost to assume a sacrosanct character, supported by an industrious clergy of interpreters and a priesthood of enforcement advisers devoted to unravelling the mysteries of their meaning and expounding upon what should or should not be done by those affected in order to achieve conformity.

Of course, comprehensive reform of any kind can be obtained only by getting new legislation through the law-making process of Parliament, so it is difficult to attain, even when there may be a sufficient consensus of view to justify it. Changes are practical usually only when they take the form of comparatively minor modifications introduced either to make some part of the system less troublesome in operation, or to calm public concern following an accident. Administrators and critics alike tend to be specialists who are too close to the operation of the system in all its details to comprehend its totality in any re-creative way, and in any case are rarely in a position to review the whole apparatus of control, or to fashion a new system.

Nevertheless, the idea that some more radical change is needed has gained a wide currency. It took shape in the minds of people engaged in carrying out the extensive public building programmes of the post world-war decades, and has continued to grow since their completion, perhaps reinforced by a general feeling that an occasion when the production of buildings has fallen to a low ebb, is opportune for introducing more fundamental reassessments.

At present, it is a time when critical transformations are affecting social and industrial affairs in the world at large. As groups of collaborating nations become larger, and modern methods of communication break down traditional barriers, two main kinds of change can be seen as fitting. The first is internal to the nation-state: to ensure that building controls serve the modern purposes of its people with apt efficiency; the second is external to it: to fit each country to its place as a partner in the international community. Standards should be in parity for all, and anachronisms or imbalances should be eliminated where possible, to avoid any unnecessary barriers to the development of economic and social exchange.

This book is part of an attempt to examine national systems of building control fundamentally, as instruments of the public will. With this objective, it avoids dealing with the kind of unquestioning interpretation of detail which is the role of the commentaries on building regulations, and concerns itself instead with the basic principles of theory and practice. It begins by exploring whether it is necessary for building to be controlled, proceeds with investigations of how control has been exercised and is now being carried out, and concludes with a study of the options available for its future. The fact that a new Bill dealing with changes to the system in the UK should be under debate in the British Parliament during the period of the publication of the book, gives more point to its subject and its projections about what might lie ahead in the practice of this kind of control; but does not affect the validity of its central theme.

Building Control by Legislation: the UK Experience is the first book in a series which will examine the main systems of building control used in the countries of the western world, assessing each in relation to its own traditions and its present international environment. The series will concentrate on systems that are characteristic of a particular form of control. For example, the practice in West Germany will be studied as an example which relies heavily upon control by public bodies; where standards are set with a scrupulous attention to detail, and imposed by technical inspectorates whose function is not unlike that of a constabulary. A different type of system to be explored will be that employed in France, where the public and the law are perhaps less involved than the insurers, in a complexity of constraints serving different purposes; and where the need for indemnity is expressed constitutionally, so that the insurers exert a powerful influence on the nature and quality of the built product. Another example will be the type of control used in America, where complications arise from the interplay of federal and state authorities, and where the separate skills of the legislator and the insurer are deployed in more equal measure.

In the first volume there is a brief review of the various methods employed in the countries of Europe, but the main subject is the building control system which operates in the United Kingdom. The book takes this as a model for analysis in order to elucidate the main principles involved in the public control of building. The British type of system is based on control by legislation, and uses public authorities in their traditional roles of central and local government. Any formal use of insurers as a component of the system has hitherto been avoided, though there are now signs of change arising from recent decisions taken in the courts of appeal and from the new proposals before Parliament that seem to reflect the growing influence of consumers' rights in contemporary society. This reliance on the protection of the common law has produced a type of control whose pattern can be traced in the methods in operation throughout the English-speaking communities of the world, and in other countries with kindred traditions. Consequently it is convenient to use the British method to explore how the various components of control are used, and what these might imply for the design of a system if it is to work satisfactorily in modern situations.

Taking the view that a control system should itself be designed to suit its purpose, the book discusses the user requirements that might theoretically form the briefing information for such a task of design, looking at the requirements of the public and its agents as controllers, and at the needs of the building owners and builders as those who are subjected to the control.

It endeavours to establish a good brief for the design of a building control system in much the same way as an architect who is trained in user-requirement analysis might try to establish a brief for the design of a building.

One of the main formulative influences on the series has been the work of the group of enquirers and enthusiasts who made up the membership of the Building Control Committee of the Royal Institute of British Architects through the decade of the nineteen-seventies. They became as a group both focus and catalyst for the feelings of discontent and frustration that ran (and may still) like a powerful, if confused, undercurrent through the ranks of the professional members of the construction industry during those years. The idea—if not heresy—that building control could be designed as a management system properly suited to its purpose, rather than endured as an ever-growing accretion of stipulated constraints around the caddis of tradition, took shape in those times. On occasions the outlook of that group became evangelical, and often their work seemed endearingly repetitive, when in so many conferences held in different places throughout the land, the same questions were answered and the same ideas expounded. Perhaps those influences remain to be manifest in the following pages. Be that as it may, it is hoped that this study will contribute to a better understanding of what building control is for, and how it might work the better to achieve its ends.

J.H. Garnham Wright
Greenway Court
1983.

General principles

INTRODUCTION

Building control seems always to have been an unpopular subject, especially with the designers and technologists who make up the membership of the various professional bodies involved in the construction industry. Perhaps that is not surprising, since it is concerned with constraints; tends to lay down requirements for building that many think should be obvious; and is by reputation tedious in matter and expression. It seems also to be an obscure subject, at least in the sense that it has always been difficult for anyone affected by building control to develop an objective and comprehensive understanding of the system as a whole.

These statements apply to the arrangements for building control in any country, and the United Kingdom is no exception. The obscurity is engendered by the way that any system having its basis in legislative compulsion seems to have three distinct aspects of operation, each producing its own kind of expert who sees the rest of the system only as a background to that particular part. These specialists are, of course, the legislators, the administrators, and the enforcers; otherwise known respectively as the lawyers who help to devise the statutory instruments; the bureaucrats who manage the system; and the inspectors who help to ensure that the technical requirements are met, in practice.

The situation is analogous to that described in the story of the three wise men of the East, who, never having seen an elephant, were put in the dark with one and asked to describe what it was. The first of the trio touched a leg and said it was a tree; the second grasped an ear and claimed it was a fan; and the third felt the trunk and declared it was a snake. All could claim to be justified in reaching their conclusion by their own past experience, but none could conceive the totality of the phenomenon called an elephant; nor could anyone construct from their three descriptions any comprehensive and accurate picture of the animal. The whole truth, as it were, escaped ungrasped.

The story in many ways provides a good illustration for the subject of building control. It shows how historical experience is not a good guide for predicting the future, a view already well established by distinguished philosophers, and worth remembering when dealing with projected reforms in the systems (though it might well be set aside occasionally for the sake of other arguments later in this book). It also shows how the whole may be very different from its parts, and, therefore, not readily inferred from them. And an elephant is an apt metaphor, because like most building control systems it has a long life deriving from obscure origins, is cumbersome, difficult to influence, slow to change, and is possessed of a long memory.

Yet in all countries the building industry, over which such control is exercised, is an important producer of national assets, and while using traditional technologies, has to be responsive to varying demands, and, therefore, needs to benefit from technical developments of all kinds. As a national industry it is in the broader sense a servant of the public, so that, if its activities are to be controlled, it is in the public interest that the constraints should be applied in a way that does not unreasonably impair its efficiency. The public should be able to get the safeguards it needs without undue extra cost. This means that the control system should be well-designed for its purpose; an objective that is unlikely to be achieved unless there is a clear understanding, widely held, of what it is required to do, and how it can best function.

The purpose of this book is to help towards such an understanding, by providing guidance for a comprehensive view of building control.

BUILDING CONTROL

Its aims

For whatever reasons there may be, it would appear that there has been some form of control over building throughout the whole period of the recorded history of human settlements. During the recent post-war period of extensive reconstruction, when the need for some further reform in the control system had become apparent, a favourite reference for lecturers on the subject wishing to illustrate this point was the Babylonian King Hammurabi, who was reputed to have had building regulations during his reign, as long ago as 1750 BC. It was claimed too that there are other references in pre-Christian writings to indicate the practice of building control. The form it took in Hammurabi's time appears to have been by the imposition of the death-penalty on any builders whose work had been so seriously at fault as to cause the collapse of a house or the death ot its owner; and the authority for this penalty was the God named Shamash, probably a figure of Shamanite antiquity, from whom the King claimed to have received his law. This probably ensured that the control was effective as a method of persuading the builders to avoid dangerously shoddy workmanship.

If this fragment of history is true, it shows how, even in those remote times, the scope of the control could be said to have been determined by a recognition of the public's needs by the ruler, on behalf of his subjects; and the method used for exercising the control reflected what would now be described as the legal and administrative competence of the community. Since then, there has been further historical evidence that systems of building control have always been an indication of the social and technical conditions prevailing in the countries where they have been in operation. They are also products of industrial development. Today it is apparent that during the present century all governments of countries claiming to be "developed" have come to impose some constraints to freedom in building, purportedly in the interests of their people. That they should be able to do so is itself evidence of an established consensus of approval for the idea that control is necessary.

The aims common to building legislation everywhere in the modern world are to do with the protection of the public from dangers caused by the built environment that might threaten the safety and health of its members. Such aims have been recognized in the first place among the more settled communities, because it has been there, at the crowded centres of population, that the hazards have occurred in the most obvious ways. Fires and plagues have been the notorious perils of urban life since towns began. Most systems of control have derived from a public acknowledgement of the physical dangers of living in communities, combined with a public awareness that something could be done to reduce them. The town dweller was the first to hold the view that buildings should be constructed safely to avoid collapse, and the dangers inherent in their normal use should and could be kept under some kind of restraint.

Urban communities could see that there were two basic dangers caused by occupational use: the burning of solid fuel to provide energy for warmth and for cooking; and the disposal of waste material. The first posed a constant threat of fire; the second, at first less obviously, was a menace to health. The undesirable effects of fire were only too readily understood from its infliction of pain and death, and the destruction of valuable property: effects that could be calamitous and against which, in the days before the invention of insurance, there was no communal protection, even though the dangers could arise through no fault of any particular individual. The effects of insanitary conditions were less obvious, and their part in the spreading of disease took longer to establish. It was not until scientific methods had been developed sufficiently to identify the significance of microbes that there was any real evidence to support the need for regulations about ventilation, lighting, and drainage. For these, among other reasons, the regulations dealing with fire were among the first to be introduced; while those dealing with health-hazards came later.

Its historical development

This sequence can be seen as readily in the development of building control in Britain as in other countries of Europe (see figure 1a). Originally, some measure of control had been introduced by the Romans, and later during the Middle Ages there existed other regulations for building in the form of local Acts, one of which, enacted in 1189, gave rise to the earliest building by-laws being made in London. In Tudor times precautionary measures of various kinds were taken in the interest of public health when plagues occurred, like the banning of meetings, or the closure of theatres, but these could not be counted as forms of building control. It took an event like the Great fire of London of 1666, which was significant enough among other urban disasters to warrant its own memorial being built, to bring about a measure of building control that was to be really effective.

During the next two years a London Building Act was passed, and the Lord Mayor and City Council were empowered to appoint surveyors to enforce its requirements. These arrangements resulted in the first properly effective control. The measures, which were then enforced by the new statutory officers, were mainly structural precautions against fire. Even so, the changes had been hard won. A century later, when further precautions were introduced by an Act of 1774 to limit the amount of exposed woodwork in buildings, there were opponents who regarded such further control as a tyranny, and denounced the measure as the "Black Act of 1774". Although these provisions were comparatively crude, it was only in London that they had effect; because only in the capital city were there available both the consensus of agreement and the administrative means to bring about a legislative response to a public danger. The general application of further by-laws was to follow as a consequence of other problems in the wake of the industrial revolution, when social philosophies were changing too.

The "population explosion", together with the shift of the rural peasantry into the towns, which went along with the development of the new technologies of coal and iron, began to make the physical dangers of overcrowding critical. Outbreaks of cholera, among other epidemics, became too frequent. There was a growing recognition that these dreadful hazards to health in the typical urban situations were connected in some causal way with physical conditions that could be controlled, or at least modified, by corporate efforts. The need for better standards of sanitation, drainage, and environmental conditions like ventilation, began to be recognized. These trends in popular beliefs became evident in the powers given to local health authorities to influence the layout of streets and to control some aspects of new building by the Public Health Act of 1848, and in other local Acts allowing some local authorities to make by-laws. The major change in the general law which reflected a positive resolve came in 1858 with the Local Government Act, which enabled local authorities to make by-laws for certain prescribed purposes, such as the layout of streets; sewerage; space about buildings; ventilation and drainage; and the construction of walls for stability and fire prevention. It also gave local authorities the right to ensure that these requirements were met by making provisions for enforcement such as the giving of notices, the deposit of plans, the inspection of work by the Local Boards of Health; and by granting statutory authority to the local Boards to alter or pull down any work begun without notice or done in contravention of the by-laws.

In effect, these were the first steps in methods of building control that were later to develop into the practices of the twentieth century. The Local Government Act of 1858 was superceded in 1875 by a Public Health Act which placed a conscious emphasis on matters of public health and safety, adding to and consolidating aspects of the previous legislation dealing with building control. It increased the scope of the former powers given to urban Authorities by enabling them to include measures for the structure of foundations, roofs, and chimneys in their by-laws.

At this time, then, as the closing quarter of the nineteenth century began, and the Victorian era reached its zenith, the public had come to accept that the protection of public health was a subject to be covered by building control, along with the stability of buildings and the prevention of fires. It remained for further Acts in 1890 and 1907 to extend to the rural authorities the powers for making by-laws and to add other subjects to their scope, like the structure of floors, hearths, and staircases, the height of rooms for human habitation, and the height of buildings and chimneys. The Public Health Act of 1936, which has survived as the basic legislation for building control in the UK, notwithstanding subsequent amendments, was mainly a consolidating measure which showed how stable the ideas had become.

6

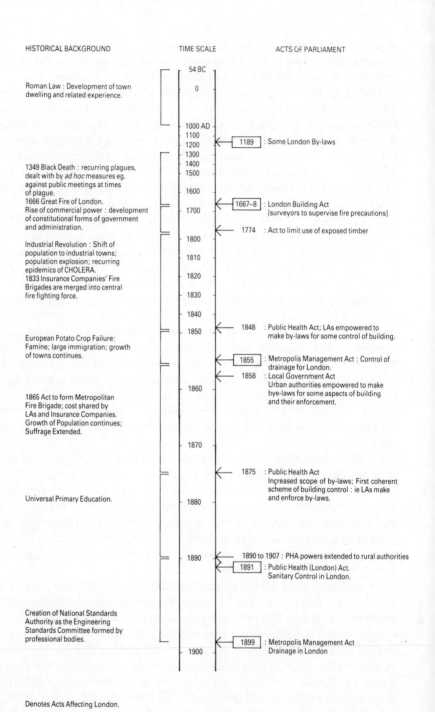

HISTORICAL BACKGROUND

TIME SCALE

ACTS OF PARLIAMENT

54 BC

Roman Law : Development of town
dwelling and related experience.

0

1000 AD
1100
1200 — 1189 : Some London By-laws
1300
1400
1500

1349 Black Death : recurring plagues,
dealt with by *ad hoc* measures eg.
against public meetings at times
of plague.
1666 Great Fire of London.
Rise of commercial power : development
of constitutional forms of government
and administration.

1600

1700 — 1667–8 : London Building Act
[surveyors to supervise fire precautions]

1774 : Act to limit use of exposed timber

Industrial Revolution : Shift of
population to industrial towns;
population explosion; recurring
epidemics of CHOLERA.
1833 Insurance Companies' Fire
Brigades are merged into central
fire fighting force.

1800

1810

1820

1830

1840

European Potato Crop Failure:
Famine; large immigration; growth
of towns continues.

1850 — 1848 : Public Health Act; LAs empowered to
make by-laws for some control of building.

1855 : Metropolis Management Act : Control of
drainage for London.
1858 : Local Government Act
Urban authorities empowered to make
bye-laws for some aspects of building
and their enforcement.

1860

1865 Act to form Metropolitan
Fire Brigade; cost shared by
LAs and Insurance Companies.
Growth of Population continues;
Suffrage Extended.

1870

1875 : Public Health Act
Increased scope of by-laws; First coherent
scheme of building control : ie LAs make
and enforce by-laws.

Universal Primary Education.

1880

1890 — 1890 to 1907 : PHA powers extended to rural authorities
1891 : Public Health (London) Act.
Sanitary Control in London.

Creation of National Standards
Authority as the Engineering
Standards Committee formed by
professional bodies.

1899 : Metropolis Management Act
Drainage in London

1900

☐ Denotes Acts Affecting London.

Figure 1a Chart of historical development of building control (up to 1900)

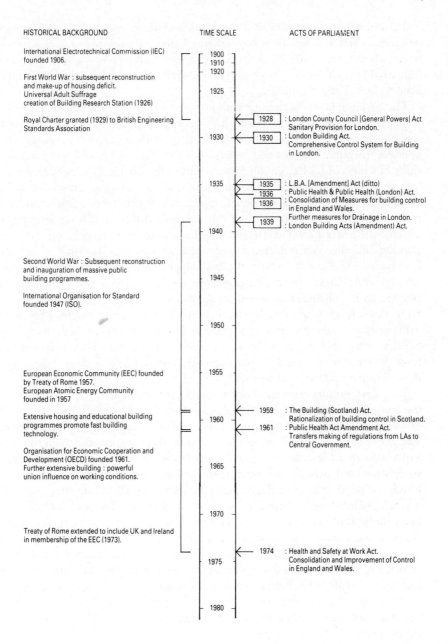

HISTORICAL BACKGROUND

International Electrotechnical Commission (IEC) founded 1906.

First World War : subsequent reconstruction and make-up of housing deficit.
Universal Adult Suffrage
creation of Building Research Station (1926)

Royal Charter granted (1929) to British Engineering Standards Association

Second World War : Subsequent reconstruction and inauguration of massive public building programmes.

International Organisation for Standard founded 1947 (ISO).

European Economic Community (EEC) founded by Treaty of Rome 1957.
European Atomic Energy Community founded in 1957

Extensive housing and educational building programmes promote fast building technology.

Organisation for Economic Cooperation and Development (OECD) founded 1961.
Further extensive building : powerful union influence on working conditions.

Treaty of Rome extended to include UK and Ireland in membership of the EEC (1973).

TIME SCALE

1900
1910
1920

1925

1930

1935

1940

1945

1950

1955

1960

1965

1970

1975

1980

ACTS OF PARLIAMENT

1928 : London County Council [General Powers] Act
Sanitary Provision for London.

1930 : London Building Act.
Comprehensive Control System for Building in London.

1935 : L.B.A. [Amendment] Act (ditto)
1936 : Public Health & Public Health (London) Act.
1936 : Consolidation of Measures for building control in England and Wales.
Further measures for Drainage in London.
1939 : London Building Acts (Amendment) Act.

1959 : The Building (Scotland) Act.
Rationalization of building control in Scotland.
1961 : Public Health Act Amendment Act.
Transfers making of regulations from LAs to Central Government.

1974 : Health and Safety at Work Act.
Consolidation and Improvement of Control in England and Wales.

Denotes Act affecting London

Figure 1b Chart of historical development of building control (1900 onwards)

These nineteenth-century by-laws, then, had dealt only with the most crude dangers to safety when they first emerged, their attention to health coming later. They were made to control a building industry on which the same industrial revolution that had brought about the need for precautions had had little technical effect, initially.

The building law was dealing with long-established technological habits for constructing buildings and which showed no perceptible signs of any revolutionary change. It was a craft-based industry with methods of training that operated through families and guilds. An elite body of craftsmen possessed skills of a high order like an inheritance, but as the demand for buildings grew the work-force was expanded to cope with it by recruitment from a population who were not yet benefiting from any general education, and at a time when universal suffrage had not yet been adopted. These deficiencies affected the general level of competence. Even in the next century, in 1930, the London Building Act reflected the remnants of this relationship between the law-givers and those to whom the law applied in its reference to provisions which should "have effect with respect to dwelling houses to be inhabited or adapted to be inhabited by *persons of the working class* ...". So, while in those early days it may admittedly have been in the public interest for local authorities to make by-laws, it seemed at the time necessary only to tell the builders what they must do by specifying what materials they may use and how the structures should be put together, without letting them know why these requirements should be met.

The same authoritarian method was also convenient for the enforcement of the law. The inspectors who were engaged by the public authorities were no different in general competence from the craftsmen employed by the builders. The use of simple controlling specifications made it possible for them to check and verify that the regulations had been complied with by a comparatively straightforward process of comparing the built product with the specified physical criteria. It may be claimed that the result, for all its primitive qualities, was a legislative method roughly suited to its purpose. By-laws were framed as a definition of means to achieve unstated ends in a way that in the prevailing circumstances made construction and checking for compliance practicable. It is interesting, in retrospect, that such changes as were taking place were principally in the arena of social affairs and were having an effect on legislation, while the building techniques remained constant or slow to alter. A century later the opposite situation applied, because the legal methods had become stable and resistant to change at a time when the building industry was experiencing a rapid development.

Its effects on industrial development

Nevertheless, it can be seen that such methods of control did have an underlying effect on the development of the construction industry itself at least in the UK. With the implementation of the development of the earlier Acts halfway through the nineteenth century, the process became customary that aspects of the built constructions were being checked as a matter of course against the basic specifications which made up the requirements of the law. This in time had the effect of promoting the standardization of the more familiar materials and some of the methods of using them, and, since the whole process was motivated by the common law, the technical experience being gained was general, and publicly available.

By the end of the century such shared practices had created a technical environment that enabled the standardization of materials and methods to be agreed on a more formal and national basis. Of course, other more powerful industrial and marketing motivations had been at work, but in 1901 the Institution of Civil Engineers and other bodies were able to set up the Engineering Standards Committee, which later was to become the recognized institution for national standards. Financed by industrialists, trade associations, and other interests, and eventually aided by government grants, it drew up and published standards for industrial materials by voluntary agreement among all concerned. As a consequence of its origins, its work was at the outset heavily influenced by the problems of manufacture and distribution, and by those whose interests were centred in such affairs. It could be said that, although the public had perhaps helped to bring about this new arrangement by making laws to control building, because by so doing it had caused attention to be concentrated on the need for certain standards to be met; yet ironically, it would not later be able to exercise much direct influence in its role of building user over the establishment of particular standards.

The work of the new Institution, in turn, played a part in creating a demand for objective assessments being made, and twenty years later the first building research station was founded in 1926. The physical problems of materials and structure were its early preoccupations, and for many years provided the main subjects for its research. During the same period, the national government, now at the centre of the work of local authorities who were creating their own building by-laws, had taken up the task of prescribing "model by-laws" in an attempt to encourage similar requirements and simplify practice from one area to another.

This could be seen as another and parallel influence promoting standardization in the construction industry, though it was not ostensibly directed to that end.

After the first World War, the building industry had been faced with growing demands, and its pace of technological change began to increase perceptibly. By the mid-thirties, when the building control legislation was consolidated, the changes affecting materials and methods of building caused the central government to advise local authorities that their local by-laws should be adjusted to keep pace. By that time it was possible for the responsible Minister of central government, through his Department, to recommend the specifications used by the Standards Institution for inclusion in the requirements of by-laws; and also to advise the local authorities to refer to the research station for guidance in connection with the use of novel materials or methods for which a national specification had not yet been issued, nor any information been made available from general practice.

In this way criteria that began as information published centrally by the voluntary efforts of the industrialists, became a powerful influence for standardizing practice in the construction industry, because it was disseminated and made mandatory through the medium of the by-laws. At the same time the system of control acted as a channel for the distribution of the findings of research. Of course, the growing availability of knowledge based on analytical studies soon began to show that the legal instruments were becoming outdated, depending as they did on fixed specifications defining what must be done; that is, expressing means rather than ends. It was soon to be recognized that more flexibility was needed than the by-laws allowed, as there were clearly more ways than one of achieving their purposes. An effect of all this was to concentrate the attention of the construction industry and its law-givers alike upon what the aims of the building regulations were intended to be. In this mood of inquiry after the second war, the topics for research became increasingly diverted to questions of user requirements, and the physical conditions of the built environment, rather than the materials and techniques of construction.

By the late sixties, the professional institutions of the industry had come to accept the proposition that building regulations should be seen as design criteria for building.

By that time it had come to be accepted that such regulations should state the minimum standards for the built environment that could be regarded as acceptable to society. In this concept, the regulations were expressions of what the public needed of its buildings; and, in view of the pressure of demand for built products, they had to be framed to take into account what its construction industry could provide quickly and economically.

The making of regulations had become recognized officially as a "complex creative act" which depended for success on a wide basis of technical knowledge and a proper balance of theory and practice. Their production and enforcement was held to be possible only by deployment of sufficient numbers of skilled administrators with their legal and technical advisers who together represented a high level of sophistication in social affairs.

In many ways these ideas were well ahead of the general level of building control practice, but they are mentioned here to show how, in a country like the UK, the earlier local practices in dealing with crude dangers to communities could develop and give rise to a national awareness of the need for a building control system. But while these ideas have emerged, many of the techniques used for the local control of a craft-based industry have survived into an era of new styles of industrial production. These have been aimed at achieving high productivity and massive output, and in turn have led to new assessments of what legislation is about, and how control systems should work to achieve an acceptable efficiency.

REASONS FOR THE WIDER INTEREST IN BUILDING CONTROL

Such attitudes are, of course, among the many changes that affect communities, and which arise from shifting influences caused by ever-developing social needs. The recent growth of a wider interest in building control is one such change and it can be traced to a number of related causes.

Patronage

Principal among these is probably the change that has taken place in the patronage of the building industry since the time when local by-law-making began, before the industrial revolution. In those days most buildings were made for rich individual clients. These have since been largely replaced by public bodies and large private corporations. The scale of the client has changed along with the increased scale of the demand for buildings. For example, in Britain during the sixties at least half of the total national expenditure on building was due to the needs of the public sector, and was commissioned by the public departments of local and central government. The remaining half was attributable to the private sector, but even here the type of client had changed from the individual to the corporative purchaser. Much of the investment funds which were used for financing construction were controlled by institutions dealing with insurance and superannuation, who could claim to have extensive popular support because they represented the interests of a universality of small investors.

Of course, in the modern world it is also true that more people use buildings, and more individuals own or share ownership of buildings than ever before, and this is further evidence of the shift from the demands of a limited sector of powerful individual owners towards the more democratically expressed needs of the populace.

Consumers' rights

In parallel with these changes, there has been a tendency for the rights of consumers to qualify for a more conscious public recognition. Modern societies have often been described as "consumer-oriented", in acknowledgement of the power of the market forces. For the construction industry, the "consumer" is the user of the built environment. As the consumer changes from the privileged individual to the public-at-large, it is perhaps true to say that the power of patronage is increasingly acknowledged, and is exercised more through the democratic processes of popular control than through the overt "market forces".

Industrial interests, too, are having a similar effect. The production of a building is an industrial event which is becoming rapidly further from the control of any individual consumer or purchaser. This is because in time of national economic growth the increase in the public demand for buildings has forced the pace of technological development. New industrial processes have been needed to achieve a matching rate of output.

Economists have pointed out, in their analyses of modern industrial development generally, that for large-scale productions like ships, aeroplanes, and motor cars, the market loses effectiveness and has to be replaced by planning.

Buildings are comparatively large consumer-products. When a purchaser wishing to acquire a building comes to place an order for it, the industrial process necessary for its production has, so to speak, long since been started up, and the purchaser's scope for choice or control is already limited. As with a customer choosing a suit within an economic price-range, who has to select from a range of manufactured cloth and a pre-selected variety of tailored "cuts", so the purchaser of a new building is bound by practical considerations of availability.

In short, the building process has become national in scale, and consequently beyond the control of the individual purchaser. If there is to be any acceptable control at all for the consumer, it will need to be exercised at community level, by means of some agency of the public that can influence the design aims of the building industry as a whole, and ensure that an acceptable standard of product-quality is maintained.

Many see the building control system as a means to this end. Whether or not this can be so, it is a matter of national importance that any system which may function as this kind of consumers' agency (which it undoubtedly is) should be properly suited to its task. At times when high productivity is a declared priority for industry, it is not only fitting that such methods of control do not frustrate that objective, but it is also wise to see that the commodity is acceptable before it is produced in massive quantities.

Such aims clearly will represent difficulties. The pace of administrative and legal change seems always, at such times, to be outstripped by the pace of technological development. The relationship of administration to technology can be said to be like that of Reason and Energy in Blake's *Marriage of Heaven and Hell*. "Reason", in the form of legal administration, produces an inertia of tradition resisting change, and in consequence constrains the "Energy" of industry. But the speed of change in modern methods of production can be unprecedented. It is not simply that new materials and ways of constructing them are being introduced, but that the methods of design and management, and applications of new forms of energy, are adapting to electronic aids, so that criteria of great complexity can be dealt with in less time than was previously needed for the simplest of basic assessments.

The influence of industrial needs

In these circumstances, the needs of an industry faced with the emergence of user-militancy in the public building programmes, were influences that brought further changes towards standardization in the building control system in Britain.

This movement towards uniformity in all countries may be only one aspect of the general development of building control, but it is made evident enough in the trends illustrated by the changes that have affected the British system.

In the United Kingdom from a time when by-laws were introduced independently by the municipal authorities in the early days of the industrial revolution, developments have moved increasingly towards the involvement of the Departments of central government. At first the changes were small and widely spaced in time, extending through the nineteenth and early twentieth centuries, but since the thirties the system of control has been the subject of reform at an increasingly rapid rate of change. The Public Health Act of 1936 gave local authorities the power to make regulations, and to enforce them. This meant that there were over twelve hundred sets of by-laws in operation, and the same number of authorities were involved in enforcement. The central government encouraged uniformity as best it could by making model by-laws; and in doing so it made use of the new technical authority it derived from the information produced at its research establishment.

After the Second World War the construction industry again became involved in meeting the massive demands for reconstruction, and for carrying out the building programmes for popular social aims. This soon revealed that methods for achieving high output cheaply could be frustrated by control-criteria that varied from place to place. In 1961 the Public Health Act to amend the earlier enabling Act, gave the power to make regulations to a Minister of central government, leaving only the task of enforcement with the local authorities. By 1965 the first national set of Regulations had been issued affecting all building in England and Wales, and replacing, in one document, the numerous sets of local authority by-laws.

In the same amending Act, the public was given the right to appeal to the Minister if any enforcement decision seemed likely to cause hardship, a change that can be seen as a reflection of the growing influence of the consumer to establish the user's rights and needs.

The Amendment Act had the effect of concentrating attention on the Building Regulations as the focal point of the building control system, through a period when a great deal of building was in progress. The Act had not changed the scope of the Regulations, and the topics about which the Minister could make regulations remained as it had been stated in the 1936 Act. In that document the aims were implied rather than set out as clear terms of guidance. As a consequence, all through the sixties and seventies the call became more urgent for the construction industry's legal terms of reference to be clarified. The professional institutions were foremost in expressing this need.

During this period there was a clear-cut demand for a greater uniformity; a reform which, it was suggested, should be achieved by a specially prepared new Building Act, which it was thought should be sponsored by that

Department of the central government which dealt with the affairs of the construction industry. This new Act would replace all others having some control over building, and provide a single point of reference for all matters of building control. The task was largely accomplished, perhaps unexpectedly, in 1974 by a new Health and Safety at Work Act. Significantly it was laid before Parliament not by the Department dealing with "Building and Public Works" but by the Home Office; a fact that gave further evidence of the growing influence of the *users* of buildings in the increasingly "consumer-oriented" society. The Act contained statements which set out more clearly than previous instruments had done what the Minister could make regulations for, and what subjects could be included in them; and it also introduced important options for the reform of enforcement.

The influence of wider international markets

By this time the growth of interest in the need for larger multi-national markets to stimulate greater industrial efficiency was affecting the policies of all major governments, whether subscribing to centrally-planned, or free-market economics. Many of the ideas for using "industrialized systems" for house construction which began to be developed at that time in Western Europe, had, in fact, been originated in the USSR.

These were ambitious long-term aims for the concentration of industry on a grand scale, and were never specifically formulated, but such trends had the effect of moving the demands for standardization from out of the confines of the local national setting to the broader dimensions of the international arena.

In Britain alone there were three separate (though related) systems of building control, one each for London, Scotland, and the area of the joint administration of England and Wales. Yet by the late sixties each had been subjected to reform, and the terms of reference had been well established that the technical criteria applying in each system should be brought into alignment by the co-operation of the responsible authorities. Another indication of the expansion of interest from the national to the international scene was contained in the fact that, by 1970, the major topic in progress at the British Building Research Establishment at Garston was the study of the control systems in use in the countries of Europe and Scandinavia, and in other nations, on the pretext of Britain's interest in its projected membership of the European Common Market.

Indeed, the wider interest in the international context of national systems of building control, which was reciprocal in the developed countries of the world, could be said to have been promoted in no small measure in Europe by the remarkable increase in the amount of research activity relating to building. Since the end of the Second World War there had been a proliferation of national building research organizations, and a growing sponsorship of international co-operation in such affairs, as made evident by the work (among other bodies) of the International Council for Building Research Studies and Documentation (known as the CIB).

BUILDING CONTROL IN EUROPE

Judging by the reports of these professional analysts, the systems in use in Europe could be seen as having emerged from a background of varied national experience, from which different influences could be discerned. Although there were social and technical differences affecting each country's practice of building control, there could also be seen a background of the shared heritage of European experience. From these factors it could be inferred that the least obstacle to the achievement of a workable international conformity for building control lay in the subject of the technical criteria, because the standards of performance generally acknowledged as desirable for the construction of the environment were already compatible. The more formidable problems lay in the different methods in use for making the constraints effective, because these were influenced by the more characteristically entrenched political, social, and legal habits of the different countries.

The common elements contributing to what might be described as the European heritage were seen to be: the shared experience of structural techniques and the materials relating to them; the modes of thought deriving from such diverse influences as the Renaissance, and the philosophy of the scientific method (which later, from the early twentieth century, gave rise to the reassessment of some of the principles of design); the social reform movements, especially relating to housing policies from the 1920s; and the development and growth of building research activities.

The basic disparities which were thought to have caused some divergences in building law and its administration were equally tendentious and difficult to define. In the distant historical background there were differences between areas that had been under Roman jurisdiction, and those not so affected, as regards language, law, and methods of administration. Later there were differences between Catholic and Protestant Europe which affected the traditions and modes of local government. These seemed to be polarized on a north and south basis. Finally, and perhaps more pronounced of all in the practice of building control, there were differences between the countries that had formed part of the Napoleonic Europe and those which had not, due to the ideas of government that had been developed between 1805 and 1815 in France and had become known as the Code Napoleon. This system of administration, devised under Napoleon's auspices to give the people "public order, equitable administration, and efficient organization" had given rise to very distinct differences in the building control systems that had since developed in modern Europe; and these were differences that were seemingly more pronounced because they exemplified an attitude to the use of authority that coincided with attitudes broadly associated with the traditional religious orientations affecting the same areas. The mode of government that had prevailed in pre-revolutionary—that is, pre-Napoleonic—France, when the power to make law had been a privilege of a perhaps undeserving and ultimately discredited aristocracy, and when powerful authority had been exercised in very personal forms, had resulted in the people coming to believe that the very *apparatus of the law* itself was a force alien to their interests, and not to be trusted. It was seen, perhaps perversely in comparison with other European countries, *as a force against which the individual needed protection*. In countries outside the influence of this Napoleonic Code, where remembered experience had been different, the idea had prevailed that the law was an embodiment of the *will of the people*—not of the privileged few—and that the authority of the law, which was vouchsafed to the trustworthy institutions of the public, could be relied upon for the safeguarding of the individual. In such countries, the community had come to regard the law as the proper basis for building control.

The BRE study

The Building Research Establishment's (BRE) report contained comparisons of the various control systems based on studies of their scope and the way they worked. In an analysis of the subjects covered in regulating documents, the countries included were England and Wales; Scotland; Denmark; Holland; Sweden; West Germany; Canada; the United States (two codes); New Zealand; and some tropical countries, for whom model regulations had been prepared by the UK Research Station itself. France was not included in the comparison of the documents because that country had no single main regulating document, and the method of exerting control there was different enough to make the same comparative analysis too difficult to be valid.

The scope of regulations

The documents studied showed that all the countries had regulations of one sort or another to cover safety in the form of structural strength and stability, and structural fire protection; and almost all to cover safety in the form of escape from fire; and the fire safety of appliances, including that of hearths and chimneys. In regard to the subject of health, almost all the regulations covered ventilation, daylighting and illumination, and the control of moisture.

The regulating documents of the countries of north-western Europe were classified as having the special characteristic of covering the amenities of the community and the convenience of the occupants of buildings. The degree of detail in which the thermal conditions in buildings were controlled seemed to relate, understandably, to the nature of the climate of the countries involved. The analysts formed an impression that in north-western Europe the regulations had the general implication that they were created to encourage good building; while those in England were devised rather to prevent bad building; and in America were intended to safeguard the owners and insurers of buildings.

Methods of control

In regard to the method of control, there were broad similarities of style in the English-speaking countries, and the countries of north-western Europe. In the UK an enabling Act of Parliament gave power to a responsible Minister of central government to make and issue national regulations, which were then enforced by the local authorities at district level [see figure 2(1)]. The system was the same, though separate laws applied, in Scotland and in central London. In the US and Canada the regulations were created separately by each municipality or local authority, but followed the pattern of common models, which were made by institutions at the national level. This arrangement resembled the English system which had operated prior to 1961. In Canada the

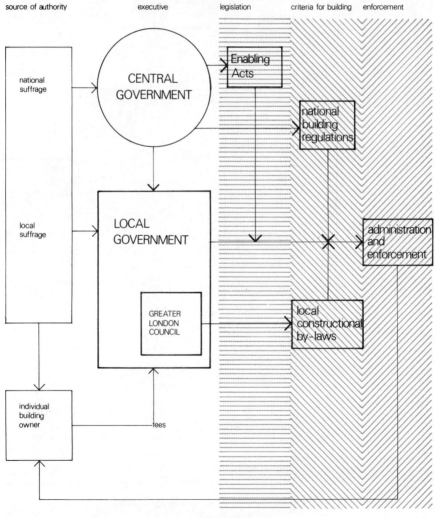

Figure 2 European systems of control
(1) United Kingdom

18

National Research Council made the National Building Code; and in the US the American Insurance Association and the International Conference of Building Officials each made a model code, entitled respectively the National Building Code and the Uniform Building Code.

In these countries the requirements for the construction of buildings, especially in relation to the safety of structures, the prevention of fire, and the protection of health, were dealt with in detail, but separate legislation covered questions of land-use and development.

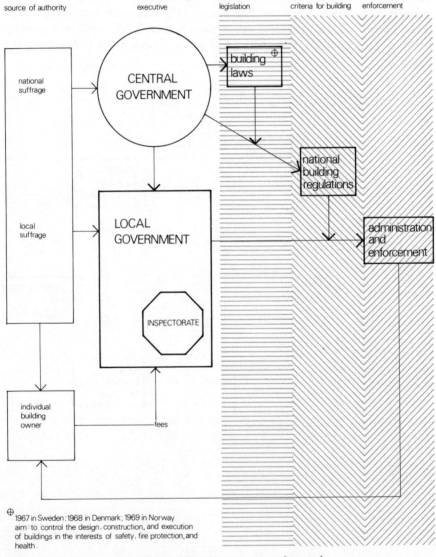

Figure 2 European systems of control
(2) Scandinavia

The Scandinavian system

In the Scandinavian countries of Denmark, Norway, and Sweden, the national building laws were also made by central government, and administered by the local authorities [see figure 2(2)]. The regulations were national and made by a central authority; in Denmark this being the Housing Ministry and in Sweden the Board of Urban Planning (the Statens Planverk). The laws in each country were comparatively recently enacted, having been made in 1967 (Sweden), 1968 (Denmark), and 1969 (Norway) with stated aims "relating to the design, construction and execution of buildings in the interest of safety, fire protection and health". A feature of the legislation was that regulations should be made, too, for small dwellings, dealing with the convenience of internal layout, and the standardization of components and fittings for housing and some other building types.

The administration of the regulations and the tasks for their enforcement were delegated to the local authorities, who were able to make by-laws about local matters concerning procedures and quality control; and who issued building permits, checked the designs, inspected work on building sites, and sanctioned occupancy certificates after completion. As regards finance, fees were paid by the building owners towards the cost of these services, which were provided by a well-organized inspectorate deploying highly qualified technical personnel.

The system in the Netherlands

In the Netherlands a basically similar system was in operation, albeit of independent origins [see figure 2(3)]. The Dutch Housing Law and others affecting building, enacted by central government, empowered the Ministry of Housing to make national regulations, which would be enforced by local authorities. Under the influence of local government, however, an agreement had been reached with the central authorities whereby a set of model by-laws was drafted by a technical committee of the Association of Netherlands Municipalities (VNG), and widely adopted by the local authorities throughout Holland. The local authorities made by-laws based on the model, and also covering other local matters, and deployed building inspectorates similar to those in Scandinavia, for which fees were also charged to building owners.

The arrangements in West Germany

In West Germany the system was similar in general concept, though there were differences in the executive process, arising from the existence of a Federal authority with State (or "Land") governments, motivated by the traditional notion that the "State" authority had direct responsibility for the "public order", and consequently for the maintenance of public health, safety, decency, and welfare [see figure 2(4)].

20

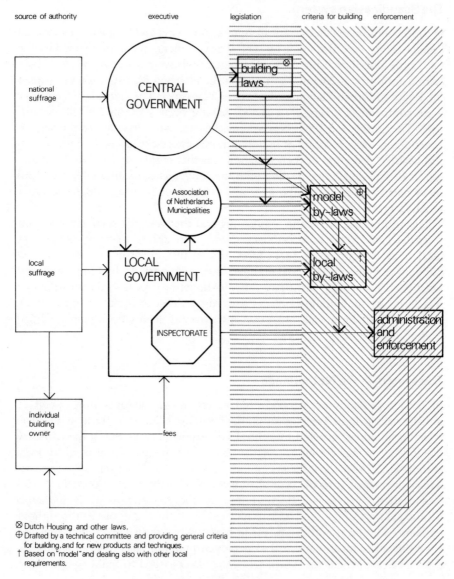

Figure 2 European systems of control
(3) Netherlands

The Federal Government produced legislation which included a model-building ordinance (*Musterbauordnung*), and this in turn was adopted and enacted separately by each State (or "Land") government. The subsequent administration of the system was performed, not by the hierarchical tiers of local authorities as in other countries, but by departments or building

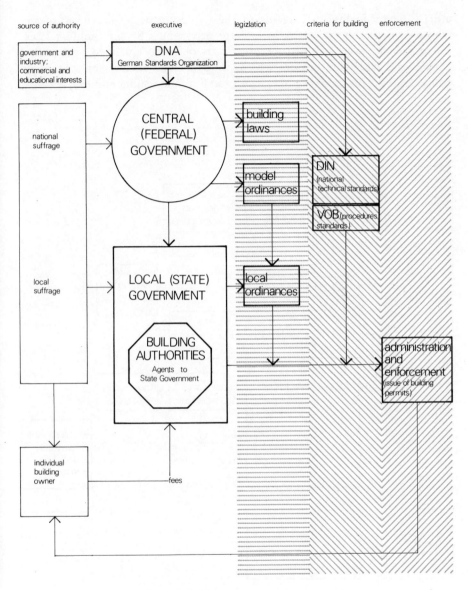

source of authority   executive   legizlation   criteria for building   enforcement

Figure   2   European systems of control
(4)   West Germany

authorities acting as agents of the State governments. The State system was
preoccupied with providing a framework for building approvals rather than
with the creation of detailed rules. Legal orders were made by the State
Building Ministries, enacting ordinances based on the national model, and
adopting technical standards (DIN) also created nationally. The State Building

officials were deployed as agents of the Government by the inspectorate, whose constitution and procedures were determined by the building laws. These agencies were manned by large staffs of highly qualified professional people, and had wide powers which, though civil, nevertheless resembled police departments, carrying out checks and tests and issuing building permits,

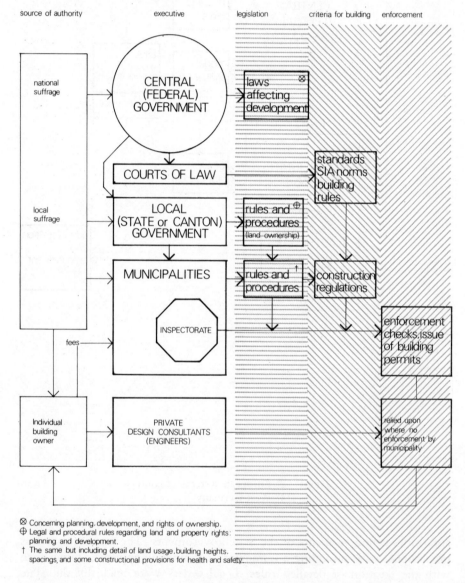

⊗ Concerning planning, development, and rights of ownership.
⊕ Legal and procedural rules regarding land and property rights: planning and development.
† The same but including detail of land usage, building heights, spacings, and some constructional provisions for health and safety.

Figure 2 European systems of control
(5) Switzerland

for which fees were charged to the building owners. One consequence of this formal deployment of authority seemed to be that the State authority had come to assume direct responsibility for the safety of the buildings in its area.

The Swiss system

In Switzerland the controls exercised at federal level were to do with planning, development, and the rights of ownership [see figure 2(5)]. The Canton (or State) governments and the municipalities, representing two levels of administration, varied in their allocation of power and scope in different localities. In general terms the Canton-made laws affecting their separate areas provided for rules and procedures about land ownership, property rights, planning, and the designation of land for development; and within their areas the municipal authorities would supplement these with more detailed ordinances about land usage, the heights and spacings of buildings, and perhaps also some constructional regulations in the interests of the safety and health of occupants.

For the latter, more reliance was placed on Standards (known as SIA Norms), which were made by Courts of Law as legal codes, or "rules for building", which applied generally. The larger municipalities had well-organized inspectorates for checking, testing, and issuing building permits, for which fees were charged; but elsewhere greater reliance was placed on the structural engineer as being responsible for the structural safety of buildings.

Some conclusions

It could be seen from this kind of information that there was a family resemblance among the systems of building control in use in the German-speaking countries and Scandinavia. Based on the law in each country, there was a comprehensive framework of building control, covering land ownership and development; the constitution and powers of building authorities; the procedures for inspection and approval; and the general requirements for construction. These latter related mainly to structural fire precautions; escape from fire; and hygiene; and were supplemented by instruments containing criteria for construction, such as national regulations (as in Scandinavia); or standards (in West Germany and Switzerland), which could be more flexible than the law itself.

The French method

In France the method was so different as to make comparisons difficult [see figure 2(6)]. Several different influences were at work in parallel, making a complex structure of control that caused the French construction industry to complain of protracted delays. Certain ministries of the central government produced town planning and other legislation affecting building, which controlled some aspects of planning; the internal arrangements of buildings for

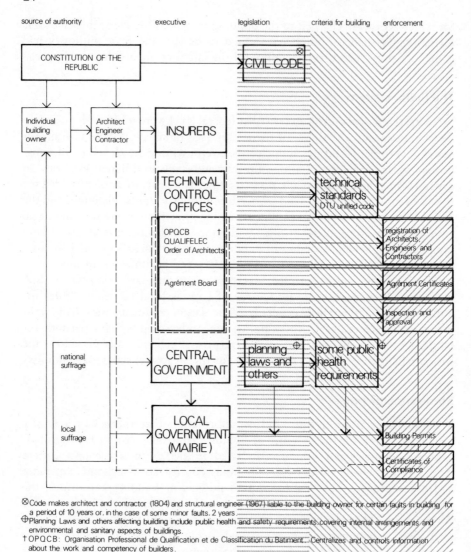

source of authority   executive   legislation   criteria for building   enforcement

CONSTITUTION OF THE REPUBLIC

CIVIL CODE ⊗

Individual building owner

Architect Engineer Contractor

INSURERS

TECHNICAL CONTROL OFFICES

technical standards
DTU unified code

OPQCB †
QUALIFELEC
Order of Architects

registration of Architects, Engineers and Contractors

Agrément Board

Agrément Certificates

Inspection and approval

national suffrage

CENTRAL GOVERNMENT

planning laws and others ⊕

some public health requirements ⊕

local suffrage

LOCAL GOVERNMENT (MAIRIE)

Building Permits

Certificates of Compliance

⊗ Code makes architect and contractor (1804) and structural engineer (1967) liable to the building owner for certain faults in building for a period of 10 years or, in the case of some minor faults, 2 years.
⊕ Planning Laws and others affecting building include public health and safety requirements covering internal arrangements and environmental and sanitary aspects of buildings.
† OPQCB: Organisation Professional de Qualification et de Classification du Batiment. Centralizes and controls information about the work and competency of builders.

Figure 2   European systems of control
(6) France

the purpose of public safety; and in regard to housing, certain environmental and sanitary aspects of dwellings. These laws also specified that permits for buildings had to be obtained from local authorities, so in this respect the system had some likeness to others making direct use of the common law processes. However, the central and most powerful influence on the structure, materials, and workmanship for building was exercised by a provision in the Civil Code, which was embodied in the constitution of the Republic, that architects and contractors should be liable to the building owner for any major faults in the building after the completion of the work, for a period of ten years.

The statement of this liability, unique in systems of building control, was contained in articles 1792 and 2270 of the Code of 1804, which had been amended in 1967 to include the structural engineer, and to reduce the period of liability to two years for certain minor failures. The architects, engineers, and contractors were compelled to protect themselves with insurance, and as a consequence, the companies of insurers who provided their indemnity had become involved not only with framing the technical requirements, but also with the processes of inspection and control. Their influence operated in many ways, affecting alike the people and products of the construction industry. They sought protection by means of the obligatory registration of designers and contractors; and by the certification of products by testing, under an arrangement known as the Agrément system. Builders were restricted by registration to certain classes of work for which their insurance cover was valid. This scheme for registration had been introduced in 1949 and its operation was also supervised by a department of the central government, which also had a hand in the production of the DTU (Documents Techniques Unifies) containing standards and codes of practice. Architects and engineers were registered in a scheme which was linked with their membership of their professional institutes.

As regards the materials used, and the techniques of applying them, these were governed by tests and specifications which came under the surveillance, either directly or indirectly, of the same insurers. In the case of new or complex work, there was the further involvement of an independent technical office (known as a "bureau de controle"), which was also concerned in the establishment of the criteria. These bureaux would charge a fee for checking and inspection, but there appeared to be no official charge for a building permit.

The scheme, which seemed to have grown in complexity far beyond its original form, had been designed with the aim of establishing the rights of the individual as building owner under a written constitution—the Napoleonic Code—as made clear by the legal statement of where the responsibility for any major faults would lie. But it seemed to have had the unexpected effects of removing from the building owner any ability to control the quality of the buidings, and of giving this instead to the insurer whose only interest in the matter was the incidental one of finance; and also of directing the control of building toward the protection of such purely financial interests rather than towards the protection of the interests of the public-at-large in respect of its health and safety.

More conclusions

That this system, which began with an unusually clear statement defining who should be held responsible for buildings, should have suffered such unintended consequences, prompted the researchers to the conclusion that the systems under study could be classified to some extent by the way each dealt with the crucial issue of responsibility. For this purpose it would be necessary to set aside the separate role of the professional designers in countries where these experts could be employed by clients under their own conditions of engage-ment that governed their liabilities by private contract. In a strict theoretical sense, *their* direct responsibilities were to their individual clients, not the public-at-large. Placing such questions in parentheses, and examining the general question of responsibility in relation to what the public might want, it could be seen that there were two broad categories of control systems, one relying on *public authorities* to act rather in the role of policemen, and the other relying on the *private sector* to operate incentives and constraints.

As regards the first, of which the prime example was the West German system, it was clear that the more the public authorities became involved in enforcement, and the more power they wielded in exercising control, the greater was the liability they had to assume for the work they approved. In this sense they could become trapped in a cycle of events, from which escape would be difficult, because the more they felt the burden of liability, the greater would be the inclination to exert tight and careful control.

As regards the second, the French system was at the other extreme because it assigned responsibility for the work-product to the designers and builders, who became preoccupied with protecting their own interests in a financial way. The public authorities were left with little part to play in deciding what was needed or in supervising the working of the industry, and a minimal share, if any at all, in the liabilities. This left them with little influence to safeguard the interests of the public, and implied that matters of health and public safety had low priority.

In reviewing these systems, the team at the Building Research Establish-ment identified too that certain fundamental problems of comparison arose because there were different *types* of control, *representing different aims*, inter-woven like strands of non-compatible material in the patterns of the various systems. Also, the same subjects could be controlled in each country, but by different devices.

The most common subjects generally controlled were: town planning; housing standards; and the construction of buildings; but these were dealt with in different ways. For example, in the UK each subject was controlled separately (that is, by different Acts of Parliament administered by different Departments of government) in a way that in theory had the advantage of allowing for each to be dealt with thoroughly; but in practice gave rise to disadvantages due to overlapping controls or lack of co-ordination. In other countries these subjects, or aspects of them, could be contained in different sections of a single code for building control. Thus, in Denmark the criteria to establish road-widths and building lines were contained in the national regulations; and in Holland (as also in Germany and Switzerland) aspects of site layout were covered in the model by-laws. In Scotland, housing standards were set in the national regulations, and provisions to the same end appeared in different forms in the Danish regulations and the German ordinances, though there were also separate orders for certain other requirements of housing. In the Netherlands and Sweden, housing standards were defined by separate central authorities, rather in the way that applied in the United Kingdom.

Central problems

This BRE study had been carried out during the aftermath in Britain of the Ronan Point disaster, which had caused a special concentration of interest on the subject of building control, and a prolonged debate between the governmental administrators and the members of the various institutions of the construction industry. Consequently, it again brought under review the problems identified in that affair. Themes central to the disputed issues were those of responsibility, the complexity of regulating documents, and the frustrations of enforcement. These problems have remained predominant, especially that of *responsibility*, which assumes increasingly critical importance as the costs rise for repairing any damage in buildings due to faults of construction. Through the ensuing decade attention was focused on where the public's reliance should be placed, and where the liability should stop. At the time of the study, the national expenditure on building was running at a high level, and the public building programmes were extensive. This sharpened awareness of the rivalries between the industry itself and the administrators; and between central and local authorities. Conflicts of interest included such topics as the complexity and sophistication of the regulations, which seemed to have increased since their production had come under central control; the opposing claims of those involved in technological innovation against those concerned with traditional methods of enforcement; and the levels of qualification needed for a competent inspectorate.

The two main styles of control

From the reports, reviews, and discussions following these activities, there emerged the acknowledged theme which has already been referred to, namely that it was possible to discern two main styles of building control in use in Europe and America. One placed reliance on the common law to enable public authorities to set rules and enforce their compliance; the other depended in effect upon insurers offering indemnity and setting their premiums according to the standards agreed with public bodies, and consequentially designing measures to protect their own interests for checking the performance and adequacy of producers and manufacturers (see figure 3).

These same two kinds of control could be seen in different ways, according to the analysis used. It could be said, for example, that the first type was one in which the society seeking protection used inspectors, or law enforcement officers, like policemen, to ensure that the public legal requirements were met; while the second was one in which society relied upon the designers operating under professional codes of practice and conditions of engagement, and liable to their clients under private contracts for their actions. (This analysis begs certain important supplementary questions in each case, but is stated here in its essentials in order to establish the general ideas involved.)

The two methods could be claimed to have different effects on the nature

1 Reliance on common law

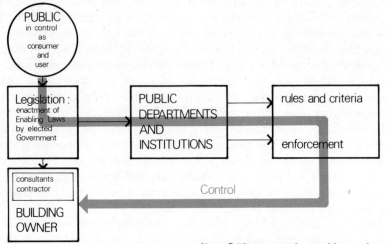

Note: Building owner seeks own defence and recovers any loss through private action in civil courts

2 Reliance on insurance indemnity

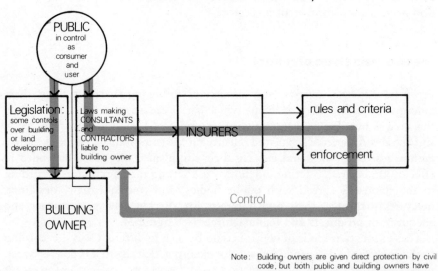

Note: Building owners are given direct protection by civil code, but both public and building owners have diminished control over the built product in terms of quality.

Figure 3 Two methods of control

and quality of the built environment. Where constitutional authorities placed reliance on common law and the system of policing by inspectorates, regulations had of necessity to be detailed and specific. In consequence, the role of the professional designer was reduced by limitations of choice. The result was the frustration of any real scope for variety and development in the techniques of construction and the form of buildings.

On the other hand, the systems that relied upon designers could be seen to have two possible effects, both due to the need for the designers to shift from themselves the burdens of their responsibility. How they did this depended upon the social and political environment in which they practised. They could reduce their burden either by turning to insurers for indemnity, or by relying on public authorities for guidance and support. Each of these in turn would rely upon the use of scientific methodology, as deployed by the research or testing establishments under their patronage, to provide reliable information upon which to base judgements. Broadly speaking, it could be claimed, the system that depended primarily on insurers tended to return the responsibility ultimately to industry itself (because that bore the cost of the safeguards), and so the industry, in this case, could be said to be setting its own rules; while, according to the same theory, the system that looked to the public authorities was in effect returning the burden to the public, and the main influence over the control system, together with its cost, to the community.

Such opinions, of course, were only interpretations of the studies of building control as it then existed in the international scene. But the review itself, which admittedly was synoptic and historical, provided a more valuable opportunity for assumptions to be made, on reasonably factual evidence, about what were the basic common components of building control systems. The comparisons that became possible gave a hint of the shortcomings that might be encountered if communities who had to deal with the needs of their consumers and producers in the contemporary world, placed too much reliance too rigidly upon the traditional modes of legal, administrative, and technical control.

Traditions are always precious, and have undoubted value provided that they are clearly recognized and properly understood. Unfortunately, those traditions which affect administrative and legal practices tend often to become so familiar as to be indiscernible, so that communities are not aware of the methods they employ to achieve quite straightforward modern objectives, much less their inadequacies and impediments to efficiency.

THE NATURE OF BUILDING CONTROL

If building control systems are to be effectively improved, it is essential that there should be a wider understanding among all who have some involvement in the construction industry, either as customers or participators, of how existing systems work. The subsequent chapters in this volume are intended, among other purposes, to help anyone concerned with building control to see what principles underlie all effective forms of it, so that it might be possible to review the theories and techniques in operation, and establish ways and means of unifying and improving the methods.

The BRE study has been a useful introductory reference in helping to throw some light on the popular assumptions about the subject of control. Certain principles emerge from it that are shown to have wide support among the nations examined, owing to natural selection rather than to any active canvassing. In a much earlier study relating to human affairs, the United Nations had already established a commonly accepted contention that all communities have three essential needs: for food, clothing, and shelter. In the context that shelter represents the built environment, it follows that one reason for building control systems being in use everywhere lies in the fact that they are dealing with one of these basic necessities.

Whatever the truth of that supposition, it is evident from the review that in all countries, communities have resolved that they need protection, *in the interests of public health and safety*, from the hazards of defective building. It is everywhere apparent that it is for this reason that the control systems exist, though once created they may also serve other ancillary purposes.

Controllers and controlled

This objective everywhere necessitates a system in which there are two participating groups, or collective role-players; that is to say, the *consumers*, or *users*, of the built product, who are the CONTROLLERS; and the *owners* of that product, who are the CONTROLLED. Of course, in the broadest sense the consumers, or users, are the public-at-large; and the owners depend upon the building industry to supply their needs, so that the main axis of control lies between the public on the one hand and the construction industry on the other.

Wherever it exists, this control is made effective by methods which make use either of constraints or inducements.

Types of constraint

Building control systems everywhere employ three devices to constrain or induce, which can be summed up for reference as relating to *law*; *finance*; or *privilege* (see figure 4). All are used in all systems, but in different degrees, and with differing emphasis. Reduced to their basic terms, these can be said to function as follows.

The concept of *law*, in its essential form, as a rule of action established by authority, involves the notion of the law-givers ordaining what is right and punishing those who do wrong. In reference to building control systems, the use of the term *law* here as a constraint is intended to mean the use by the public, as controller, of the system of common law to establish rules, and to punish those who break them as criminal offenders under the penal code. Of course, building control makes use of other forms of law as well, for example in cases where the civil courts are used to adjudicate between contestants. But these are ancillary functions, and do not form the basic determinants of the

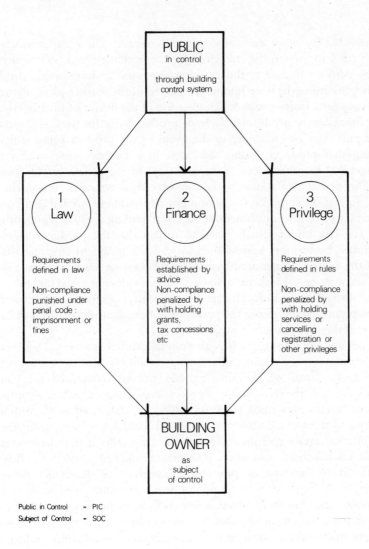

Figure 4 Types of constraint

relationship between the controllers and the controlled, as in the case when the rules are created as an integral part of the penal code.

The device of *finance* as a constraint or inducement does not have the same moral connotations, namely invoking right or wrong, but can be seen to operate in several different ways. One direct form is commonly used by government departments, who represent the public as consumers, and who have statutory responsibilities for certain types of buildings, like schools, houses and hospitals, which are financed partly by the central governments and provided by other authorities or undertakers. These departments will publish rules to govern the standards for the buildings, and will enforce the rules by denying finance to those undertakers who do not comply. In doing this, they are using the time-honoured method of the market-place, namely of not paying for a faulty product. Another use of the device of finance takes the form of making the producers of a built-product liable for the losses sustained by the purchaser or consumer in the event of the product being faulty, by exposing that producer (using this term in a generic sense to cover the designers and manufacturers of the industry) to the penalty of meeting the cost. This process, of course, would involve legal activities, but in the civil courts, so that the common law is brought into action (if needed at all) only in a secondary role, as a punishment of the court's ruling if a case is not complied with. The law might also be used to ordain that the producer should be indemnified by insurers against such losses, as a means of ensuring that the cost of the damages can indeed by met. In this case, as has been seen, a special status devolves on the insurer, who is able to set rules not based on law, which can be enforced by the financial expedients of denying insurance cover to those not complying; or increasing the premiums of those producers who make too many mistakes and too often incur losses.

The device of managing *privilege* also can take different forms. That which is most commonly used consists of selecting certain types of person to perform chosen tasks, from which other persons not so recognized are banned. Examples include the recognition of professional designers as being competent to accept certain prescribed responsibilities; the classification of contractors according to their tested ability to cope with contracts of approved size; the acceptance of certain persons to function as inspectors if they have acquired requisite qualifications; and so on. The management of privileges in this way can effectively function as providing incentives or deterrents for those involved in the protection of the public. It is commonly used in all building control systems. Another, rather different, form of privilege-management is that which is used by the suppliers of services like electricity, gas, or water, who may make rules governing the construction of installations, which they will enforce by withholding the supply of their service from those who do not obey.

THE THREE COMPONENTS OF BUILDING CONTROL

Whatever the kind of constraints that may be employed, there are three components in all types of system which together make up the whole of the apparatus of control (see figure 5). These exist together in some form or other, though with different degrees of emphasis or balance.

The enactment of the will of the people

The first component is the expression of the will of the public by means of the enactment of a law. It is the establishment by an appropriate authority of

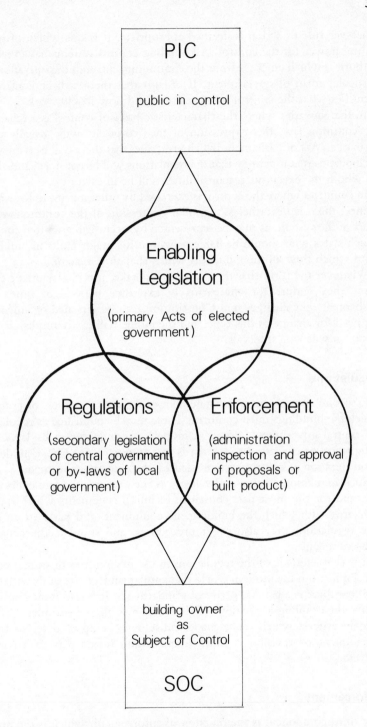

Figure 5 Components of building control

whatever rule of action is deemed appropriate. It is this which provides the central power for the control. All building control systems have this basis of authority, which emerges from the community through the operation of their particular form of government. It ordains that there will be control, and it identifies what the control will consist of and how it will work.

In the countries where the characteristic basis of control is a reliance upon the common law, this expression of the "corporate will" usually takes the form of an Act of Parliament which prescribes that there will be regulations for such purposes as it defines; that the regulations will be enforced; and also states on whom the executive responsibilities will lie in each case.

In countries where the control is exercised by other means, as for example in France, there is nevertheless a similar expression of the common will at the heart of the system, as may be represented by a clause in a written constitution which states who should be liable to whom for major faults in building, and from which flow all the influences which shape the system.

Whatever the form that these enactments take, it is characteristic that once made they endure for comparitively extensive periods of time. Acts of Parliament, like changes in a Constitution, can be repealed or amended; but the need for change of this type, and the public will to accomplish it, seem to occur only at long intervals.

Regulations

The second component is the statement of regulations, rules, or criteria with which the buildings must conform. These may be published as regulations by the central government; issued as models; promulgated as by-laws by local authorities; or expressed as standards by insurers or producers; all depending upon the type of control system used by the country concerned.

Such regulations, rules, or by-laws, as the case may be, are everywhere in use, and for the most part consist of technical statements which specify the standards with which the building, its equipment, and parts are to comply. The regulations may also cover procedures, and stipulate the penalties for non-compliance.

It is characteristic of the regulations in use in countries of similar economic development in the modern world that similar subjects are dealt with in them, and that there is a general parity of standards set. It is also worth noting that, unlike the enabling legislation referred to above, these instruments of control contain criteria which, once made, must be kept up to date, so that their amendment or revision is more frequent and forms part of a continuing process.

Enforcement

The third component is the function of enforcement, which is the process of checking that the rules or regulations have been or are being complied with. It has been shown that this is carried out in many different ways, by public servants, consultants, or inspectors employed by private bodies like insurers, according to the mode of control. It also covers different aspects of the requirements laid down. For example, in some systems of control the checks are made only on the drawings and specifications which are to be used for the construction; while in others the inspections are aimed at checking the built product itself, which cannot be taken into use until its compliance has been certified. The enabling legislation, referred to as the first component above, usually determines where the responsibility for enforcement should lie; and the mode of enforcement is often contained in the regulation or other rules of procedure. In all systems the act of enforcement involves the use or deployment of large numbers of people, and is the main element of the cost of building control.

The parts and the whole

Each building control system is a product of these components, which are interdependent and together determine its style.

For example, the nature of the governing criteria—whether expressed as regulations, by-laws, standards, or rules—is closely linked with the type of enforcement in use; and both are dependent upon the question of where the community places its reliance, whether on a public inspectorate, or upon the building industry, to ensure that its requirements are met. If reliance is placed on inspectors, their level of competence must be matched with the type of criteria used to define what the law prescribes. The more a system depends upon separate inspection, the more the requirements tend to be stated as specific descriptions which are capable of straightforward verification, with the minimum use of subjective judgement. If the criteria, by contrast, are drawn up so that there are many options available for their requirements to be satisfied, so that technical innovation is not frustrated, it follows that the onus for compliance tends to rest mainly with the designers, because if a complex design of a large building should prove to be wrong, the cost of putting it right after completion would be too disproportionate to be acceptable.

In general, it can be seen that the design criteria, in whatever form they are produced to suit the style of enforcement, need themselves to be designed to suit the needs of their two main users: the public as "controllers" of the built environment, who need to be protected; and the construction industry who are to be controlled in their production of it.

For the controllers, such regulations need to cover all aspects of the performance of the built environment that are important to the health and safety of the users; for those controlled, their contents should be expressed in technical terms and legislative techniques that allow for efficient compliance and enforcement. Allowance must be made for the controllers wanting to improve their standards of health and safety from time to time; and for the industry under control wanting to introduce new materials and methods. At any time, the standards set must be those which can be met by the industry within the currently acceptable boundaries of cost. The industrialists will claim that decisions affecting design are also decisions affecting the economics of building, and consequently govern choice in every detail; and therefore, that any design criteria set for the purpose of building control can be practicable only when this condition is taken properly into account. All these prerequisites serve to show how much depends upon the level of social and technical competence for the design of a control system to be apt and successful.

With regard to the function of enforcement, equally important considerations apply if it is to work well and efficiently. It needs to be recognized that in modern times, even allowing for periods of recession, the demand for buildings is greater than it was in the past; building programmes are larger; buildings more complex in terms of fabric and mechanism; and the pace of technological change is faster. In the process of responding to the demands made on it, the modern construction industry has developed its own framework of design and management, comprising an array of professional experts who operate independently or as members of large organizations, and who generally decide what is to be done and how it is to be carried out.

In view of this, the industry would claim that any system of enforcement can be effective in its aims *only* if it operates through this existing framework of management. In theory, the number of buildings in production at any one time, and their complexity of design, is sufficient to mean that their inspection cannot be carried out with real efficiency unless the inspectors are also the designers and managers of the work of construction. It can be argued that it is increasingly uneconomical to change such large products as buildings *after* they are built, or even to change their design once the design is complete; and in consequence there are unacceptable disadvantages in relying upon inspection after completion as an economic method of checking compliance. What is needed instead is an efficient system of enforcement that can give the public a means of management that will enable it to achieve its own aims effectively and economically, without disrupting the management of the supplying industry that it seeks to control.

All these functions of legislation and enforcement need to be examined and described objectively if a theory is to be established for designing the systems used for building control. This will be done in subsequent chapters.

THE CHANGING STANDARDS

Among the many difficulties of attempting to administer, much more reform, a building control system, is the tendency for the public's requirements which lie at the heart of the matter as its main motivation, to be themselves subjected to constant change. Like any organizational method that attempts to manage human affairs, the systems of control are never static, and the attempts to identify what exactly is happening are easily confused by the shifting circumstances and the mounting variables of practice and opinion. The principles that might have been the basis of some of the original decisions that shaped the system, become disguised or obscured as the years go by. But at the centre of the activity is the problem that the needs which generate the demand for the controls change and modify almost imperceptibly, and over longer periods of time will transmogrify into different concepts, which make the safeguards obsolete. For example, while it has been shown that the public everywhere has concluded that it wants safeguards in the interests of *health* and *safety*, and is prepared to exercise some form of control over building for those purposes; the ideas about what the dangers are, what can be accepted as safe, and what is meant by health are themselves constantly changing and developing.

Standards of health

Ideas about health, for example, have changed radically since the inception of building control. In those times health was thought of in terms of meaning the absence of disease and pestilence, and the law was preoccupied with the disposal of refuse and effluent, and other hazards likely to spread infection and plague. Later, in more recent times, health has come to be thought of in terms of the *presence of human well-being*, and the capacity for enjoyment. If the law is to take account of this, it will become concerned with the standards for the provision of space, light, warmth, clean air, and humidity; and the degree of protection needed from noise, glare, fumes, dust, and other detractors from human comfort. In the modern world an awareness of the human condition has been developing rapidly, informed by medical research and such objective studies as have accompanied activities like space exploration. In consequence there are implications that new controlling criteria may be needed for the environmental conditions inside buildings and around them. If regulations are to cope with such changing standards affecting buildings, they will need to be capable of being readily updated. The instruments of control, too, if they are to deal with environmental issues, may have to cross traditional boundaries of jurisdiction, and will need access to the kind of research information that may be considered necessary for dealing with the task.

Standards of safety

The standards of safety demanded by the public may remain constant in principle, but the hazards may continue to multiply, and become different in kind.

Buildings consist increasingly of a complex array of structures, fabrics, and mechanisms. The services supplying water and energy, the installations for their provision in the form of fluids, electricity, solids, and gas (to say nothing of the development of solar or nuclear energy) are likely to become as much a part of the built end-product as were the solid-fuel appliances that had been so familiar when by-laws began. They represent other hazards to safety than the threat of fire, and can include such extremes of danger as radiation and explosion. All such systems can become integral parts of the built product, whose design and construction becomes, as a consequence, more dependent upon multi-professional teamwork. The safety of the building as a whole will need to be dealt with as depending not only on the security of each individual part, but on the control of the way they interact with each other. The relevant criteria must be available for guidance or to form the basis of the legally enforced information that makes up the paraphernalia of control.

It must be borne in mind, too, that value-engineering and similar scientific methods of designing have led to a new consciousness of the priorities and their balance in the provisions. Legal safeguards to secure reasonable standards of safety should not result in disproportionately high costs in the final products of building.

Their relative value needs to be adequately assessed, and the degree of risk involved in each case needs to be evaluated so that expenditure on protection from them in the completed building can be sensibly proportionate; or decisions that high expenditure is unavoidable can be properly justified. In the national spectrum the safety standards imply an expenditure which can be seen as the national insurance premium for protection from disasters.

The public, in dealing with the safety of other built products in general use, is already using more sophisticated forms of assessment of dangers and methods of protection, which might provide ideas for use in bringing the building control systems up to date. For example, in the aircraft industry a scientific terminology is used for cateloguing the hazards, which are categorized as "occurrences", consisting of failures, events, or errors, and their "probability", which may be frequent, reasonably probable, recurrent, remote, extremely remote, and extremely improbable. Such degrees of probability can be given numerical values, depending on known evidence of their eventuality. The "effects" of an occurrence can be described as minor, major, hazardous, or catastrophic, each condition being defined in terms of its severity affecting the aeroplane and its occupants.

Along with such methods of assessment of dangers, there go matching concepts of designing the safeguards, so that the aircraft cannot be operated without a certificate of airworthiness, or some such classification, and the considerations cover not just the construction of the product itself, but also a triumvirate of requirements including the product, its maintenance, and the methods of operating it, all of which must attain a prescribed standard of acceptability.

Although buildings may not be susceptible to such dramatic dangers as aircraft, there are many points of similarity in principle when they are considered as artefacts that may cause threats to the health and safety of the public. It may be the time when the systems of building control could be designed to take account of the methods used for these other more modern forms of public protection, and become much more specific and efficient for their own more modest purposes.

In this series of books each of the main types of building control will be examined in turn, by describing an example of each as practised in a country where the system is most typical. In this volume the system described is that which is based on the use of law, and in particular is characterized by its reliance on the common law, or the penal code, for its effectiveness. A prime, if not archetypal, example of this form of control is to be found in the United Kingdom, and so the systems operated in this country are examined in detail in the following chapters.

CHAPTER TWO

Building control in the UK

THE GENERAL NATURE OF THE UK SYSTEM

The system of building control used in the United Kingdom is representative of one of the main generic types of control discussed earlier. It places reliance on the common law, using the penal code, and employs a type of enforcement that is based on inspection. Historically, it can be seen as an originator of one system of building control, because those which now operate in the English-speaking countries have developed from it; while methods in use in the sea-board states of north-western Europe, particularly in Holland, Denmark, Norway, and Sweden, bear a close family resemblance. Characteristically, too, it avoids extremes and is seemingly somewhat vague in its definition, so that although it exemplifies the type of system that depends on common law, the authoritarianism that forms the core of this method of control is muted. The "inspectorates" are less like police departments and there is no special tradition for their members to be screened by high qualifications, except in London. Reliance is also placed on professional designers for compliance, but in a round-about way involving the civil courts. The designers can be held responsible for any failure to comply by their clients, and are liable to actions for damages. In turn, this can involve insurers who indemnify designers and contractors against such risks, though without themselves exercising any particular influence over the legal system or the content of the regulations that define the public's requirements. To add to the variety, if not the inclination to confusion, there are three forms of the system in operation separately in the UK, namely one each in the areas of England together with Wales, London, and Scotland. For the purposes of study this is an advantage, because important variations within the general context of the method can be examined.

THE STRUCTURE OF CONTROL

In the UK the control of building is exercised through Acts of Parliament. These give powers to a nominated authority or person for the making of regulations; describe the purposes for which regulations can be made; state what matters relating to buildings can be regulated; and provide for the function of enforcement by establishing where the executive responsibility lies. These Acts and the regulations arising from them together make up the "legal instruments" for the constraints on building. The whole apparatus of control, however, includes the legal instruments and the system of enforcement. It can be seen as a structure of two parts, comprising documentation and the activity of ensuring compliance.

The three administrative areas of the UK each have their own version of this two-part structure. *In England and Wales* the legal documents consist of the Public Health Acts of 1936 and 1961 as amended by Part III of the Health and Safety at Work, etc. Act of 1974; and the national Building Regulations, which are the statutory instruments arising from them made by the nominated secretary of state of the central government. The responsibility for enforcement lies with the local authorities as empowered by the Acts. *In London*, the enabling powers are contained in the London Building Act of 1930, as amended in 1935 and 1939, and the regulations arising from them are the Constructional By-laws made by the Greater London Council. Enforcement is delegated by the Acts to district surveyors who are officers of the Council but whose appointment is governed by criteria contained in the Acts, which also describe their duties. *In Scotland*, the documentation consists of the Building (Scotland) Acts of 1959 and 1970, and the Building Standards (Scotland) Regulations made by the Secretary of State as prescribed in the Acts. The responsibility for enforcement is given to Building Authorities, whose constitution is defined in the Acts and whose appointment is related to the local authorities.

In each case, then, the relevant Acts of Parliament, which are known generally as the enabling Acts, provide the terms of reference for the making of the regulations (or by-laws, as the case may be), and also determine where the responsibility for enforcement lies and how it should function. Since the sixties there has been an acknowledgement by the central government of the need for the three sets of regulating documents to prescribe comparable standards for technical purposes throughout the UK.

THE SYSTEM IN LONDON

Historically, the first steps in building control were taken in London. There had been local Acts of one sort or another there as early as AD 1189, but the major incentive for control was brought about by the Great Fire of London. After that disaster the Lord Mayor and City Council were authorized to appoint surveyors with statutory powers to control building, with particular reference to structural precautions against fire. From such origins came the method of control that has been unique to London. Although the main structure of the legislation is familiar, because it consists of enabling Acts of Parliament together with by-laws made under them, the practice of control in London differs from that in the rest of the country in respect of the regulations themselves, which are contained in different sets of by-laws, and in the manner of their enforcement (see figure 6).

The criteria

In the country at large, anyone who intends to build is able to look at one set of national Building Regulations to find out what the law requires in respect of the building; but anyone intending to build in inner London must look in several places for these instructions. The provisions are prescribed in three sets of by-laws, one dealing with the constructional requirements and two with drainage and sanitary measures; and in addition the Acts themselves contain provisions resembling by-laws dealing with open spaces near buildings, the height of buildings, the construction of buildings, and means of escape in case of fire. These diverse requirements are enforced in different ways, and it is one method among them, involving the use of District Surveyors, that has given the capital its special character in the practice of building control.

The by-laws dealing with *sanitary matters*, however, are not enforced in this way, but come under the jurisdiction of the London Boroughs. There have been two sets for some considerable time. There were drainage by-laws made by the former London County Council in March 1934, under Section 202 of the Metropolis Management Act of 1855 and the Metropolis Management Acts Amendment (By-laws) of 1899; and by-laws made with respect to "water-closets, urinals, earth closets, privies, and cess-pools" in May 1930 under Section 39 (1) of the Public Health (London) Act 1891, and Section 24 of

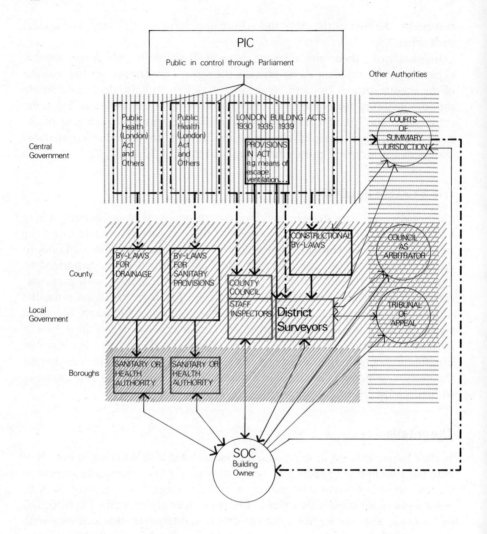

Figure 6 Building control in London

the London County Council (General Powers) Act of 1928. The drainage by-laws in current application were made in 1962 under the Public Health (London) Act of 1936. As may be expected these provisions are cast very much in the mould of building specifications, and generally cover the same subjects as are dealt with in the national Building Regulations. The City of London differs from other parts of the capital in that it has its own drainage by-laws.

The more familiar form of the *Constructional By-laws* is a product of the Greater London Council, made under the powers given by the London Building Act of 1930, and the London Building Act (Amendment) Acts of 1935 and 1939. As already mentioned, these Acts themselves contained requirements similar to some of the provisions included in the national regulations, for which they probably provided models. There are stipulations about the space at the "rear of domestic buildings", dealing ostensibly with lighting and ventilation; and about courts outside the "windows of habitable rooms", and about the heights of buildings in relation to the widths of streets; provisions about the construction of buildings, dealing with their structural framework, wall thicknesses and heights, chimneys and flues, ventilation, heights of rooms and windows in habitable rooms; means of escape, and other matters of detail which have since come to be regarded as being more appropriate to regulations than to the enabling Acts.

In respect of these matters, the Acts require that the Council is notified of an intention to carry out work, and as far as the provisions for "means of escape" are concerned, the owner of the building is required to deposit a set of plans and particulars at the County Hall at the same time as the building notice (which is also required under Section 161 of the Act of 1930) is served on the District Surveyor. This means that the enforcement, even though the surveyors may be involved, is dealt with separately within the bureaucracy of the Council.

Enforcement

The method of enforcement in regard to the Constructional By-laws is unique to London. To a greater degree than has applied in the rest of the country under the Public Health Act of 1935, the system of control used in London has placed reliance upon inspection by an elite group of persons whose powers are defined by the statutes, which also set out the terms of appointment and qualifications applying to the inspectorate.

Under the London Building Act of 1930, the London County Council was empowered to make by-laws "for the better carrying into effect the objects and powers" of the Act, which has been made "for the purpose of securing the proper width and direction of streets, the sound construction of buildings, the diminution of the danger arising from fire, the securing of more light, air and space round buildings and generally with respect to the control and regulation of streets and buildings". The by-laws could deal with a miscellany of requirements such as the forms of notice, foundations and sites, the thickness and substance of walls, the dimensions of joists, woodwork in exeternal walls, and, significantly, could also cover *the duties of District Surveyors* and the imposition of penalties in the form of fines.

The Act prescribed that every building or structure should be "subject to the supervision of the District Surveyor" appointed to the district in which it was situated. Such persons could be appointed only after they had been examined by the appointees of the Royal Institute of British Architects (RIBA), and had received a certificate of competency from that Institute.

The mode of control was clearly defined in the Act in relation to these officials. Before work on any building was begun a notice had to be given by the builder to the District Surveyor together with certain specified information about the proposed building, and the District Surveyor was required to "survey any building or work thereby placed under his supervision and cause all ... provisions and byelaws to be duly observed". In the event of a contravention, the surveyor was empowered to serve a "notice of irregularity" on the builder or owner requiring the fault to be remedied; and, further, to complain to a sessional court for an order requiring the defaulting person to comply if nothing was done. If that order was not carried out, the Council were able to enter the premises and do all that was needed by "direct action".

The power of the inspectorate

These were formidable powers, and were different in two fundamental ways from the control exercised in other parts of the country. First, the District Surveyor was endowed with an exceptional authority. His powers were provided directly *by statute*; and since the by-laws stated that all work should be done to his satisfaction, his *opinions* were given the status of the law itself. For these privileges, of course, it was fitting that he should be highly qualified. *Secondly*, the certificates of compliance issued by him were related to the *building itself*, not to the drawings, and to this end work had to be inspected by him on the building site.

The amendment Acts of 1935 and 1939 maintained the strength of the District Surveyor's position. The 1935 Amendment revised the list of matters which could be the subject of the by-laws made by the Council. The former miscellany was brought more up to date, and set out in a sequence more logically related to the building processes, dealing with building and structures, and administrative matters like the information needed on the deposit of plans and the duties of the surveyors.

The 1939 Amendments added more items to the list, such as the control of lifts and escalators, and of gas meters, but were principally concerned with the revision and restatement of the Council's powers to appoint District Surveyors, and of the scope of their authority. The task of examining candidates for these appointments was transferred from the RIBA to a board whose members were to be appointed by the Council, and provision was also made for appeals by owners against a decision of a surveyor to be made to the Council for determination; but the upshot of the amendments in general was to give clearer and more detailed directions about how these officers should be appointed and what their powers were in a way that would strengthen and consolidate their position.

Summing up

Although subsequent legislation in the UK has sought to achieve a greater measure of uniformity in the three major national areas of jurisdiction for building control, the system in use in London has remained in a form that distinguishes it from the national pattern. Yet it is not fundamentally at variance in terms of legal practice. It is based on enabling Acts which empower the making of regulations (known as by-laws because they are made by a local authority and not by the central government); and it relies upon the local government to enforce them. It sets out the requirements in less convenient ways for the building owners who have to comply, but in regard to the enforcement of the main provisions for *construction* it is more specific about the nature and quality of the inspectorate and its mode of operation; and this gives the system a more personalized and authoritative character. This probably reflects the severe nature of the disasters of fire and plague that led the people of the great conurbation of London, so long ago, to the conviction that control was necessary.

THE NATIONAL SYSTEMS

The systems in use in England and Wales, and in Scotland, are more alike, fundamentally. The Acts require a Secretary of State of the central government to make regulations which apply nationally; and enforcement lies with the local authorities. There are differences in scope, but a detailed study in each case will identify how the same principles apply. It should be made clear first, however, that in the UK generally, town planning and accommodational standards for such social building programmes as housing and education have been covered traditionally by separate legislation, enforced in different ways. Building control as examined here is a central system aimed at dealing with the basic requirements of all types of building, whatever other standards of accommodation or cost may apply.

England and Wales: the enabling Acts

In England and Wales, the Public Health Act of 1936 consolidated "with amendments, certain enactments relating to public health", and gave to local authorities (which it defined) responsibilities and powers covering matters of health and safety. The duties which it defined included those concerned with sewage disposal; drains and sanitary convenience; nuisances and "offensive trades"; water supply; the prevention and treatment of disease; the provision of hospitals, laboratories, baths, and wash-houses; the protection of maternity and child welfare; and other provisions of equal importance, among which were those that set the pattern for building control. These included some requirements that were clearly concerned with the safety of buildings, such as those dealing with dangerous or dilapidated buildings, with entrances and exits from buildings used for public purposes, and with means of escape from fire for certain high buildings. But there were also stipulations about "bylaws with respect to buildings and sanitation". Eleven of the sections of the Act, numbered 61 to 71, set out the provisions which, for ensuing decades, governed what the by-laws should deal with and how they should be enforced. There were no reasons given for the making of by-laws, but the scope for them was contained, as far as it went, in Sections 61 and 62.

Every local authority was permitted, or if directed by the Minister, *required* to make by-laws regulating the following matters: "*as regards buildings*"—their construction and the materials used in building them; the space about them, their lighting and ventilation, and the dimensions of rooms intended for human habitation; their height, and the height of chimneys; and "*as regards works and fittings*"—sanitary conveniences; drainage (including surface water); cesspools and other means of disposing of foul matter; ashpits; wells, tanks, and cisterns for supplying water for human consumption; stoves and other fittings (not electric) in so far as by-laws were required "for the purpose of health and the prevention of fire", and private sewers and drains. Of such by-laws, those made "as regards buildings" (that is, not those covering works and fittings) were to be applied to existing buildings, but only in the case of structural alterations being carried out, or changes of use being effected.

All this meant that the regulating by-laws were limited in purpose to matters of health, because that was what the Act itself was about; and matters of safety, because some of the requirements of the Act dealt with this too, and by implication made this a subsidiary purpose. But the by-laws were able to cover only specific aspects of the construction and form of buildings and such of their fittings as related to water supply, sanitation, and the traditional stoves for burning solid fuels.

By comparison with the information then being used by the designers of buildings, derived from building research and issued as guidance by the British Standards Institution, these requirements seemed already outdated, and appeared to have the limited intention of fixing the very minimum standards for the protection of the public against only the most basic dangers. At the time, however, it could be argued that this level of precaution seemed appropriate and acceptable, especially as the by-laws were effectively legal instruments which formed part of the penal code, so that any failure to comply with them or to attain the standards set by them would constitute a criminal offence, for which heavy punishment could be imposed.

Apart from its dealing with the making of the by-laws, the Act gave power to the local authority (with the consent of the Minister) to relax the requirements where they might be thought unreasonable in particular cases; and it gave exemption to certain buildings from by-laws made under the Act, such buildings being those constructed by Education Authorities or local authorities in accordance with other requirements, and buildings belonging to statutory undertakings.

The enforcement of the by-laws was imposed on the local authorities as a statutory duty, but the Act dealt with this only in the most rudimentary way.

The first section of the first part of the Act stated that "it shall be the duty of" certain authorities as described "to carry this Act with execution". In the section which dealt with building by-laws, the Act required local authorities to pass or reject the "plans of any proposed work", and gave to them the power to require the removal or alteration of work not in conformity with the by-laws, or executed notwithstanding the rejection of the plans; or ultimately to "pull down or remove the work in question" themselves, if the owner did not comply. Indeed, any work that contravened a by-law could be removed even if it had been built in accordance with plans that had been passed by the local authority.

The Act also allowed any question or dispute arising between the local authority and the person executing the work to be referred to the Minister for determination, provided that the application to him was made jointly by the authority and the person concerned, in which case the Minister's decision would be final. It also gave power to the Minister to make building by-laws in the case of default by a responsible local authority, and enabled him to resolve unreasonable by-laws.

Thus, at the outset, the 1936 Act, while establishing where the responsibility lay for carrying the Act with execution, left the question of how it should be done largely to the discretion of the local authorities. It told them what their sanctions were: simply the removal of work that did not comply; and it instructed them to pass or reject the plans of any work proposed, but gave no directions about the inspection of completed work.

After the Second World War there was a large increase in the amount of building during the late 1940s and 1950s due to the need for reconstruction after extensive war-damage, and also for the making up of the deficiencies due to the inactivity of the construction industry during the period at hostilities.

One consequence of this experience of heavy demand for national investment in building was that the Act was amended by the central government in 1961; though only to transfer the responsibility for the making of regulations from the local authority to a Minister of the central government, and to modify some aspects of enforcement.

The purposes for which regulations could be made were left as they were, being "all or any of the matters set out in sections sixty-one and sixty-two of the Public Health Act 1936". With regard to enforcement the amending Act was explicit that it should be "the function of every local authority to enforce building regulations in their district", but otherwise it applied the functions governing the enforcement of by-laws in the previous Act to the enforcement of the new regulations [see figure 7(a)]. No other substantial changes were made, excepting to allow the Minister to relax or dispense with any requirement in the building regulations if that requirement appeared unreasonable in relation to a particular case; and also to enable applications to be made to him by direct appeal in writing, if necessary, thus dispensing with the previous requirement that such applications were permissible only if made jointly.

48

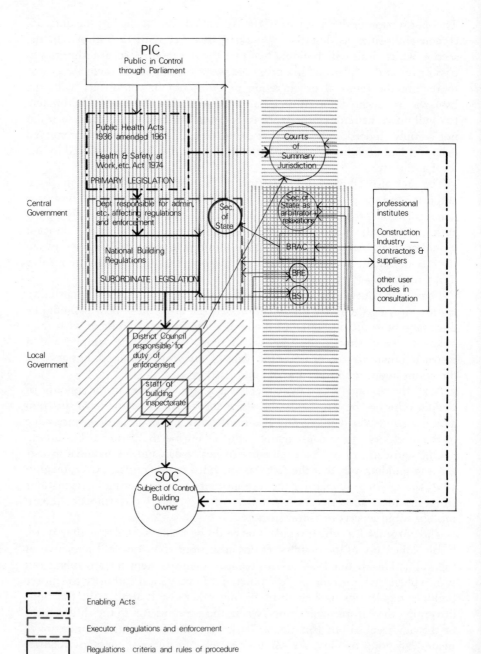

Figure 7a Building control in UK: the system in England and Wales

The Advisory function

The reforming zeal (if such it was) that helped bring about the amending Act of 1961 came largely from the construction industry itself (including, in this definition, its professional designers) (see figure 8). The industry was faced with new demands and ambitious building programmes at a time of a reduction of its labour-force, and in order to achieve new levels of productivity it could see the need for more clarity in the legal instruments and more uniformity in their enforcement. Acknowledgement of this influence seemed to be indicated by one of the amendments that required the Minister to "appoint a committee, to be known as the Building Regulations Advisory Committee", for the purpose of advising him "on the exercise of his power to make building regulations", and to consult the Committee, among other bodies with an interest in the subject "before making any building regulations".

The new committee was appointed in April 1962 with a membership predominantly representing the professional community of architects, engineers, and surveyors who made up the management sector of the industry. The committee had eleven members, of whom seven were from these disciplines; another was chairman of a firm of builders; and the others were respectively a fire officer, a health inspector, and a town clerk in the public service. There were also eleven assessors, two from the national building research station, five from the Ministry of Housing and Local Government, three from the Ministry of Public Building and Works, and one from the Home Office. All of these officers were members of the professional or administrative branches of the Civil Service, and much involved in the affairs of the construction industry, either as "clients" or executors of the large government-financed building programmes.

By the early sixties, of course, the designers of the construction industry had already become accustomed to the use of the "Codes of Practice" that were issued by the British Standards Institution as comprehensive briefing criteria to guide their work. These publications had set out the "Codes of the Basic Data for the Design of Buildings", as being those aspects of the function and performance of buildings that, in the opinion of their authors (who largely represented the professional technical institutions), were important to good design practice. These designers were coming to see the national regulations as design briefs for the basic minimum requirements of the public; and so the catalogue of purposes for which regulations could be made (as contained in the Act of 1936 and still in use), seemed to them to be seriously out of date.

Scotland and the Scottish reforms

Added point had been given to this belief by the publication of the Report of a Building Legislative Committee in Scotland, under the chairmanship of Lord Guest, and the new Building (Scotland) Act of 1959, which, together with the

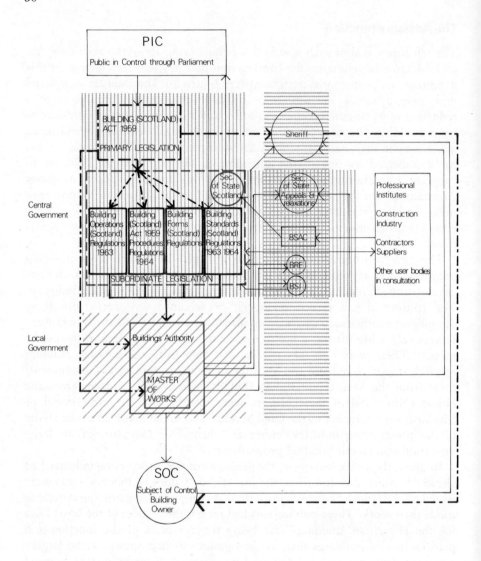

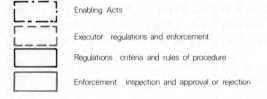

Figure 7b Building control in UK: the system in Scotland

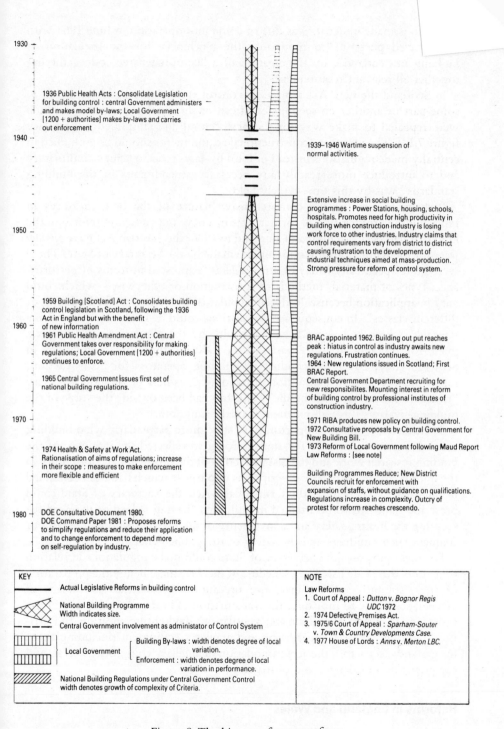

1930

1936 Public Health Acts : Consolidate Legislation for building control : central Government administers and makes model by-laws; Local Government [1200 + authorities] makes by-laws and carries out enforcement

1940

1939–1946 Wartime suspension of normal activities.

Extensive increase in social building programmes : Power Stations, housing, schools, hospitals. Promotes need for high productivity in building when construction industry is losing work force to other industries. Industry claims that control requirements vary from district to district causing frustration to the development of industrial techniques aimed at mass-production. Strong pressure for reform of control system.

1950

1959 Building [Scotland] Act : Consolidates building control legislation in Scotland, following the 1936 Act in England but with the benefit of new information.

1960

1961 Public Health Amendment Act : Central Government takes over responsibility for making regulations; Local Government [1200 + authorities] continues to enforce.

1965 Central Government issues first set of national building regulations.

BRAC appointed 1962. Building out put reaches peak : hiatus in control as industry awaits new regulations. Frustration continues.
1964 : New regulations issued in Scotland; First BRAC Report.
Central Government Department recruiting for new responsibilites. Mounting interest in reform of building control by professional institutes of construction industry.

1970

1971 RIBA produces new policy on building control.
1972 Consultative proposals by Central Government for New Building Bill.
1973 Reform of Local Government following Maud Report
Law Reforms : [see note]

1974 Health & Safety at Work Act.
Rationalisation of aims of regulations; increase in their scope : measures to make enforcement more flexible and efficient

Building Programmes Reduce; New District Councils recruit for enforcement with expansion of staffs, without guidance on qualifications. Regulations increase in complexity. Outcry of protest for reform reaches crescendo.

1980

DOE Consultative Document 1980.
DOE Command Paper 1981 : Proposes reforms to simplify regulations and reduce their application and to change enforcement to depend more on self-regulation by industry.

KEY

Actual Legislative Reforms in building control

National Building Programme
Width indicates size.

Central Government involvement as administator of Control System

Local Government
    Building By-laws : width denotes degree of local variation.
    Enforcement : width denotes degree of local variation in performance.

National Building Regulations under Central Government Control width denotes growth of complexity of Criteria.

NOTE

Law Reforms
1. Court of Appeal : *Dutton* v. *Bognor Regis UDC* 1972
2. 1974 Defective Premises Act.
3. 1975/6 Court of Appeal : *Sparham-Souter* v. *Town & Country Developments Case.*
4. 1977 House of Lords : *Anns* v. *Merton LBC.*

Figure 8 The history of recent reform

regulations made under it, was due to come into operation in June 1964 with the avowed purpose "to modernise the machinery for the regulation of building in Scotland", by the creation of a "comprehensive code gathering together all relevant requirements".

In Scotland the new Act replaced a control system that had been based in some part or another on sections of fifteen or more other enactments which were repealed to make way for the new central and simplified system [see figure 7(b)]. The idea that "constructional requirements should be embodied in centrally made regulations instead of local by-laws so as to achieve uniformity and to introduce more readily any necessary amendments of the building standards" was by this time widely held.

Perhaps because of the comprehensive nature of the new measures in replacing the proliferation of former Acts in a new and sweeping reform of the kind that had been attempted in England in 1936, the Scottish Act gave a *wider scope* for the regulations it required to be made by the Secretary of State. These were quite specifically to lay down *standards* "expressed in terms of perform-ance, types of material, methods of construction or otherwise", which could vary in application because "different standards" could be set "for buildings of different classes". In consequence, regulations could be made to cover *housing standards*, which had never been dealt with by the regulations and by-laws made for building in other parts of the UK. Furthermore, regulations in Scotland could cover the conduct of building operators for "construction, repair, maintenance or demolition of buildings", as may be thought necessary "to secure the safety of the public". This too had been outside the scope of the building by-laws throughout the rest of the kingdom.

The new Act took the opportunity to state more particularly what building control was thought to be for, and in doing so reflected the influence of the buiding research work and the dissatisfaction of the professional community in the outmoded and imprecise descriptions of purpose which had been contained in the earlier Acts. Under the terms of the Act, the Secretary of State could prescribe standards to be attained in buildings "having regard to the need for securing the health, safety and convenience of the persons who will inhabit or frequent such buildings and the safety of the public generally".

For these purposes the Secretary of State could make regulations in relation to matters that were listed in a schedule of the Act, these being: the preparation of sites; strength and stability; fire precautions (structural and means of escape); resistance to moisture; the transmission of heat and sound; durability; resistance to infestation; drainage; ventilation; daylighting; heating and arti-ficial lighting; services, installation and ancillary equipment (including those for gas and electricity); the accommodation of ancillary equipment; access; and the prevention of danger and obstruction.

Reforms in England and Wales

In other parts of the UK these terms of reference were seen to have the advantage of being comprehensive. It was argued that any central regulations made under them could include all the design information that might be considered necessary. Even though the list contained some of the old, traditional terminology, the criteria to be prepared could take the form of specifications of performance or other sophisticated data, which would not limit the designers to one solution; and all of the modern hazards against which safeguards might be thought to be necessary could be provided for. The inclusion of the open-ended purpose of "convenience" was also seen as an advantage by many (though not all), because it offered scope for introducing new industrial reforms aimed at achieving higher productivity or faster building (like dimensional standardization); and it also would permit the imposition of accommodational standards (specifying area and equipment per person per unit of cost) that might otherwise be difficult to justify on grounds of health or safety alone. It was yet to be recognized that there might be serious disadvantages, which might for example include future legislators being able to produce regulations of encyclopaedic proportions, as a consequence of their wider terms of reference, with consequential difficulties for designers and inspectors alike.

With this example of centralization so recent and prominent, the new Building Regulation Advisory Committee in the UK was quick to give expression to a continuing concern about the scope of the regulations affecting England and Wales, notwithstanding the amending Act of 1961, and to point out the remaining complications of enforcement due to the large number of different controls and the many authorities that were still operating in the general control of building.

The views of the advisers

In its first Report, presented to Parliament and published in 1964, the Advisory Committee in London found it necessary to refer to the limitation of purpose of the regulations as governed by the Public Health Act of 1936, and to explain that, while in Scotland under wider powers, regulations could be made to encourage efficiency in the building industry, or to deal with the "convenience" of building owner or user, and covering the whole of the building and its services, in England and Wales the matters for which regulations could be made were "specific and restricted". The terms of reference for making regulations which had been "unaltered since 1936 save in respect to clean air", did not cover piped water, electrical appliances or wiring, fuel storage or pipes, or means of escape from fire.

Furthermore, the committee complained, there remained too many diverse controls and authorities concerned in the business of regulating building. These were listed in the Report, and showed that the new "*national* regulations" with which the Committee itself was concerned, formed a type of control that was only the first item among sixteen others. There were eight controls administered by the Building By-law Authorities, but other controls were administered by those Authorities jointly with Fire Authorities; by Fire Authorities alone; by Water Authorities; Electricity Authorities; the Factory

Inspectorate; the Home Office; and the Education Authorities. Yet there was no statutory control at all for "oil-fired equipment other than stoves; engineering installations (lifts, ventilating plant, etc.); means of escape from fire in private buildings under three storeys, and from small shops and offices" (although control of the last two items named was being undertaken under the Offices, Shops and Railway Premises Act of 1963!).

The Committee went on to make general recommendations which were to set the pattern for debate about reforms through the next decade. It defined the main regulating techniques and concluded that the method of specifying performance standards was clearly "the ultimate objective" but that its adoption for all regulations would take time to achieve because its success depended upon a high level of technical competence and expensive testing facilities. It pointed to some of the pitfalls and difficulties of enforcement, and discussed the form that regulations should take, laying emphasis on the need for a convenient working document that was comprehensive though not too bulky, did not work against technological developments, and though couched necessarily in legal language should remain effective without having "unnecessarily complicated provisions". It also discussed the relationship between regulations and the British Standards and Codes of Practice, pointing out that, because of their different objectives, these latter were "rarely suitable for mandatory provisions". It reviewed problems of administration and in a final and significant recommendation spoke of the urgency of ensuring that highly-trained inspectors should be available to the local authorities if the control system was to evolve in the way it should. With sufficient persons of the right qualifications it might well "be possible to encourage the evolution of the control from a large assembly of detailed requirements to a system based on more generalised principles".

The views of the professional institutions

These opinions echoed round the deliberating committees in the various professional institutions through the remainder of the sixties and into the seventies. The Royal Institution of British Architects created a standing technical committee which prepared a policy statement about building control that was published in 1971, in which it set out its guidelines for a new "Building Bill". A document of rare clarity and succinctness for so complex a topic, it was reputed to be among the few statements of policy ever to have received the unanimous approval of the RIBA Council, and it remained central to the Institute's campaign for a further ten years.

The RIBA had managed to distill from the opinions and recommendations of the Guest Report and the new Building Regulations Advisory Committee the main essence of a theory for the design of a building control system suited to the UK experience and based on an insight of its practice.

Its report called for a single Act, dubbed the "Building Bill", which would replace all other measures affecting the construction industry. This would express its own aims clearly, and enable a Minister of the central government to have responsibility for the national regulations. The report included proposals for the form and content of the regulations, suggesting how best they could be designed and kept up to date; and outlining the use that could be made of the national Standards and Codes of Practice as a support to legislative provisions. The question of enforcement was dealt with carefully. It was suggested that the Minister should delegate this to local authorities, but that the task should be given to the larger formations, like the County Councils, that would emerge from the planned reorganization of the local government structure; and performed by highly qualified personnel working under the direction of a chief officer in each case. It recommended that these enforcement inspectorates should form an elite body of administrators in each area of jurisdiction who would call on the local chartered consultants of architecture, engineering and surveying to augment their efforts in checking and certifying compliance.

The RIBA was arguing for a simpler and more unified system of building control to take account of the interests of the construction industry, the public, and the UK in relation to Europe. It wanted the new system to replace the existing forms of control in England and Wales, Scotland, and London, and asked for three reforms to be put into effect. The first would be the passing of the new Act to provide for the making and enforcing of the new regulations, which should be designed to affect "the built environment in all its uses, for the purpose of public health and safety". Among its provisions, the Act should ensure that the Secretary of State would be able "to grant relaxation (to mitigate hardships); to grant waivers (to promote experiments in the interests of research and devleopment for the improvement of environmental standards or constructional techniques); and to delegate powers to local authorities to appoint chief officers and suitably qualified professional designers to aid in enforcement". The second reform would be the introduction of the new set of regulations for the whole of the UK which should "deal with all aspects of the performance of the environment as affecting public health and safety; should be classified in relation to management systems of the construction industry, and use regulating techniques suited to diverse design and construction methods". The third reform was to be the new organization for the task of enforcement "comprising the central government department working through the larger local authorities, and using chief officers with delegated powers and suitably qualified professional designers of the construction industry to aid in enforcement".

At the time of the pronouncement of this policy by the RIBA, there existed a joint consultative committee of the professional institutions of the construction industry dealing with the subject of building legislation and meeting at the RIBA under the chairmanship of an architect. This gave general support to the aims of the policy, and also produced its own statement about the "form and content" of the regulations, so that the RIBA was able to feel that its advocacy was on a firm basis of support. Its own Building Regulations Committee also had kept in touch with the Department of central government concerned with the administration of building control, and could claim that there was "general sympathy" expressed there for the principles of the policy.

The official proposals

This confidence was borne out in 1972 when the newly formed Department of the Environment issued, in July, a consultative document giving proposals for a Building Bill. The main features of such a Bill were described in seven paragraphs, and included: the widening of the scope of existing powers to cover, *inter alia*, building services and equipment; the rationalization of control by the concentration of all requirements in the one set of regulations; the repeal of other local Acts; the removal of exemptions; changes in enforcement procedures to achieve more flexibility; provision for appeal to the Secretary of State rather than to the magistrates' court on questions of contravention; and (possibly) provision for charging fees for applications.

It seemed at the time to those members of the professional institutions and others involved with the activities of building who had concerned themselves with the campaign to reform the building control system, that the essential changes were at last within reach. Consultation might yet take time, but the desired reforms would soon be accomplished by the long-advocated Bill.

The eventual action: a reforming Act

In spite of the strength of this belief, the reform, when it came, took a different shape. The government of the day was not able to promote new legislation having the hoped-for singleness of purpose of the projected "Building Bill", but instead, deriving some political motivation from the interest of people in their working conditions, was able to prepare legislation to deal with their health and safety at work. Yet, as if to give emphasis to the belief that politics is the art of the possible, the administrators and others within the circle of governmental service were able to include many of the proposed reforming provisions for building in the new Act, even though it was not a measure sponsored by the Department responsible for building matters, but emerged from the Department dealing primarily with home affairs. Consequently, the first steps in the fulfilment of the aims of the building reformers were taken in one of the Parts of an Act dealing with the safeguarding of working conditions which went before Parliament in 1974.

The Health and Safety at Work, etc. Act was added to the Statutes in 1974 and gave further change and new shape to the Enabling Acts of 1936 and 1961, together with which it would provide for the control of building. As its introduction stated, the new measure was

an Act to make further provision for securing the health, safety and welfare of persons at work, for protecting others against risks to health and safety in connection with the activities of persons at work, for controlling the keeping and use and preventing the unlawful acquisition, possession and use of dangerous substances, and for controlling certain emissions into the atmosphere; to make further provisions with respect to the employment medical advisory service; *to amend the law relating to building regulations, and the Building (Scotland) Act 1959: and for connected purposes....*

The Act conformed with the principles of an enabling measure by granting to the Secretary of State the power to make health and safety regulations as described in Part I for its main purpose, and laid the duty for their enforcement on a new body corporate which the Act also created, known as The Health and Safety Executive *and also on local authorities* "to such extent as may be prescribed". But it made no fundamental change in regard to the enforcement of the building regulations, leaving the clauses 4(1) and (3) of Part II of the Act of 1961 unchanged in stipulating, among other things, that it should be "the function of every local authority to enforce building regulations in their district". But it allowed for certain important changes to be made in regulations about the way authorities could go about their task of enforcement.

The new terms of reference for regulations

The most significant change in the Act of 1974 was the substitution of the clauses of the 1936 Act which described what matters could be covered by regulation, and how regulations could be applied to existing buildings, with entirely new sections; which applied also (in ways given in a schedule) to the more recent Building (Scotland) Act of 1959.

For the first time, the enabling Act gave in a full and coherent form the *purposes* for which regulations were to be made and what their *scope* should be, in a form that went as far as possible to meet the requirements of the construction industry whose techniques of design and construction had developed so far since the pre-war era of the original Public Health Act.

The new terms of reference gave the Secretary of State power to make regulations for "the design and construction of buildings and the provision of services, fittings and equipment", for the purposes of (to quote in full), "(a) securing the health, safety, welfare and convenience of persons in, or about buildings, and of others who may be affected by buildings or matters connected with buildings; (b) furthering the conservation of fuel and power; and (c) preventing waste, undue consumption, misuse or contamination of water". Furthermore, these regulations could be made with respect to alterations and extensions of buildings and their services, fittings and equipment; and to new services, fittings and equipment; to the whole or part of any building with its services, fittings and equpment where there was a material change of use; and in this connection the meanings of the terms "building" and the "construction or erection of a building" were defined.

As to the matters that regulations could cover, these were given in a comprehensive schedule entitled the "*Subject-matter of building regulations*", and dealt in full measure with what previously had become conspicuous by its absence. Regulations were now to cover

(1)   preparation of sites;

(2)   suitability, durability and use of materials and components (including surface finishes).

(3)   structural strength and stability, including—(a) precautions against overloading, impact and explosion; (b) measures to safeguard adjacent buildings and services, (c) underpinning.

(4)   fire precautions, including—(a) structural measures to resist the outbreak and spread of fire and to mitigate its effects; (b) services, fittings and equipment designed to mitigate the effects of fire or to facilitate fire-fighting; (c) means of escape in case of fire and means for securing that such means of escape can be safely and effectively used at all material times.

(5)   resistance to moisture and decay.

(6)   measures affecting the transmission of heat.

(7)   measures affecting the transmission of sound.

(8)   measures to prevent infestation.

(9)   measures affecting the emission of smoke, gases, fumes, grit, dust or other noxious or offensive substances.

(10)   drainage (including waste disposal units).

(11)   cesspools and other means for the reception, treatment and disposal of foul matter.

(12)   storage, treatment and removal of waste.

(13)   installations utilising solid fuel, oil, gas, electricity or any other fuel or power (including appliances, storage tanks, heat exchangers, ducts fans and other equipment.

(14)   water services (including wells and bore-holes for the supply of water), and fittings and fixed equipment associated therewith.

(15)   telecommunication services (including telephones and radio and television wiring installations).

(16)   lifts, escalators, hoists, conveyors and moving footways.

(17)   plant providing air under pressure.

(18)   standards of heating, artificial lighting, mechanical ventilation, and air-conditioning, and provision of power outlets.

(19)   open space about buildings and the natural lighting and ventilation of buildings.

(20)   accommodation for specific purposes in, or in connection with buildings, and the dimensions of rooms and other spaces within buildings.

(21)   means of access to and egress from buildings and parts of buildings.

(22)   prevention of danger and obstruction to persons in and about buildings (including passers-by).

(23)   matters connected with, or ancillary to any of the matters mentioned in the preceding provisions of this schedule.

Clearly, such a comprehensive list seemed to remove, finally, any obstacle from the path of reformers who wanted to see regulations take the form of comprehensive technical briefs. The way was clear, so far as the terms of reference went, for provisions being made in the pattern of design criteria of a more sophisticated kind than they had ever been, like the briefing guidance data for designers published by the BSI in the Codes of Practice.

Changes in enforcement

With regard to the activity of enforcement, the new Act introduced important administrative reforms with the aim of improving scope for efficiency. It gave authority for the regulations to prescribe materials and methods of construction as being "deemed-to-satisfy"; to make reference to or otherwise use separate documents or authorities for framing requirements; and to exempt prescribed classes of building services. It also allowed the regulations to authorize local authorities to accept certificates (as evidence of compliance) from persons "of any class or description" prescibed, or from anyone nominated by the Secretary of State; to permit the issue of certificates as evidence of compliance by the local authorities; to give sanction for the charging of fees by these authorities for the performance of their functions of enforcement; and to impose on building owners any continuing requirements as the Secreary of State may decide to be necessary.

Local authorities would also, under the Act, be permitted to pass plans by stages with or without conditions; or pass plans provisionally subject to modification; or to require tests to be carried out to check compliance (or to do the tests themselves).

The Secretary of State was given power to exempt any building or type of building from all or any of the regulations; to relax any requirement of the regulations in relation to any type of building matter, with or without conditions; to approve any *type* of building (either in general or in any particular case) as being in compliance with any requirement; or to prescribe any material, component, type of service or fitting as unsuitable for use in permanent buildings. Also, in dealing with appeals to him made under Section 64 of the 1936 Act and Section 7 of the 1961 Act, he could appoint another person to hear the case put by the appellant and the local authority before giving his decision, against which the appellant or the local authority could appeal to the High Court on a point of law.

On more general issues, the new Act stated that those sections of the Acts of 1936 and 1961 which provided the power to make regulations should apply throughout Inner London; affirmed that building regulations should also apply to Crown buildings and buildings of the United Kingdom Atomic Energy Authority; and, in regard to civil liability, pointed out that a breach of a duty imposed by the regulations would be actionable if it caused damage.

At the conclusion of Part III dealing with building regulations, the Act laid down that all of the provisions of the Public Health Acts of 1936 and 1961 that related to building regulations, together with those in the new Act itself (i.e. in Part III), should be construed as one. In this way, the Act neatly identified the whole of the apparatus of the law relating to building regulations in the United Kingdom.

As a consequence of the new Act there were now provisions to enable most, if not all, of the reforms regarded as essential by the Advisory Committee and the professional Institutions to be carried out, given the will of the Secretary of State. Indeed, the elements of the control system, as shown in the following summary, were now in theory more like the kind of effective instrument of management needed for the control of a large modern industry.

The modified shape of the control system

Under the 1936 and 1961 provisions it was the task of the central government (in the person of a prescribed Secretary of State) to make regulations, and of the local authorities (as defined) to enforce them. Any person who intended to erect or alter a building, or carry out works in connection with it or change its use, had first to give notice or deposit plans with the relevant local authority, who was required to pass or reject them. If the operation of any requirement seemed unreasonable, either the person or the local authority could appeal to the Secretary of State.

The new Act: (a) *extended the scope* of the regulations to cover the provision of services, fittings, and equipment as well as the design and construction of buildings; (b) *defined the purposes* for which regulations could be made, that is to say: (i) to secure the health, safety, welfare, and convenience of persons; (ii) to further the conservation of fuel and power; and (iii) to prevent the waste or contamination of water; (c) extended the coverage to affect all buildings uniformally so that requirements in all parts of the UK could be brought into alignment; and (d) introduced administrative reforms to improve enforcement. These included allowing for (i) prescribed materials or methods of construction to be deemed satisfactory; (ii) reference to be made to separate documents in framing regulations; (iii) prescribed classes of buildings or services to be exempt; (iv) the passing of plans provisionally or by stages; (v) the carrying out of tests to check compliance; (vi) the acceptance of certificates from prescribed persons as evidence of compliance; (vii) the charging of fees; (viii) the exemption of buildings by the Secretary of State; (ix) the relaxing of requirements, and the approval of particular types of building by the Secretary of State; (x) the prescribing of materials or components deemed unsuitable for use in permanent buildings; (xi) the imposing on owners or occupiers such continuing requirements as the Secretary of State considered necessary; and (xii) the appointment of persons by the Secretary of State to hear appeals.

Such reforms, however, did no more than provide the opportunity for the effective changes to be made, but it was clear that these would not become manifest in practice until the Secretary of State had done what he was now empowered to do. In the view of the management sector of the construction industry the three most important steps to be taken, constituting major reforms, were still seen to be: (1) the replacement of all other Acts affecting building by the one new Act; (2) the replacement of the outmoded building regulations with one up-to-date instrument; and (3) the establishment of a high-quality enforcement service of equal capability throughout the land, which might include (as now permitted by the new provisions) for reliance to be placed on professional designers for the issue of certificates of compliance [see figure 9(a)].

Background activities

Shortly after the introduction of the Health and Safety at Work Act, the responsible Department of central government was seen to be active in minor ways in connection with these three aims. It had set up a small research study to explore the practicality of replacing all other Acts affecting building. It had collaborated with an equivalent Department in Scotland to investigate what form an updated set of regulations could best take, having regard for future harmonization with other control systems in the EEC; and it had asked the Local Government Training Board to investigate what qualifications were needed for building control inspectorates.

CONCURRENT REFORMING MOVEMENTS

But other events were taking place coincidentally that were affecting the control system in different and drastic ways in the sphere of local government. The reforms set in train by the Royal Commission on Local Government under the chairmanship of Lord Redcliff-Maude, which had been contained in a report of which a short version had been presented to Parliament in June 1969, were put into effect in a nationwide reorganization of local authorities at the end of 1974.

Through the same period, the growing pressures of public opinion about the importance of consumers' interests were apparently having an effect in the separate province of the Courts of Law. In these precincts the decisions in court by learned judges were changing the legal aspects of building control in ways that were to have profound repercussions on the liabilities of enforcing authorities and professional designers.

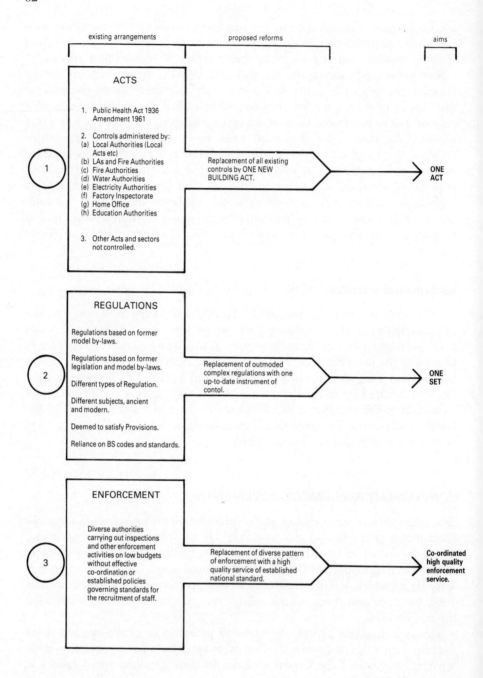

Figure 9a Major aims for the reform of the building control system in the UK in the early seventies

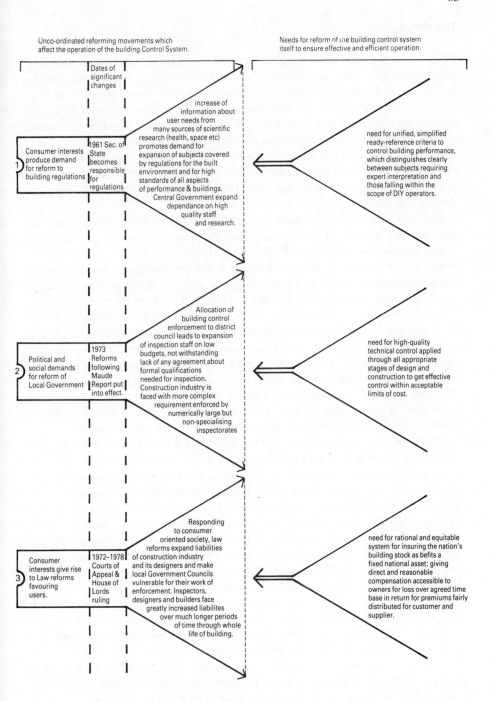

Figure 9b Three reforming movements and their effect on building control

The three aims

These three separate reforming movements, namely to update the building regulations, to change the structure of local government, and to modify the law by court decisions to protect consumers' interests, were together to have an effect on the affairs of building control, bringing about a new and unforeseen condition of crisis. Such self-inflicted injuries, borne out of good intentions, deserve more particular mention [see figure 9(b)].

We have seen how the idea of *reforming the regulations* themselves had been a preoccupation of the client–authority and the construction industry since the growth of building programmes after the war. Other reforming ideas were also having effect.

The *changes in local government* had been designed to deal with the faults of the previous pattern of 79 county boroughs and 45 counties (for England alone) which had tended to divide urban from rural affairs, producing an administrative structure which no longer fitted the modern social, economic, and technological scene, and preventing the efficient development of public services. It had been claimed that this had reduced the faith of local communities in their ability to control local affairs, and weakened relationships between local and central government. The solution was to replace the existing local authorities of various shapes and sizes and numbering some twelve hundred with a new basically two-tiered structure of regional authorities and local district councils. The responsibilities for local government services would be allocated so that those concerned with the strategy of economic planning and social development would go to the larger authorities while the district councils would deal with the "nuts and bolts" of local public services.

Unfortunately, and much against the wishes of the professional institutions of the construction industry, when the changes were put into effect in 1974 the responsibility for the enforcement of building regulations was allocated to the district councils, being the smaller authorities making up the lower tier. During the second half of that decade, then, these councils began recruitment to deal with their duties of inspecting plans and buildings, but in doing so were bound to comparatively small budgets by their financial limitations. At the time there were no statutory requirements for any special qualifications being necessary for these staff appointments, and the central government had only just begun to investigate what the qualifications for a building inspectorate staff should be through the means of the Local Government Training Board. The cut-back in the national spending on building programmes meant that the construction industry was shedding its less permanent employees, and as a consequence the new inspectorates were created during the latter half of the decade on insufficient budgets. The consequential lack of quality for these key organizations was directly contrary to what had been advocated by all those who had been seeking to improve the system of building control.

Meanwhile *changes* had begun to develop *in the law* which, during a period between 1972 and 1978, were to have a drastic effect on the system, and especially on how local authorities dealt with their responsibilities. The changes began with the case of *Dutton v. Bognor Regis UDC* which enabled the owners of buildings to take action against enforcement authorities to recover damages when a building which had contravened the regulations had nonetheless been built and had proved faulty. In 1974 the Defective Premises Act came into force, placing some special duties on anyone involved in the provision of a dwelling; and in the same year the Health and Safety at Work Act set out that any breach of a duty which had been imposed by building regulations would be actionable if it caused damage. That Act also, in Section 6, placed a duty on anyone who designs articles for use in a place of work to ensure that it is "so designed and constructed as to be safe and without risks to health when properly used". This implied that a designer responsible for a piece of equipment like a heating system, which proved to be dangerous, had contravened the law and could suffer the imposition of criminal sanctions as well as being sued for damages by anyone who had been injured as a result of a breach of statutory duty. Since the same Act had included the provision of services, fittings, and equipment in buildings as a subject about which regulations could be made, such legal changes were of profound significance.

In 1975 and 1976 actions in the Court of Appeal included the judgement in the *Sparham-Souter and Country Developments* case in which Lord Denning suggested that the limitation period for action for damages should start from the time of the discovery of the damage; and in 1977 the decision of the House of Lords in the *Anns v. London Borough of Merton* case brought about the fundamental change in the responsibilities of local authorities in relation to building regulations. It is established that although a local authority does not *need* to carry out an inspection of a building for the purpose of regulation approval, *if it does so* and approves it and the building is later found to be defective, causing damages, it is liable for negligence; and the cause of action would arise when (in Lord Wilberforce's words) "there is present or imminent danger to the health and safety of persons occupying it",

Previously, where there was a cause to sue, the period when the building owner could sue had been confined by the Limitations Act 1939 to a period of six years beginning when the building itself had been accepted, and such action was possible only when there had been a contract between the parties, as between a client and his professional adviser, or between a purchaser and a builder. After the *Anns and London Borough of Merton* case many others followed until in 1980 a new Limitation Act made the period of six years begin from the date "on which the cause of action accrued", so that local authorities could become liable for this period starting from the appearance of a defect, which in practice would make them liable for the lifetime of a building. For public bodies who had previously been considered immune from any such actions when carrying out their "duty of care", if only by virtue of the absence of any formal contract with a member of the public involved, this was a new, stern discipline, which could hardly have come at a worse time.

Until these legal changes, local authorities had been accustomed to dealing with regulation enforcement within reasonably low-key budgets. These local councils had been well acquainted with the contents and criteria of regulations because until 1961 they had been responsible for making their own by-laws; and since that date they had been enforcing national regulations whose texts were based largely on the same models. Their duties, too, had been discretionary. They had needed to take reasonable care to see that laws were generally complied with, and their *statutory* obligation had been only to approve or reject plans. They needed to see that adequate resources were deployed to this end, but the amount of inspection had been a matter for their judgement. If mistakes were made the authorities had traditionally been able to resist any claims for compensation from aggrieved individuals, because a remedy by action in the civil courts existed only if the damage suffered had resulted from a breach of contract, and as the statutory duties did not involve contracts with individual owners of buildings, authorities had felt themselves to be protected from actions concerned with private interests. Now everything had changed in that respect, and the changes would affect both the policy and execution of enforcement.

The question of what might be construed as negligence would clearly affect the judgement of how much an authority's resources should reasonably be devoted to inspection for enforcement, and what might be regarded as an appropriate level of qualifications for the inspectors. With regulations being changed to bring in new requirements for services, environmental conditions, fire precautions, and modern concepts of structural safety, the difficulties mounted. The days of brief consultations and the prompt approval of plans were gone, as the local authorities, newly created to their particular role in the changed hierarchy, began to take precautions against possible accusations of negligence and an infinite possibility of future actions. The process of enforcement became painstakingly careful, and in the eyes of the applicants slow and expensive for all concerned.

Their general effect

It is strange that these reforms should have been coming to fruition at the time when the efforts to improve the system of building control seemed to have achieved their culmination in the new Enabling Act of 1974, and that this total effect should have been so frustrating for the reformers. The aim of the legislators in transferring the responsibility for making regulations from the local authorities to a Minister of central government in 1961 had been to unify and simplify. The first set of national Building Regulations had been issued in 1965, but these had not introduced many new provisions, beyond requirements for fire safety and sound insulation. Later in that decade the work in central government became preoccupied with amendments resulting from the Ronan Point disaster and the need to convert all of the regulating criteria to metric values. None the less, the result of the transferance of these tasks to a Department of central government, and of depending upon the same Department for the general administration of building control, had been very different from that now affecting the local government departments after their reorganization. The central government Department had been able to create a staff of highly qualified professional advisers, and to rely upon consultations with the newly constituted Advisory Committee and with other representatives of industrial management.

Their interest in establishing modern regulations in the form of sophisticated design criteria was reflected in the innovations of the 1974 Act itself, which was intended to provide the terms of reference for the new provisions. All this was taking place against a background of considerable technical change in the construction industry. Computer technology was affecting structural design, and the codes of practice for structural design and for dealing with wind loading and "progressive collapse" were being rewritten by specialists. Experts on such subjects as energy conservation, thermal and sound insulation, and other aspects of environmental conditions were being informed by a growing body of research. Consequently, the regulations began to grow in size and complexity as new requirements were specified. No comprehensive revision of the form and content of the regulations had been possible, so that new requirements had to be grafted on the historic and outmoded framework. By 1976, when a new edition of the building regulations was laid before Parliament, the document had become a strange compendium of the old and the new. Requirements specifying the maximum U-value of walls, and the limits for the transmission of airborne sound were to be found along with others for the ventilation of larders "for the storage of perishable foods", and the provision of earth closets.

In short, the seventies witnessed the confluence of different currents of reform which soon produced a turbulence which defied the skill of all pilots.

In central government, the highly trained theorists were bent on producing complex, modern building regulations, based on scientific information about the performance of materials and the needs of people. In local government the newly formed inspectorates were recruiting large numbers of comparatively unqualified artisans whose task was to ensure that the requirements were met in practice. As though this mis-match was not enough, in the interests of the consumer the development of the law was towards broader and stricter liability for those involved in designing, constructing, and inspecting buildings and their equipment, making an "unduly heavy burden" (Law Reform Committee) of the duty of care.

Voices of protest

Awareness of this problem soon became evident. At professional meetings, lectures, symposia, and conferences throughout the latter half of the seventies the topics were increasingly preoccupied with the unsatisfactory state of building control, and the voices of protest were increasingly strident. In an RIBA talk-in in 1976 there was reference to the profession being "entangled by a complex and confusing mass of planning law and building regulations", and legislation being "a maze of confusion". At a regional meeting in East Anglia in 1977 a paper dealt with "Fighting your way through: the complexities of national regulations and the methods at present adopted for their enforcement", and later, at an annual conference of building surveyors, a paper humorously referred to "patron, designers and public in Twentieth Century Wonderland", drawing parallels between the inspector and Alice in her topsy-turvy world. By 1979 the RIBA had come to organize a seminar on the future of the Building Regulations, which brought together representatives of the central government's Department, the construction industry and its professions, clients, and enforcement authorities, to consider "the options available for simplification of the Building Regulations". There were opening addresses from the Minister and the chairman of the Building Regulations Advisory Committee.

The response of the law-makers

By the end of the decade, as though in response to this unrest, more positive action began to emerge from the central government. In December 1979 the Secretary of State for the Environment made a speech advocating a radical review of the whole system of building control. He established principles which he thought any new arrangements should be guided by, these being "maximum self-regulation; minimum Government interference; total self-financing, and simplicity in operation".

There was a wide response to these suggestions, and the Department of the Environment outlined some specific possibilities for change in a Consultation Document issued in June 1980. These included some familiar proposals, like the recasting of the regulations in the form of functional requirements; the "certification" of plans and construction by prescribed persons; the exemption of public bodies from formal control; and other less familiar but equally welcome proposals such as: a review of the law concerning latent damage and liability; the local adjudication of appeals; and a wider exemption for minor works and certain industrial buildings. When the Document was circulated it received over five hundred submissions of comment from the construction industry and its professions, and from local authorities, thereby demonstrating a wide measure of general agreement.

The climax to this activity came in the form of a Command Paper on *The Future of Building Regulations in England and Wales*. It was presented to Parliament in February 1981 by the Secretary of State for the Environment and the Secretary of State for Wales, and set out "firm and detailed proposals" in answer to the "persistent criticisms" that the building control system had become more "cumbersome and bureaucratic than it need be". The firm proposals concerned a revised form of regulations, exemptions and simplifications for dealing with minor works, exemptions for public bodies, and new arrangements for appeals. The Paper also described a certification scheme for greater self-regulation by the industry and the building professions, calling for views on these proposals in relation particularly to the certified works, the selection of certifiers, and the definition of their responsibilities. In relation to these the Paper pointed out the need for certifiers to have adequate indemnity insurance, which might mean that a new type of cover would have to be devised. It asked for the views of the insurance industry on how this might be done.

On the vexed question of liability, the Consultation Document commented that the legal issues went wider than building control and consequently the Lord Chancellor had referred the question of latent damage and negligence to the Law Reform Committee under the chairmanship of Lord Scarman.

Designers and builders had claimed that the present state of the law had caused over-caution and unnecessary costs and delays affecting the industry and the consumer, and a general view had been expressed that the open-ended liability had imposed undue burdens. Consequently, the Law Reform Committee had been asked "to consider the law relating to (i) the accrual of the cause for action; and (ii) limitation in negligence cases involving latent defects (other than latent disease or injury to the person), and to make recommendations".

The Paper concluded by re-affirming the Government's belief that the system of building control would be improved by the changes it proposed. The regulations would have more clarity, the procedures of local authorities more simplicity, and the construction industry would have more freedom for self-regulation. All this would save money without reducing the existing standards of safety. Consequently, the Government proposed to get ahead with the changes, some of which could be put in hand without new statutes, though others would require legislation.

This, then, was where matters affecting building legislation stood in the United Kingdom at the turn of the decade bringing in the 1980s. That this account should break off at this time is of no essential importance. The description has shown that the building control system is in a continuing state of evolution. Changes affect it constantly; though perhaps unlike a living organism which it might resemble it does not always maintain a condition of balance. Even when the structure of the system might enjoy a period of stability, the interpretation of its rules adapts to the state of development of the society it protects: what is meant by "health" and "safety" and what aspects of them have priority, are at all times a reflection of public opinion.

THE ESSENTIAL PRINCIPLES OF THE UK SYSTEM

Though this story of change may seem unending, the essential nature of the control system itself remained intact. This can now be described more specifically, while reviewing the underlying principles (see figure 10).

The public and its legislation

It has been shown that in the UK there is a long-standing belief that some control of building is necessary, and that the construction of buildings needs to be regulated in the public interest. Traditionally the objective of such control has been to secure the health and safety of persons; though more recently other secondary purposes have been added dealing with the welfare and convenience

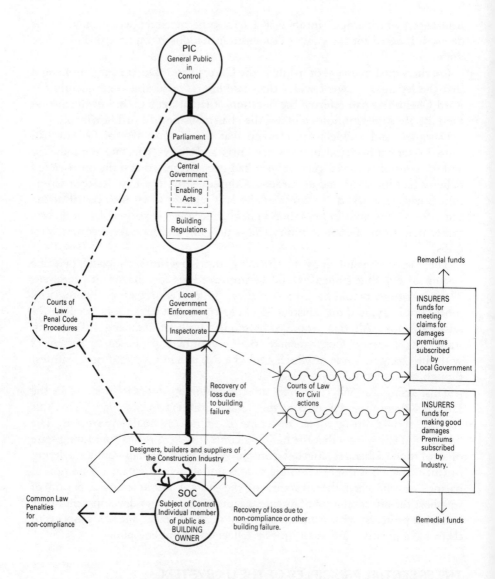

Figure 10 Synoptic diagram of building control

of people affected by buildings, and with the conservation of the national resources of energy and water. Although building is carried out by private transactions between owners (or clients) and builders, the imposing of constraints is held to be justified by this need to protect the interest of the community as "third party". This is done by placing reliance on the penal code.

The contraints take the form of laws created for the public by Parliament. These are made as *primary legislation*, consisting of statute law, and *subordinate legislation*, in the form of building regulations. The two levels may be regarded as "positive" and "negative" forms of law-making. That is to say, the *enabling Acts* are *positive decisions* of Parliament, taken after the due process of debate in both Houses. They give power to a representative of the central government to make regulations, and define their scope and the purposes for which they are to be made. They also place the responsibility for the enforcement of regulations on local authorities, describing what this implies and laying down the sanctions that may be imposed for non-compliance. Such *building regulations* are made by the delegated Secretary of State in the form of statutory instruments, by a process of *negative resolution*. They are laid before Parliament (while it is in session) for a period of forty days, and become law if they are not annulled by either House during that period.

The Enabling Act of 1961 describes this process precisely in Part II, Section 4 (7) with the words: "The power of making regulations shall be exercisable by statutory instrument which shall be subject to amendment in pursuance of a resolution of either House of Parliament".

Of course, other Acts made for different purposes also have an effect on buildings. Indeed, the wide range of legislation that affects the design and construction of buildings is catalogued in a guide which was prepared by the Departments of the Secretaries of State for the Environment and for Wales and published in 1973, entitled: *Design and Construction of Buildings—Guide to Statutory Provisions* [CI/SFB (A3j)]. But the existence of these provisions is extraneous to the central apparatus of control, and it is generally acknowledged that efficiency and economy would be better served if all were consolidated.

The central system of control consists of primary and subordinate forms of legislation which together provide a form of constraint that in *legal* terms is theoretically well-suited to its purpose. The "positive" type of statute law is not easily made. It needs a wide measure of public support, and must take its place among other measures that compete for priority in a government's parliamentary programme. It is appropriate then that the enabling Acts, made in this way, deal with firmly established principles. Their enactment is a ponderous process and their modification or amendement tends to be needed only after comparatively long periods of time. On the other hand, the subordinate legislation, which is used for making building regulations, can be made more economically in terms of parliamentary time. The Secretary of State adopts a procedure for preparing regulations which entails having the draft proposals considered by the Building Regulation Advisory Committee and then circulated for comment to interested bodies (representing the interests of the industry, professional institutions, trade, local and central government departments, and agencies who may be affected) before the final version is drawn up and laid before Parliament. This can be a lengthy procedure, but its progress can be controlled and urgency can be given when necessary. The regulations are made as technical design criteria which can be affected often by the emergence of new information or the adoption of new techniques or standards, so it is appropriate that they should be readily changeable. Alterations to them are made by the same process, amendments taking the same form of statutory instruments which are laid before Parliament.

The role of the Secretary of State

The Secretary of State, then, has the task of producing the building regulations which apply nationally, and for this purpose takes advice on legal and technical matters. He maintains information about industrial development from research establishments, and also the occurrence of accidents affecting people in buildings, or other difficulties that might cause hazards to health and safety or affect the application of the regulations in practice. He is empowered to make decisions about problems arising from the regulations in certain particular cases, by virtue of the provisions in the Acts. That is to say, he can (under Section 67 of the PHA 1936), when a joint application is made to him by an applicant and a local authority, determine what regulations should apply, whether plans are in conformity with them, and whether the work carried out accords with the plans. Under Section 6 of the 1961 Act he is able to delegate to local authorities the power to dispense with or relax regulations in particular cases when applications are made, and to reserve to himself such powers in special cases; and under Section 7 of the same Act he can deal with appeals from persons who have had an application for relaxation refused by a local authority.

These responsibilities cause references to be made to the central government department which can produce information day by day on how the building regulations are working in practice. As a consequence, the department becomes a co-ordinator of information and experience on the practical application of regulations, and is able to supply advice to local authorities in the form of letters, memoranda, and published circulars. These are issued for guidance and are authoritative, but are not enforceable in law.

Although the Secretary of State is able to make regulations, once they have been laid before Parliament and come into operation as statutory instruments they have become part of the body of the law, and any problem of meaning or interpretation can only be resolved in the courts of law. Section 64 of the 1936 Act, which provides for local authorities passing or rejecting plans, states that "any question arising under this section between a local authority and the person by whom or on whose behalf plans are deposited as to whether the plans are defective, or whether the proposed work would contravene any of the by-laws, may on the application of that person, be determined by a court of summary jurisdiction".

As a consequence, any statement about the meaning of a regulation by the department of central government, or the local authority, or the owner of the building, has no more validity than an expression of opinion in respect of the law. The courts alone have authority to interpret the law, and their decision, once made, itself becomes embodied in the legislation as case law.

This problem of interpretation has an important effect on the composition of the regulations, as will be seen below. The aim of the legal style of writing is to avoid ambiguities, and this often leads to a cumbersome mode of expression and a complexity of language that is unfamiliar to all except those familiar with the law. The system also leads to a reluctance on the part of the officials in the departments of central and local government to express an opinion about the interpretation of a regulation, in case a subsequent court ruling might show them to have been wrong and expose them to action for damages. The position is different where (as in Central London) the inspectors are themselves referred to in the regulations. The requirement that the work must be carried out "to the satisfaction of the District Surveyor" gives the opinion of that person as inspector the authority of the law itself.

Of course, other institutions with governmental backing (in the form of financial rather than legal support) provide information for advisory purposes. Foremost among these in relation to the control of building is the British Standards Institution. This body has the aim of promoting standardization in British industry. So far as the construction industry is concerned, it seeks to do this by issuing Codes of Practice and Standard Specifications. The codes are prepared by committees consisting of professional advisers and describe what is regarded as a good standard of practice in design and construction. The specifications are produced by committees drawn from the professional, industrial, and commercial communities and prescribe materials and components in common use. These documents have no legal aspirations, but can be referred to in the regulations when the standards of quality or performance which they recommend are suited to the purpose of the legislation. In this way, documents not designed for legal purposes are incorporated into the statutory instruments as supportive statements of acceptable practice.

The building owner

These laws which control building are applied essentially to building owners; or, as the building regulations themselves specify, to "any person who intends to erect any building, or make any structural alteration of or extension to a building; or execute any works or install any fitting in connection with a building; or make any material changes of use of a building...". That person is required by the regulations to give notice of such intention, and to submit plans, sections, specifications, and written particulars to the local authority responsible for enforcement. The regulations continue with the requirement that such person, or the "builder", must give not less than 24 hours' notice of the start of the operations and of the covering up of foundations or drains, and at least 7 days' notice after the laying of a drain has been carried out, or after the erection of a building has been completed. This is intended to give the local authority an opportunity to inspect the work, though the law does not direct that it must do so.

If any work is found to contravene any regulation, the local authority has the power to "require the *owner* either to pull down or remove the work" or alter it to make it comply (PHA 1936,S. 65). In the 1974 Act this power was extended to enable the authority to serve the notice requiring this to be done on the occupier, builder, or anyone appearing to have control of the work, in addition to or instead of the owner.

Nevertheless, it.is this implication that the owner will be required to remove defective work that is at the core of the control. It is for the owner to obey the law, and consequently to see that anyone carrying out the work does likewise. The building must comply with the regulations, whether it is inspected or not; and even if it has been inspected and approved, and is still found to be faulty, the same penalty applies. Of course, if an authority has had an inspection made and approved a building which later proves to be in contravention of a regulation, it may be liable for damages, but it is for the owner to take action in the civil courts to seek that remedy.

In the light of this liability under the common law to comply with regulations, the owner needs to have appropriate contracts with designers or builders, or both, which clarify his reliance upon them to ensure that there are no contraventions. These private contracts can be drawn up in a way that makes the specialists liable for actions for the recovery of damages due to negligence, so that the placing of reliance upon them in this way will enable the owner to recoup his losses if he suffers penalties for breaking the common law.

In effect, then, the *owner* must obey the laws of building control, so a wise owner will safeguard his interests by having contracts with the technical experts to ensure that he can take his own action to recover damages if he is found not to have complied. As to the question of who decides whether he has contravened, this is for a magistrate in a court of common jurisdiction to do. Others may inspect, but their decision in relation to the law is an opinion which can be challenged. Thus, if an owner is sure that his building complies, there is nothing in law to prevent him (after submitting plans and giving notices appropriately) from completing the work, unless there is a regulation requiring that the work must be to the satisfaction of the local authority's inspector. In the absence of *that* stipulation, the onus would be upon the enforcing authority to prove to a magistrate presiding in court that there had been a contravention.

The designers and builders indemnify themselves against actions for damages by insurance, so that the ultimate cost of a contravention may be borne by the insurers, though it may also be reasonable to say that the financial burden is borne by the designers and builders as a community through the level of their insurance premiums upon which the insurance industry depends.

Responsibilities

Thus, reduced to the most basic terms, the ultimate responsibility in respect of the common law controlling building lies with the *building owner*. The owner is the one who might have to remove the building, or be fined. And, depending upon the arrangements made by the owner, it is the insurer who takes the final responsibility in respect of the cost. The public, as "third party", has always been protected by the law functioning as a deterrent against malpractice giving rise to dangerous buildings. In 1983 there is added protection from the new consumer-oriented legislation arising from case-law which enables action to be taken against a local authority for negligent inspection to recover damages due to a defective building. Indeed, if any member of the public becomes an owner of a building which proves to be defective, action can be taken against all who might have been concerned with its design, building, or inspection.

The local authorities have traditionally been responsible for enforcement and have discharged this as a statutory duty. Their powers have been discretionary. They had a statutory obligation to pass or reject all the plans of any proposed work submitted to them, though they were able to grant relaxations. They could also carry out inspections of the work, though this was not obligatory, and the regulations to this end required that they should be notified when foundations and drains were about to be laid or covered up, in case they wished to check compliance. Their task of enforcement implied that they should take reasonable care to see that the laws were generally complied with. They had discretion to decide what proportion of their resources would be expended on enforcement, and how it would be done within the requirements of the Acts. They had to see that the resources were equal to the task of dealing with plans because it was a duty imposed by statute, but the amount of inspection was a matter for judgement. In theory, this function in this respect was similar to other aspects of their law enforcement, namely that of general surveillance to encourage the public to be law-abiding and to deter potential offenders, rather than that of apprehending every transgressor. Before 1972, when a process of legal change began, they were regarded as having these discretionary powers for the general protection of the public. They were not thought to be liable to actions for damage in the event of a building failure because they had no contractual duty to any particular individual. Even where a contractual duty did exist between individuals, as between a client and a builder, the Limitations Act of 1939 precluded any action after a period of six years from the time when the cause of action accrued, and this made action even less likely ever to affect a local authority's building inspectorate. After 1972 the changes made these authorities more at risk to such actions. It became acknowledged in law that the enforcement authorities owed a duty of care to individual building owners, and were liable to actions by such individuals to recover loss. Furthermore, the damages recoverable were not confined to physical loss alone. It was also established that the limitation period should begin from the time when any damage from defective work became manifest, an innovation that made local authorities virtually at risk throughout the complete life of any building that had been inspected.

Of course, these modifications of the law, while strengthening the position of an individual as "consumer" or building owner, did not change the basic function of the local authorities in regard to the system of building control. It remains for them to enforce building regulations in their district. But the policy and execution of enforcement were affected radically. The questions of what might constitute negligence became ominous in the minds of these responsible for enforcement: How much should an authority spend on inspection? Which buildings should it inspect? Who should carry out the inspection? What qualifications are adequate? What records should be kept against the possibility of future actions? It is not simply that the authorities can be faced with the prospect of actions against them at some time in the future by the owner of a building, but that any member of the public who has relied upon the inspecting authority for protection may have cause. As a consequence, and also because in addition the regulations are drawn up in respect of new dangers and different standards, the process of enforcement has become more cumbersome, more expensive, and more affected by delays.

Summary and conclusions

The building control system in the UK, then, is operated by living communities and, being subject to change and development, is more like a living organism than a static structure. Yet its character remains constant enough to have significance as an archetype or model. It protects the public against identified hazards by means of community-enacted laws which place restraints on individuals when they act in the role of building owners (see figure 10 above).

The restraints are enforced through the penal code by public bodies, who in turn owe a duty of care to individual members of the public, who have their own remedies in civil law if their interests are adversely affected. The traditional priorities are reflected in this hierarchy of control: the public's interest in the need for safeguards is important enough to make the person who does not comply with the protecting statutes guilty of a criminal offence; while the private interests are acknowledged by the individual's right to take action in the civil courts if given cause for grievance by the community's actions.

This description, which is intended to simplify the definition of the system to its basic principles, is also fitting for the form of control used in London, notwithstanding that more emphasis is placed on the quality and power of the inspectorate. Ultimately, even these differences may disappear as the methods in use are merged in the efforts to achieve a more uniform method of control built on the experience gained from long practice.

Regulations

THE ROLE OF REGULATIONS

The central feature of any building control system is the statement of the public's requirements in the form of building regulations. In the UK, where regulations are statutory instruments, their definition must be stated without ambiguity, in order to facilitate their interpretation in courts of law. Such instruments of administration must be designed to suit their purpose aptly, like all other artifacts which have been created to serve particular ends. To fashion them well so that they function precisely and economically is a task of daunting sophistication requiring great skill. The knowledge needed must rest on experience of legal, administrative, and technological affairs, plus an acquaintanceship with consumer requirements and the problems of designing and constructing buildings with due regard to convenience and cost.

Yet, surprisingly, there have been few aids to the creation of satisfactory regulations. Existing requirements seem to have had their origin in the bureaucratic commandments which, once written down or encoded in legal documents, have grown by accretion. Modes of expression which had their origin in the nineteenth century remain in use in modern times. Not only the style of writing, but the typography and format of the statutes are governed by the traditions of legal practice. Yet in theory the rules that enable regulations to be well-designed for their purpose are readily identified.

The first steps in recent times to review the techniques employed in making effective regulations were taken after the passing of the Public Health Amendment Act in 1961, which transferred the responsibility for making regulations to a Minister of the central government, so that a department of its administration was faced with the task of replacing the numerous local by-laws with a single set of national building regulations.

The act required the Minister to appoint a committee to advise him, and the Building Regulations Advisory Committee, which was appointed a year later, broached the question in their first Report to Parliament in 1964, as already mentioned, a year before the first edition of the new Regulations appeared. In discussing the techniques of regulation the Report began with the truism that "the objective of any form of building control is a finished building which conforms to the rules", and went on to make the general statement that "the form of regulations used should be tailored to the circumstances - the state of design practice, the level of technology, the complexity of the requirements, the quality of administration, and (wherever this can be of consistent with the enabling powers) the economic importance of preserving feasibility or an incentive to new methods".

The Report identified three legislatory techniques which then existed for the purpose of giving force to the mandatory requirements. It named these as the *specific requirement*, the *functional requirement*, and the *performance standard*. All were then in use, and remain so almost 20 years later, giving point to the Report's opinion that there would be "room for a long time for all the variants, and combinations of them...". These three types of regulation have a chronological sequence from the "specific", which is the earliest and most traditional and most readily enforced, because it relies mainly on visual inspection; to the "performance standard", which is later and more difficult, because any checks of compliance rely upon more scientific methods of testing.

THE BASIC RULES FOR THE DESIGN OF EFFICIENT REGULATIONS

Such techniques must themselves be judged according to their ability to fulfil the basic rules governing the design of effective regulations. These rules depend upon the nature of the constraint to be used in making the control system work, and also upon the type of enforcement to be employed (see figure 11). For the type of control used in the UK, where regulations are an integral part of the penal code relying on the courts of law, and are enforced by

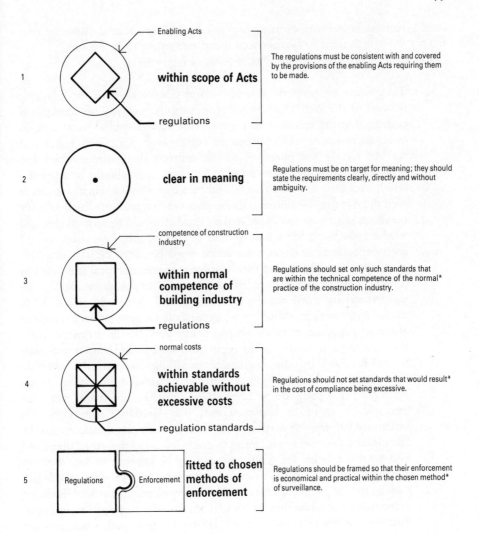

Enabling Acts

1 **within scope of Acts**

regulations

The regulations must be consistent with and covered by the provisions of the enabling Acts requiring them to be made.

2 **clear in meaning**

Regulations must be on target for meaning; they should state the requirements clearly, directly and without ambiguity.

competence of construction industry

3 **within normal competence of building industry**

regulations

Regulations should set only such standards that are within the technical competence of the normal* practice of the construction industry.

normal costs

4 **within standards achievable without excessive costs**

regulation standards

Regulations should not set standards that would result* in the cost of compliance being excessive.

Regulations Enforcement **fitted to chosen methods of enforcement**

5

Regulations should be framed so that their enforcement is economical and practical within the chosen method* of surveillance.

*This assumes that the regulations are kept abreast of the hazards to safety and excludes the situation that might arise if they are not and an unpredicted disaster occurs which makes drastically new measures unavoidable.

Figure 11 Basic rules for designing regulations

local government authorities using some form of inspectorate, there are five main rules which need to be followed if difficulties are to be avoided.

Regulations need to comply with the following criteria.

(1) They must be properly related to and consistent with the enabling powers of the Act which requires them to be made. This implies, of course, that the enabling Act itself must be well-suited to its task in order to promote well-constructed regulations. An effective Act will set out clearly the purposes of the control, the matters which the regulating Authority is to provide for, how they should be administered, and how the constraints and penalties should work. However well the Act may be suited to its purpose, any regulation which calls for measures which are not mandated by the Act would be unworkable and would soon bring the whole system of control into disrepute.

(2) Every requirement of the regulations must be stated clearly, directly, and without ambiguity, so that its meaning is unequivocal and never in doubt. This clarity is needed because the requirement has to be understood by those who must comply and those who must check compliance, so there should be no grounds for argument between them about its meaning. In cases where a controversy results in court action the meaning and validity of the regulation are among the first questions to be resolved by the magistrate presiding. Indeed, the ultimate interpretation of a regulation can only be obtained in the courts. It can be argued that there are refinements or subtleties about this rule. For example, a word in common use, like "building", may be left undefined in the regulations, so that its current meaning can be identified whenever a case comes to court featuring the use of that word, and by this process the requirements may be kept up to date without the regulation itself being amended. Similarly, the use of the words like "adequate" or "suitable" may enable the regulations to reflect changing standards of acceptability by similar means of interpretation in court. But for the practical purposes of day-to-day use, such vagueness can cause serious dispute between the controller and those who are controlled, resulting in expensive delays. As the financial penalties for non-compliance are constantly rising in modern practice, it is becoming more and more important that requirements as stated are not obscure. This principle of clarity, then, remains as a primary rule ·for the practical success of the regulation, notwithstanding the niceties of legal theory.

(3) All requirements should be within the technical competence of the construction industry to provide through the means of normal practice. That is to say that the standards of safety and the level of protection from hazards to health must be set with due regard for the condition of design practice and the state of the technology of building production. This implies that an authority responsible for making regulations should have not only a means of assessing the dangers against which the public needs safeguarding, but also an ability to judge accurately what

the industry can do. Of course, *safety must be achieved* and the regulations must set standards that are acceptable as well as reasonable. These must obviously be attainable in all of the buildings (which are the nation's fixed asset) to which they are applied. In judging what is technically possible, the law-makers must remember that it is not the objective of building control to promote technological development, but rather to state requirements in a way that will not frustrate it. It should be possible for the industry to comply using different solutions, so that it has flexibility to use new methods of construction or new ranges of material where appropriate.

(4) Similarly, regulations should not normally set standards that would result in compliance only being possible at excessive cost. This principle is of particular importance when the penal code is used as the constraint. In *other instances*, for example in the case of an authority wishing to set standards of accommodation in terms of space per occupant for a particular kind of building, and withholding funds from those not complying as a means of enforcement, *it might be reasonable to ask for higher standards* than have been provided previously. But where statutory requirements are in use, implying that non-compliance would be a criminal offence, it is necessary that the standards set should be at the minimum level reconcilable with adequacy. This will not prevent higher standards being attained by good practice, but it will ensure that the quality of provision remains within the national means at any one time. Again this indicates that a regulating authority needs to be able to exercise well-informed judgement as to what is attainable within national budgetary limits in setting its legal standards. Of course, there may be times when disaster in a new form makes new precautions obligatory, and in such exceptional circumstances a high cost is unavoidable: but for normal times prudence is needed in establishing suitable levels of safety.

(5) All regulations should be framed in a way that makes enforcement practicable within the competence of the *chosen methods of surveillance*. There are a number of aspects to this rule that need to be recognized. First, the meaning of the regulations should be clear to everyone, so that those seeking to comply and those checking compliance have an equal understanding of what is being called for. Secondly, the *standard of safety* which is set should not be left to the judgement of any individual, since this would result in standards varying widely according to the number of persons involved and the nature of their prejudices. Reliance on personal judgement may be unavoidable in decisions about whether *compliance* has been attained, but if the criterion itself is a matter of personal judgement there are too many variables for most practical purposes. Thirdly, it should be possible for compliance with a regulation to be checked properly and in a practical and economical way. Unless extreme dangers call for exceptional measures, the requirements should be stated in a way that will not require expensive tests on inspection in every case, or result in the cost of

checking being seriously out of scale with the aim of the provision. Finally, it is desirable that the regulations should call only for those standards that can be embodied in the finished product through the use of design methods that have predictable results. That is to say, it would be impractical to set requirements whose attainment is beyond the range of predictable design techniques, because it would mean that it would not be possible to check for compliance until after the completion of a building. This would imply that every building would have to be modified or "tuned" to the requirement after completion, or even taken down and rebuilt until it met the standard. The best illustration of this principle is available by reference to the field of structural design. Where tested theories of structure exist and there are formulae for calculating the performance of materials used in certain combinations, it is possible for designers to predict with reasonable surety what standards of performance will be embodied in their completed construction. Until they are able to do this, any regulation that requires more knowledge than the existing experience provides to attain its end, would result in all attempts to comply being experimental. Of course such empirical methods are not compatible with the use of the penal code to ensure compliance.

THE THREE TECHNIQUES OF REGULATION

These general rules will be referred to again in the discussion of methods of enforcement and in the examination of how the system of building control relates to national standards and research activities. With regard to the practical problems of drafting regulations as statutory instruments, the three techniques of regulation referred to previously as having been identified by BRAC, are described below.

THE SPECIFIC REQUIREMENT

Description

The technique of the "specific requirement" has long been established as a traditional method of expressing what is wanted in regulations. As its name suggests, if *specifies* in direct terms what is needed or what is to be done, using the language of the specification writer that is so familiar to the construction industry (see figure 12). Historically, the earlier regulations, which were prepared as by-laws by local authorities, were composed almost exclusively in this form, and many examples remain in use in present editions of the national regulations, particularly in the parts dealing with traditional subjects, like rising damp and drainage. The style of such regulations is authoritarian. It is most commonly in use in the by-laws of the Greater London Council made under the London Building Acts, where the system of enforcement depends upon highly qualified individuals acting as inspectors, in a way that owes much to the practice of architects in carrying out the supervision of building

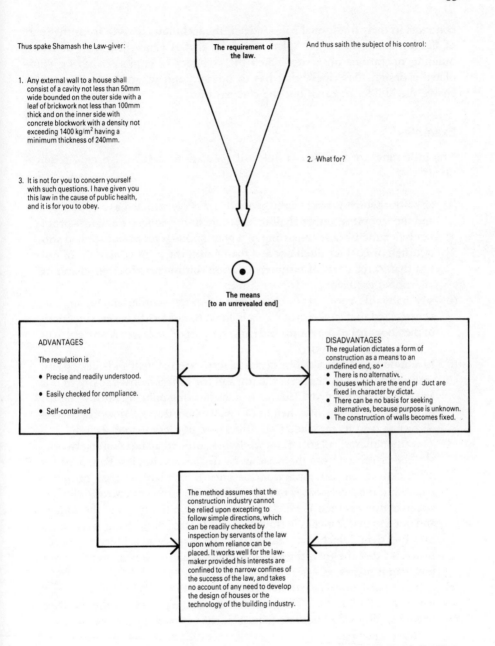

Thus spake Shamash the Law-giver:

1. Any external wall to a house shall consist of a cavity not less than 50mm wide bounded on the outer side with a leaf of brickwork not less than 100mm thick and on the inner side with concrete blockwork with a density not exceeding 1400 kg/m^2 having a minimum thickness of 240mm.

3. It is not for you to concern yourself with such questions. I have given you this law in the cause of public health, and it is for you to obey.

The requirement of the law.

And thus saith the subject of his control:

2. What for?

The means [to an unrevealed end]

ADVANTAGES

The regulation is

• Precise and readily understood.

• Easily checked for compliance.

• Self-contained

DISADVANTAGES
The regulation dictates a form of construction as a means to an undefined end, so
• There is no alternative.
• houses which are the end product are fixed in character by dictat.
• There can be no basis for seeking alternatives, because purpose is unknown.
• The construction of walls becomes fixed.

The method assumes that the construction industry cannot be relied upon excepting to follow simple directions, which can be readily checked by inspection by servants of the law upon whom reliance can be placed. It works well for the law-maker provided his interests are confined to the narrow confines of the success of the law, and takes no account of any need to develop the design of houses or the technology of the building industry.

Figure 12 The specific requirement

contracts in their traditional role. Indeed, the technique derives from that part of the normal professional "plan of work" that is concerned with directing building operations on a site, when the architect or engineer, having completed a design, describes what has to be used and what has to be done to enable the builder to carry out the construction.

Examples

The following are typical examples of regulations cast as "specific requirements".

(a) any floor which is next to the ground and is constructed as a solid floor and incorporates timber shall incorporate in the concrete a damp-proof sandwich membrane consisting of a continuous layer of hot applied soft bitumen or coal tar pitch not less than 3 mm thick, or consisting of not less than three coats of bitumen solution, bitumen/rubber emulsion or tar/rubber emulsion....

(b) any habitable room shall...have one or more ventilation opening so constructed that (i) their total area is equal to not less than one twentieth of the floor area of the room; and (ii) some part of such area is not less than 1.75 m above the floor.

(c) In a building of the warehouse class every external wall and every party wall shall have a thickness at the top and for 16 feet below the top of not less than 13 inches: provided that (i) a wall having only one storey height; or (ii) the top-most storey height of a wall where the wall does not exceed 30 feet in height; may be of any thickness not less than 8 inches....

(d) ...in any building, all structural steelwork, other than internal steelwork, shall be protected from the weather by (i) concrete not less than 3 inches in thickness, or (ii) brickwork, stone or similar material properly secured, if the steelwork is protected from the effects of corrosion by (a) concrete not less than 1½ inches in thickness on the edges of the flanges and not less than 2 inches in thickness on the faces of the flanges but in no case less than 1 inch over any projecting rivet-heads, bolts or splice-plates, so that the total thickness of encasement to the steelwork is not less than 4 inches.

(e) ...the constructional hearth shall (i) be not less than 5 inches thick in every part, (ii) extend not less than 6 inches beyond each side of the fireplace opening; (iii) extend not less than 20 inches in front of the jambs of the fireplace openings....

Advantages

It is a primary advantage of such specific requirements that the practical tasks of administration and compliance are not likely to cause difficulties. This type of regulation is expressed as a specification in a form which is in common use in the construction industry, so it is readily comprehensible to designer, builder, supplier and inspector alike. As a consequence it can be put into effect without undue trouble, and its application easily checked. Drawings that show the construction as detailed in the specification with proper descriptive notes can be "passed" as not showing any contravention of the law. On site, a straightforward inspection will confirm whether the construction complies with the specification. In *principle*, all regulations should be as clear, and as readily understood and enforced.

A further advantage is that regulations cast in this form are self-contained, and, therefore, convenient to use. No other references need be made, and if all the regulations are framed in the same way, then the instructions relating to the requirements of the law can be contained in one document.

Regulations of this kind were devised, however, when the construction industry was "craft-based" and when an isolated objective could be met by one standard and obvious solution. As long as the ranges of materials available were limited and the methods of construction were traditional, the rigidity of the technique could be accepted as reasonable. When the construction industry began to make use of new materials and evolve other ways of putting them together, the limitations of the method made it inappropriate and obsolescent.

Disadvantages

The disadvantages have been revealed through decades of practice, and are readily catalogued. A regulation in this form admits of no other solution in law to the problem it is dealing with, and industrial practice is forced to remain locked into a particular form of construction using the specified materials. Furthermore, the *aim* of the requirement is not expressed, so there is no justification *in law* for conjecture that it has any objective. The drawback here is that without a legally recognized aim, there are no valid grounds for seeking alternatives.

This is illustrated by the case of the first example requiring a damp-proof membrane in a solid floor. The specification does not tolerate anything else beyond the materials placed in the manner defined, so that it has the effect of frustrating the development of water-proofing technology or damp-resisting structure. Of course, this is to assume that its aim is the protection of a floor from rising damp, but in law such assumptions are irrelevant. Since the regulation does not explain that its purpose is to prevent moisture from the ground rising through the floor and becoming a hazard to the health of the occupants of the building and to the safety of the structure, the designers have no mandate to suggest other solutions, and the inspectors have no terms of reference for considering alternatives.

The practical way of dealing with the rigidity of specific requirements has been to allow "relaxations", or "waivers", in order to permit new solutions to be introduced. This can be done more conveniently in some cases than others, and a great deal depends upon the system of enforcement in operation. The original form of a specification in professional practice would allow the builder to adopt another material or method "equal and approved" *by the supervising architect or engineer* as the case may be, so that a decision to accept a change could be taken promptly. The enforcement system used in Central London places the District Surveyor in a similar position in relation to specific requirements in the by-laws by requiring the work to be done to his satisfaction, so that in theory it is possible to obtain an approval or a waiver more promptly, by direct reference to the responsible person. But when a great deal depends upon the view of one person, as it does in the operation of such a system, then disagreements can arise and soon cause deadlock and acrimony. In other parts of the UK, where the authority to enforce is vested in a Council, the decision to accept a change or an alternative solution is more difficult to obtain, and can take much longer. On the other hand, the decision, when reached, might seem more acceptable because it has followed from debate and arbitration. In either case, however, the process is cumbersome and can add to the time and cost of building. Since technical innovations have become commonplace in the construction industry, and since delay can produce disproportionate expense, the use of the specific requirement for regulatory purposes has become increasingly unacceptable.

Problems for the designers

The primary objectors to the method have been the designers in the industry; although in times of peak demand, when special steps were called for to achieve higher productivity, the whole industrial community became alienated. The designers' objections arose from their having the professional aim of producing buildings properly suited to their purpose. To this end it has always been necessary for them first to identify the purpose, then to design a solution, then to translate this concept into practical instructions so that the builder can achieve its embodiment in the finished product. Such instructions take the form of drawings and specifications; but if a legal specification *already lays down what must be done*, it can be seen as an obstacle to the sensible and integrated solution to the main problem; and *if the purpose of the legal prescription is not made clear*, it can be especially difficult to accept.

The kind of problem that can arise due to this absence of the stated reasons for specific requirements can be illustrated by reference to a part in the national building regulations issued in 1965 which dealt with "open space, ventilation, and the height of rooms". The opening section of this part dealt with the need for "open space outside windows of habitable rooms". It is required, in specific terms, that there should be "a minimum zone of open space outside the window such as to leave adjacent to the window an upright shaft of space wholly open to the sky...the base of the shaft being formed by a plane inclined upwards at an angle of 30° to the horizontal from the wall at the lower window level and its sides coinciding with...four vertical planes". These were further defined in the same manner; for example an "outer plane" parallel to the wall had to be "...at a distance from the wall of 3.6 m, or such distance as may be required by paragraph (7), or…one half the distance between the upper window level and the top of the wall containing the window, whichever is the greatest…"; and an "inner plane" coinciding with the external surface of the wall had to have, among other stipulations, "a width such that the product of that width and the window height equals one tenth of the floor area of the room containing the window…". Further paragraphs described the projections which were permitted in front of this inner plane, which included "any projection above the upper window level extending not more than 1.5 m horizontally in front of the inner plane", and qualified this with the provision that "if any projection…extends more than 600 mm in front of the inner plane, the minimum distance between the outer plane and inner plane…shall be increased by the amount in excess of 600 mm by which such projection extends horizontally in front of the inner plane…".

It seems likely that a provision of this kind may have been introduced originally during times when towns were overcrowded and conditions were made worse by back-to-back terraced housing, so that it was necessary to take steps to try to avoid dark and airless rooms, at a time when little was known about daylight factors or air-change rates. Once the basic provision, such as "a space open to the sky outside a window", had been introduced, it would be refined and added to by amendments based on experience of its application in practice. The extension of such a requirement can become a self-perpetuating process in the normal day-to-day administration of enforcement, arbitration, and appeal, until it acquires a rich-and-strange complexity.

Nevertheless, the specification of the space required outside a window contains nothing to confirm that its purpose is to provide light and air to the room behind the window, and no assumptions about this being its purpose can be admissible in law.

In later practice, when designers have acquired a great deal of knowledge about lighting and ventilation, and have the skills to provide for them in chosen degree, and equipment to measure the standards of their provision to prove their claims, they can be expected to argue that they can meet the real requirements without having to conform exactly with the arrangements as detailed in the regulations. Their point of view is countered by the legal argument of the administrators, namely that the law describes exactly the dimensions of a space, and if it has not been provided the law has not been met: to suggest something else may not be relevant and cannot be assumed to compensate for the discrepancy. Arguments of this kind might sometimes be resolved in unexpected ways, as for example when the designer may make the scheme acceptable to the enforcer by omitting a window altogether. Such an impasse can arise if both parties to the argument are unreasonable and take extreme views. The solution that they might adopt in such cases may be far from the intention of the Act that caused the regulation to be made, because in the argument over the letter of the law they might have been persuaded to neglect its spirit. The real fault lies in the regulation itself, which withholds the aim of the provision and so denies the designer the use of his own knowledge and skill.

The needs of designers and enforcement officers

Such problems affecting the use of specific requirements can create the contention that designers and enforcement officers have opposing needs that will always be difficult to reconcile. The enforcement officer needs criteria that are direct and easy to inspect for compliance, and these will always create unacceptable barriers to the freedom of the designer. But the designer has had to acknowledge that both he and the inspector need clear statements of what is needed, and this is given undeniably in a specific requirement. This balancing factor made the traditional form of regulations acceptable enough for general application as long as they dealt only with the most elementary issues of safety and health, and were concerned in requiring minimal standards that fell *below* the normal practice of designers. When the consumer began to call for standards to be set for other aspects of the performance of buildings, like thermal and sound insulation, lighting, heating and provisions for fire safety, the traditional form of the specific requirement was clearly not equal to the task.

The example of the London by-laws

At the time when the method had been suited to the demand, the regulations had been expressed almost exclusively in this style, so they had been available as self-contained documents of moderately compact size. The best known example is the publication that was issued by the Greater London Council containing the London Building Constructional By-laws (with explanatory memorandum). As the document contained by-laws and was published by a "local authority" it did not have to conform with the standard legal format of a national statutory instrument, so it was issued in a size and with a typography that made it easy to read and acceptable as a document to its users in the industry. In this form it has long been held to be a good example of its kind, and a useful and workable instrument of the law.

Notwithstanding this reputation, the Council introduced a change in the edition produced during the decade of the sixties, apparently in an attempt to offset the disadvantages of the extensive use of the specific requirement at a time when the construction industry was working under great pressure to meet massive demands. A note was added as an introduction to each of the thirteen parts. An explanation was included in a foreword to the list of parts that these "descriptive headings which preface the parts of the by-laws are not intended to form part of the by-laws, but merely to serve as a *guide to the intention of the by-laws in that part*". It is reasonable to believe that this was intended to counter the main criticism of the Building Regulations Advisory Committee in 1964 that the technique of the specific requirement "ought rarely to be used", by giving an indication of the purpose of the requirements in each part, though without granting to that statement the same legal standing as the provisions themselves, which had always to be complied with to the satisfaction of the enforcement officers. Such a compromise might help the complier without detriment to the power of the inspectorate.

The headings were model examples of clear statements, and used a form of expression that reflected a style emerging from the newly issued national regulations, as the following examples show:

Part III. Dead and imposed load. The purpose of this part of these by-laws is to ensure that adequate provision is made in the design of a building or chimney shaft for the dead and imposed loads and the wind effects to which that building or chimney shaft may be subjected.

Part IV. Materials of construction. The purpose of this part of these by-laws is to ensure that material used in the construction of a building is of adequate strength and durability and is of a suitable nature and quality for the purpose for which it is used.

Part VIII. The structural use of steel. The purpose of this part of these by-laws is to ensure that structural steelwork is adequately protected against corrosion and has adequate strength, stiffness and stability.

The implication of these descriptions is that whatever is "adequate" for strength and "suitable" for purpose has already been determined by the author of the specific requirements contained in each part. The designer has only to comply with the criteria set, and the builder to carry out the work "to the satisfaction of the District Surveyor in a proper and workmanlike manner", and all will be well. The form seems like a direct transcript of the traditional practice of an architect, but with the Council designing the requirement and the District Surveyor adopting the role of supervisor. This practice worked well when it had been applied by an architect in the modest role of creating an individual building. As designer he could specify what was intended, and then supervise the embodiment of his criteria in the built product. But he would be the first to recognize that if the function of design were to be separated from the function of supervision, the practice would lose directness and efficiency. Ideally, the system would work most economically if the District Surveyor had designed the building, because the judgement that determined compliance would be applied during the process of design and the solution would emerge as appropriate in the first place.

Ideally, if the functions of design and inspection could be re-combined for legal purposes as they have always been combined in the process of building for the purposes of the owner as client, it would seem that the plain-speaking "descriptive heading" of the London by-laws could itself become the mandatory requirement, and the specifications forming the body of the law could be dispensed with. Of course this would be to place reliance on the *experts* to know what had to be done and to leave them to ensure that all the technical steps were taken to meet the requirements.

Until such "ideal" theories gain wide and popular support, the system of building control will be preoccupied with the need to make provision for the work of "any person who intends to...erect any building", without qualification. For this purpose, the specific requirement, by making clear exactly what is required, can be said to remain a useful, if not model, instrument for its limited goals.

THE FUNCTIONAL REQUIREMENT

Description

The technique of expressing regulations as "functional requirements" came into use later than that of the specific requirement, seemingly as a method more suitable for general purposes. It is a method that prescribes that materials or components should carry out their particular function in the building adequately (see figure 13). A regulation cast in this form is, in the plain language of the first BRAC Report, "in effect a requirement that the thing in question shall stand up to its job". Broadly speaking, it states the aim or *purpose* of the provision, without necessarily detailing exactly what has to be done. In short, it concentrates on *ends* rather than *means*, and so leaves the designer free to decide how the aim is to be embodied in the product.

Examples

The nature of the method is best illustrated by the following examples from the national Building Regulations (Statutory Instruments, 1976, No. 1676; author's italics):

(a) [Part B. Materials.] (1) subject to the provisions of paragraph (2), *any materials used* (a) in the erection of a building; (b) in the structural alteration or extension of a building; (c) in the execution of works or the installation of fittings, being works or fittings to which any provision of these regulations applies; or (d) for the backfilling of any excavation on a site in connection with any building or works or fittings to which any provision of this regulation applies, *shall be-(i) of a suitable nature and quality in relation to the purposes for and conditions in which they are used; (ii) adequately mixed or prepared; and (iii) applied, used or fixed so as adequately to perform the functions for which they are designed.*

(b) [D8 Structure above foundations.] The structure of a building above the foundations shall *safely sustain and transmit to the foundations the combined dead load, imposed load and wind load without such deflection or deformation as will impair the stability of, or cause damage to, the whole or any part of the building.*

(c) [Part G: Sound insulation.] (1) *any wall* which (a) separates any dwelling from another dwelling or from another building; or (b) separates any habitable room in a dwelling from any other part of the same building which—(i) is not used exclusively with that dwelling; and (ii) is a place used for purposes other than occasional repair or

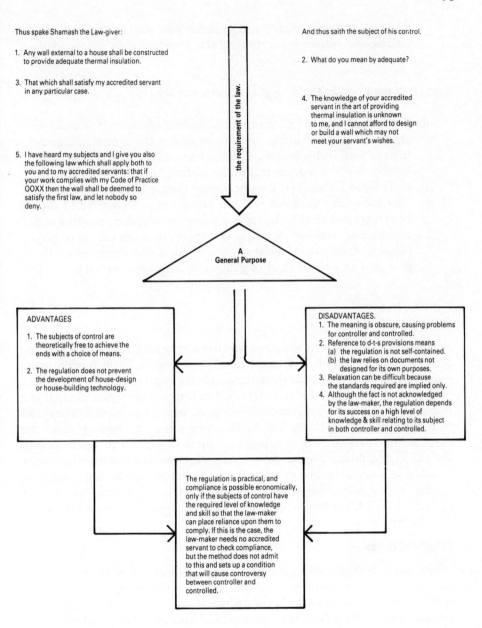

Thus spake Shamash the Law-giver:

1. Any wall external to a house shall be constructed to provide adequate thermal insulation.

3. That which shall satisfy my accredited servant in any particular case.

5. I have heard my subjects and I give you also the following law which shall apply both to you and to my accredited servants: that if your work complies with my Code of Practice OOXX then the wall shall be deemed to satisfy the first law, and let nobody so deny.

the requirement of the law.

And thus saith the subject of his control.

2. What do you mean by adequate?

4. The knowledge of your accredited servant in the art of providing thermal insulation is unknown to me, and I cannot afford to design or build a wall which may not meet your servant's wishes.

A
General Purpose

ADVANTAGES

1. The subjects of control are theoretically free to achieve the ends with a choice of means.

2. The regulation does not prevent the development of house-design or house-building technology.

DISADVANTAGES.
1. The meaning is obscure, causing problems for controller and controlled.
2. Reference to d-t-s provisions means
   (a) the regulation is not self-contained.
   (b) the law relies on documents not designed for its own purposes.
3. Relaxation can be difficult because the standards required are implied only.
4. Although the fact is not acknowledged by the law-maker, the regulation depends for its success on a high level of knowledge & skill relating to its subject in both controller and controlled.

The regulation is practical, and compliance is possible economically, only if the subjects of control have the required level of knowledge and skill so that the law-maker can place reliance upon them to comply. If this is the case, the law-maker needs no accredited servant to check compliance, but the method does not admit to this and sets up a condition that will cause controversy between controller and controlled.

Figure 13 The functional requirement

maintenance, or is a machinery or tank room, *shall in conjunction with its associated structure be so constructed as to provide adequate resistance to the transmission of airborne sound."*

and from the London Building (Constructional) By-laws

(d) [3.03 Wind Effects.] (2) Every roof shall be constructed so as to be capable of *safely* resisting, without exceeding the apropriate limitations of permissible stresses, the simultaneous effects of pressure and suction due to wind, normal to the surface, specified in Table 4".

(e) (3.03 Wind Effects.] (4) Every chimney shaft other than brick shafts constructed in accordance with the provisions of By-law 12.13 shall be constructed so as to be capable of *safely* sustaining, resisting and transmitting without exceeding the appropriate limitations of permissible stresses wind pressure in any horizontal direction on the projected area of the shaft of p'lb per sq.ft specified in Table 5."

Advantages

Regulations made like this appear at first to be very satisfactory, especially to designers, among whom they have proved to be popular. This is because the requirements make clear what the designer is being asked to achieve, but allow a great deal of flexibility for the ways and means of complying. Indeed the method appears to place reliance on the designer, who is accustomed to this kind of relationship with a client. But by the same token the method leaves the designer in a position where compliance must be proved to the enforcing authority notwithstanding that there is only vague guidance about what might be taken as acceptable. For this reason, the technique works best when it is dealing with familiar objectives about which there is a wide measure of agreement on what needs to be done to fulfil the functional requirements.

Disadvantages

Where such understandings do not exist, the method is burdened with difficulties. These serious inherent disadvantages in the functional requirement will become more acute as the law shifts towards the interest of the consumer, placing heavier liabilities on the producers and enforcers. The problems can be identified briefly as follows: (a) the *meaning* of the requirement, in terms of what must be done in practice, is obscure, so that compliance can be uncertain and enforcement can be impracticable; (b) as regards the *users* of the regulations, the method is suitable for the control of the work of skilled designers, who may be relied upon to know what has to be done; but is unsuitable for the inexpert builder or owner; (c) if this disadvantage of obscurity is overcome by the regulations making reference to approved examples of how to comply, the *regulations are no longer self-contained*; and (d) the *relaxation* of a regulation whose standards are vague can cause disproportionate difficulties.

These problems are examined in greater detail in the following:

(a) Interpretation

The most obvious problems caused by the expression of a functional requirement are to do with what is meant by the key words "suitable", "adequate", and "safely". How can it be shown that these conditions have been met and in whose judgement is the decision made?

The system, being derived from the form of specification-writing used in normal contracts drawn up by building designers, is based on the idea that there is direct personal control by an expert. It was the architect or engineer referred to in the specification whose judgement was to be satisfied. Consequently, there is less difficulty in the use of the functional requirement, in theory, when the form of enforcement has a similar authority.

In London, where the by-laws require that the District Surveyor is to be satisfied, it is that official's judgement that is the deciding factor. Yet the method is rarely used in the construction of those by-laws, which consist mainly of specific requirements. The Surveyor must be satisfied, and his judgement is the law's criterion, but he is given very precise guidance about what compliance means: a necessary precaution when the penalties that now exist for making a mistake might be too onerous for any official to be expected to bear.

Where the national regulations apply, the crucial judgement lies ultimately with the magistrate presiding in a court of summary jurisdiction, but it would be a bad regulation that had to invoke the long process by which reference is made to that arbiter to reach a decision about its fulfilment.

Consequently, the law-makers who draft the statutory instruments, in their wisdom, are expected to provide guidance in the regulations by specifying examples of what is deemed to satisfy the functional requirement. In doing so, they are following the original recommendations of BRAC that "illustrative deemed-to-satisfy specifications" would be necessary to make the "practical implications of requirements expressed in general or abstract terms...readily comprehensible to all users of the regulations". The Committee also advised that such specifications should be quoted *only* as examples, and to be most useful they should "follow good practice which is very widely encountered".

The result of all this is that it is now customary for all functional requirements to be supported by illustrations of what is deemed to comply. The "deemed-to-satisfy" provisions are themselves mandatory. This is to say that if their specification has been followed, the inspector is obliged to accept that the main provision has been met, and that what has been done is indeed "suitable" or "adequate" for the purpose defined. The benefit of this custom is that the flexibility of the system is maintained, even though precise guidance is given, because the *guidance is optional*.

A designer is informed about the purpose of the regulations, and in order to ensure compliance may follow the specific illustration, but there is freedom for choosing another solution provided that it can be shown to achieve the same standard.

Once the principle of using "deemed-to-satisfy" clauses has been adopted, it becomes possible to make reference to other solutions in common practice. The need for the examples to have a wide measure of acceptance has promoted the use of the standard specifications issued by the British Standards Institution for this purpose. In theory, these qualify by their very nature, being composed by committees of "experts" drawn from all sectors of the construction industry to describe what is seen in standard practice to be satisfactory. The strength of support for such "standard specifications" can be powerful enough to overcome the objections of the professional law-makers, namely that the language used in them is not ideally suited to legal purposes, and not precise enough to be taken into the body of the law.

The use of such documents, having wide consensus and popularity, has the useful side-effect of giving their contents a further stamp of authoritative approval. This can help to encourage the wider use of methods which are authentically held to represent good practice. As a consequence, the national regulations in the UK now contain extensive references to the Standard Specifications and the Standard Codes of Practice of the British Standards Institution, in support of the statements of functional requirements. Of the many examples, Part B, which deals with the use of materials for building (requiring that they should be "of a *suitable* nature...*adequately* mixed...and applied, using or fixed so as *adequately* to perform the functions" as quoted previously) gives as "deemed-to-satisfy provisions regarding the fitness of materials" the legal authority for "the use of any material or any method of fixing or preparing materials or of applying, used or fixing materials *which conforms with a British Standard or a British Standard Code of Practice* prescribing the quality of material or standards of workmanship...", while Part D, dealing with structural stability makes reference more exclusively to the Standard Codes. The implications of this are illustrated most particularly by Part D8 which, in legislating for the design of the "structure above foundations", makes "deemed-to-satisfy" provision by referring to codes which describe, respectively, how to design structures using steel; aluminium, reinforced, pre-stressed or plain concrete; timber; bricks; blocks; stone, flints or clunches of bricks; and composite constructions of steel and concrete.

(b) The problem of users

The use of the BSI Codes of Practice as deemed-to-satisfy provisions for functional requirements gives added point to the criticism that the technique is suitable only for the control of skilled designers by equally skilled inspectorates.

The Codes dealing with structural design are prepared by qualified civil engineers and are accordingly intended for interpretation only by other engineers of equivalent qualifications. The importance of this limitation is pointed out in their prefaces, and in a similar way other Codes are prepared by specialists in their respective subjects and addressed to practitioners of similar skills. This can have important effects on the task of enforcement, because it implies that inspectors or surveyors who have the duty of checking compliance must themselves have the requisite qualifications for using the Code. In a climate of opinion that favours consumer legislation, a local authority would be ill-advised to allow an inspection of any aspect of the performance of a building which is designed in reference to a Code by a person not suitably qualified, because it would run the risk of a charge of negligence in the event of a failure of the building to function as specified.

This problem of the interpretation of functional requirements places emphasis on the difficulties of control which are peculiar to the construction industry, especially when the controls are intended to cover the building services as well as the construction.

Building is an activity which spans a wide range of skills, from the high technology of large projects depending upon the design work of teams with mixed professional skills and the appropriate techniques of management and supervision, to the modest skills of the small builder or do-it-yourself craftsman dealing with adaptations. If building control is to be applied efficiently over the whole spectrum of this ability it is likely to present difficulties of a schizogenic character to anyone who has to create the control system. The danger is that any method which attempts to control both extremes is likely to be unsuitable for either. Regulations containing detailed instructions suited to the small builder are likely to frustrate the work of the skilled multi-professional team and obstruct the development of the full economic potential of the large project; and those providing the flexibility needed for the sophisticated project can be meaningless in practical terms to the plain operator.

The "functional requirement" is thought to be a technique which can cater for the whole of this range of skills, and in its general application it can be said to work reasonably well. But it is rather like the exercise of riding a bicycle: everyone can do it without too much trouble, until they are asked to explain how it is done; and there can be painful accidents if it is not done properly. Functional requirements can work reasonably well so long as the level of knowledge and skill of both designer and inspector are equal, and the checking can be carried out during the progress of the work of designing and constructing, so that expensive changes are not needed after the building is completed. This means, too, that the design systems in use need to be well-tried so that they can be relied upon to have predictable results, such as are obtained, for example, from the use of theories of structures to determine the size and position of the members of a steel framework. It works too if the inspector does not insist on a particular deemed-to-satisfy solution, but allows the flexible nature of the method to operate; and it works for the small builder if the deemed-to-satisfy clauses contain a straightforward specification which can be readily applied and checked. But it would have to be admitted that it does *not* work if it depends upon an inspector carrying out a check thoroughly, at the completion of a project. Unless the rules have been followed properly during the process of production, such checking becomes impracticable, especially if it is to be carried out within acceptable limits of time and cost.

Such problems have greater significance as the legal penalties for making mistakes become greater. Clearly, if the inspector is to satisfy himself that all the materials are appropriately prepared, he would need to make reference to many BSI Codes and Standards, and would need to carry out the same kind of ongoing supervision usually done by a clerk of works during the process of construction. Furthermore, if he is to satisfy himself that the structure above the foundations is safely sustaining and transmitting to the foundations "the combined dead load, imposed load and wind load without such deflection or deformation as will impair the stability", and that a design process described in a manual of practice (like a Code) has been followed; or, if it has not, that an equal alternative method has been faithfully applied, he may find the problems insurmountable, unless he can work alongside the designer and carry out the surveillance of the work in progress with the site engineer. Such a doubling-up of effort to ensure compliance would go far beyond the limits hitherto considered appropriate for the budgets of the enforcing authorities. More practical ways of seeing that requirements are met would require some use to be made of the designers themselves, and would involve the existing management structure of the construction industry in collaborative techniques of checking and making reference to an inspectorate.

(c) The question of self-sufficiency

It has always been a popular and insistent demand that what the law requires on any subject like building should be expressed in terms that can be readily understood and contained in one document. The more concise the language, and the more slender the document, the better it would be for all concerned.

Adopting the use of the technique of "functional requirements" appears to be a step in the right direction in meeting this demand. As the examples quoted previously show, a regulation cast as a functional requirement is a direct and succinct statement of aim. If all of the regulations were expressed in this way, the statements would be brief and to the point, and the size of the document containing them would be compact. Such an arrangement, however, would only be practical if the regulations were to be addressed exclusively to qualified designers who were properly trained to do all of the right things in preparing their designs. The "functional requirement" statement, in itself, presumes that building is in the hands of highly-trained specialists who can be relied upon to know how to go about providing the functions that are asked for, or achieving the aims of the regulations.

Unfortunately, this is not always the case in practice, and for this reason the

deemed-to-satisfy provisions are used in tandem with each functional requirement. These provisions substitute, for the benefit of those who do not know
how to achieve the objective, the manuals or codes of design and the
specifications of production, setting out in technical detail how the building
should be designed, or how the materials should be prepared, issued, and used.

If such prescriptions could be contained within the schedules as part of the
statutory instrument, the regulations could be published as a self-sufficient
document; but reliance upon other publications to illustrate the requirements
makes this impossible. The use of the Standards and Codes of the British
Standards Institution for this purpose means that the total number of external
documents referred to can amount to many hundreds. One result is that the
full documentation of the information needed by anyone wishing to understand the law of building control is very large and can be very costly. For
information that is needed for the plain purposes of finding out what rules
apply to building, the size of the library and its cost can seem grossly out of
proportion to a person seeking to comply.

Of course, the advantages of making reference to other documents in this
way are clear enough. As we have seen they can have wide acceptance as
reliable statements of standard practice, and bring to the regulations the
valuable asset of popular authenticity. They can be written without the
strictures which apply to legal language, and contain drawings, diagrams, and
other illustrations not normally employed in defining legal requirements. This
is widely believed to make them more popular and more easily understood,
although, of course, in practice they might give litigators more to argue about
if ever their meaning had to be resolved in court. In theory, too, they can be
revised, amended, and kept up to date without having to go through the
formal and delaying process of being "laid before Parliament" as would be
necessary for the amendment of the statutory instruments (though in practice
they may be affected by different bureaucratic delays).

Such pros and cons must be considered carefully to see where the balance of
advantage lies, but the demand for the regulations to be contained in one
comprehensive statement has always had particular force.

(d) The question of relaxations

The enabling Acts for building legislation allow for regulations to be relaxed in
particular cases, and this concession is important for a number of reasons,
especially as a means of allowing new materials or constructional techniques to
be introduced in an experimental way. Yet there can be problems about
relaxing functional requirements which can cause complications in the process
of enforcement.

When the technique was introduced it was argued strongly among the
administrators of building legislation that a functional requirement could *not*
be relaxed. This was based on the contention that it would not be possible to
relax a requirement for one function of a building to be "suitable", "adequate",

or to perform "safely", because this would amount to an admission that the function, while *not* being suitable, adequate, or safe in particular cases, could yet be acceptable: in short; unsuitable, inadequate, or unsafe conditions could, by implication, be allowed.

The fallacy of this view was that these descriptions were in fact referring to a qualitative *standard* or degree of suitability or adequacy or safety that could be regarded as acceptable for compliance. In theory, however, this standard in any particular case could be relaxed so that a different standard could be permitted, without the result being a total absence of the condition required. There were many examples of this, of which a familiar one was the load that may be "safely sustained" with different factors on safety, or margins of error, and what was suitable in one case could be relaxed in another where the particular risks being guarded against might be very different. A further, opposing, contention was that since the functional requirement was always concerned with suitability for purpose, the degree of standard of performance could always be changed to suit a different purpose, so that there would never be any need for such a provision to be relaxed.

Either way, this meant that the relaxation for a functional requirement was not more difficult than for other types of provision, though it may place a special emphasis on the question of whose judgement might be acceptable.

Further assessments

These are the issues affecting the use of the functional requirement as a mode of regulation. The inherent problems of the technique, arising from its particular characteristic of attempting to identify the aim of a constraint, were probably not recognized when it was first introduced in the way which will be described briefly in the historical note later in this chapter. As will be seen from this, it seems likely that the functional requirement was introduced in the belief that skilled designers could be relied upon to comply with regulatory objectives expressed in this way. Such dependence on designers was perhaps a natural consequence of the way that the law was applied, which was through the submission of plans and details of any proposed work for approval or rejection by the legal authority. In any case, too, the designers were responsible to their clients for seeing that the buildings complied with the law, so it must have seemed a small step to expect them to provide the same service, as it were, to the public-at-large.

The extension of this line of thought has since led to the general awareness of new problems. It can be seen to follow from the contention that the application of the technique of the functional requirement must depend, ideally, on the skilled judgements of the designers, and if this is to be accepted, then the greatest efficiency in the control system would be obtained if the roles of designer and inspector could be amalgamated.

Such contentions have since been affected by the growing financial burdens of liability for damages due to building faults, which make designers, builders, and inspectors alike unwilling to assume extra responsibilities. These same influences tend to sharpen their awareness of the need for more precise statements of what the law requires, than the functional requirement provides. Indeed, the very flexibility of this form of regulation, which was its prime commendation, comes to be seen by them, in the light of the modern consumer-oriented legislation, as a dangerous cause of contention if a building proves to be faulty, and proof has to be established in a court of law that it had complied with the "general and abstract terms" of this kind of regulation.

THE PERFORMANCE STANDARD

Description

The technique of the performance standard is theoretically an advance from the functional requirement, being more explicit and more readily enforceable. It overcomes the disadvantages of the specific and the functional requirements by combining the virtues of both into a new form made possible by the application of scientific research to the affairs of the construction industry (see figure 14). At the time of the first BRAC Report there were few performance standards incorporated in the regulations, but the committee stated categorically that "clearly performance standards are the ultimate objective".

The performance standard is a regulation which defines the performance required (of a part, component, material, or fitting used in a building) in objective terms, and which makes the attainment of that performance the actual criterion of compliance. It is like the specific requirement in the way that it *specifies* what is required, but in terms of performance rather than material content. It is like the functional requirement in that it states the ends rather than the means, but it identifies the ends as degrees of performance that can be measured and, therefore, checked for compliance.

Examples

The examples in the regulations all relate to the comparatively new subjects for which requirements have been formulated since the task of making regulations became a concern of the central government.

(1) E5 Fire resistance of elements of structure...
(2) Subject to the provisions of this regulation and of regulation E6, every element of structure shall have fire resistance of not less than the relevant period set out in the Table to this regulation....

[The Table sets out the minimum period of fire resistance in hours per maximum dimensions of height, area and volume for each type of purpose group of building.]

This requirement has to be read in conjunction with:

(2)   E1 Interpretation of Section 1...

(5) Any requirement in this Section that an element of structure, door or other part of a building shall have fire resistance of a specified period shall be construed as meaning that it shall be so constructed that a specimen constructed to the same specification, if exposed to test by fire in accordance with BS 476: Part 8: 1972, would (subject to any relevant provision in Table 1 of this regulation) *satisfy the requirements of that test as to stability, integrity and insulation for not less than the specified period*...[author's italics].

(3)   F3 Maximum U value of walls, floors, roofs and perimeter walling...

(1) The U value of any part of a wall, floor or roof which encloses a dwelling and is described in column (1) of the Table to this regulation (incuding surface finishes thereof and excluding any openings therein) shall not exceed the appropriate value specified in column (2) of that Table.

(2) The calculated average U value of perimeter walling (including any opening therein) shall not exceed 1.8....

[The Table referred to in (1) gives the maximum U-value of any part of an element for a list of nine "elements of building".]

These requirements have to be read in conjunction with:

(4)   F2 Interpretation of Part F

(1) In this Part and in Schedule 11—...U-value means thermal transmittance coefficient, that is to say, the rate of heat transfer in watts through 1 m^2 of a structure when the combined radiant and air temperatures at each side of the structure differ by 1°C and is expressed in $W/m^{2°}C$....

Advantages

The advantages that can be claimed for this method of regulating are the same as those applying to both of the previously described techniques. Because the performance standard sets the aim by describing the performance required, it is not concerned with stipulating what methods should be used to achieve it. Consequently, the designers, manufacturers, and contractors of the construction industry have the freedom to provide the performance in whatever way they may think best, so the method leaves all the opportunity needed for technical innovation and industrial development.

Equally, since the method also gives the measure of the performance which is to be achieved, it is well suited to the requirements of the enforcement officer, who knows what has to be checked. It is like a modern form of the "specific requirement" because it lays down precisely what is needed and in a form that makes checking theoretically straightforward. The difference for the

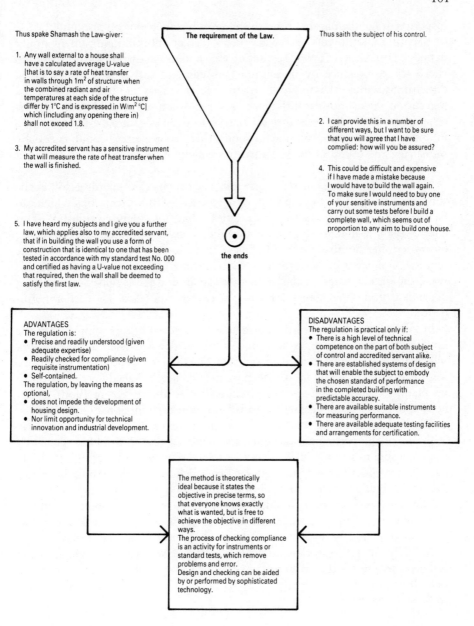

Thus spake Shamash the Law-giver:

1. Any wall external to a house shall have a calculated avverage U-value [that is to say a rate of heat transfer in walls through 1m² of structure when the combined radiant and air temperatures at each side of the structure differ by 1°C and is expressed in W/m² °C] which (including any opening there in) shall not exceed 1.8.

3. My accredited servant has a sensitive instrument that will measure the rate of heat transfer when the wall is finished.

5. I have heard my subjects and I give you a further law, which applies also to my accredited servant, that if in building the wall you use a form of construction that is identical to one that has been tested in accordance with my standard test No. 000 and certified as having a U-value not exceeding that required, then the wall shall be deemed to satisfy the first law.

The requirement of the Law.

the ends

Thus saith the subject of his control.

2. I can provide this in a number of different ways, but I want to be sure that you will agree that I have complied: how will you be assured?

4. This could be difficult and expensive if I have made a mistake because I would have to build the wall again. To make sure I would need to buy one of your sensitive instruments and carry out some tests before I build a complete wall, which seems out of proportion to any aim to build one house.

ADVANTAGES
The regulation is:
• Precise and readily understood (given adequate expertise)
• Readily checked for compliance (given requisite instrumentation)
• Self-contained.
The regulation, by leaving the means as optional,
• does not impede the development of housing design.
• Nor limit opportunity for technical innovation and industrial development.

DISADVANTAGES
The regulation is practical only if:
• There is a high level of technical competence on the part of both subject of control and accredited servant alike.
• There are established systems of design that will enable the subject to embody the chosen standard of performance in the completed building with predictable accuracy.
• There are available suitable instruments for measuring performance.
• There are available adequate testing facilities and arrangements for certification.

The method is theoretically ideal because it states the objective in precise terms, so that everyone knows exactly what is wanted, but is free to achieve the objective in different ways.
The process of checking compliance is an activity for instruments or standard tests, which remove problems and error.
Design and checking can be aided by or performed by sophisticated technology.

Figure 14 The performance standard

inspector lies in the nature of the checking, which depends on tests and the use of scientific instruments. For example, a former specific requirement might define the thickness of a wall separating two houses, so that the inspector could check for compliance by measuring the width of the wall with a scale of dimensions without having to know that the thickness had been specified as a precaution against noise transferance. The performance standard might, on the other hand, define the resistance to the transmission of sound needed for a wall in the same situation, on the grounds that an inspector could check by measuring the sound at the specified frequencies using instruments made for that purpose.

As with the functional requirements, performance standards also can be supported by examples in the form of deemed-to-satisfy provisions which can be used as a practical guide to what might be done to achieve compliance. This enables the law-makers to give the unskilled builder a passport to compliance by prescribing familiar forms of construction that are known to provide the required standards of performance. Of course, this facility may bring in its wake the disadvantage of the regulations again not being self-contained, but dependent upon an extensive library of external publications used for guidance.

In this respect, however, the performance standard brings with it from the same origins of applied research new kinds of deemed-to-satisfy provision, which are more apposite to its objectives. These are references to a prescribed test, or rule of calculations, whose existence reduces the need for references to be made to large numbers of specifications of alternative methods as are needed to provide the deemed-to-satisfy support for functional requirements.

The development of this new form of reference has countered an early criticism of the performance standard which said that it would be generally impracticable to specify performance as a legal requirement, because it would necessitate checks being carried out *after* completion, and this would be to risk great costs being incurred to modify the construction if it was shown that the performance had not been attained. In short, on this basis nobody would be able to be sure if the requirement had been met until it was too late, because *performance* would be a function of the *finished product* required by law.

An early example of this kind of deemed-to satisfy provision which makes reference to a test is the provision in G2 which deals with the sound insulation of walls, stating that the requirements of a main regulation (G1(1)) are deemed to be satisfied if:

(1)   the wall and its associated structure are identical with, or are similar to and unlikely to provide less resistance to the transmission of sound than, a wall and its associated structure, when tested in accordance with regulation G6 at all frequencies set out in the Table to this regulation limit the transmission of airborne sound so that the reduction at each frequency given in column (1) of that Table

does not fall short of the appropriate value given in column (2) of that Table by an amount which causes the aggregate of such deviations to exceed 23 dB...

The reference here to regulation G6 is to the rules specified for the measurement of sound transmission which include the requirement that "measurements shall be in accordance with Sections TWO A and THREE A of BS 2750: 1956, and the method of normalising the results for both air-borne and impact sound shall be that given in clause 3e (ii) thereof...".

A more radical version of this kind of change has already been quoted in the example referring to regulation F1 (5) previously. In this case the logical step has been taken of "upgrading" the deemed-to-satisfy provision referring to a test *to that of a substantive clause of interpretation,* which states that any requirement for a part of a building to have fire resistance of a specified period "shall be construed as meaning that it shall be so constructed that a specimen constructed to the same specification, if exposed to test by fire in accordance with BS 476: Part 8, 1972, would...satisfy the requirements of that test...".

The important principle established by these provisions is that it cancels the need for an enforcement officer to check every completed part for compliance, because the regulations accept that the construction has only to be the same as (i.e. built to the same specification as) a construction that has already passed a specified test. This promotes economy and efficiency, because *any form of construction* that has been put properly to a scientific test of performance *can be repeated in any building* where its use is appropriate, *in the full knowledge that it will comply with the regulations,* and the only check that is strictly necessary is that the construction has indeed followed the same specification.

The other new type of deemed-to-satisfy provision is one that makes reference to a rule of calculation. An example of this is to be found in the "deemed-to-satisy provisions regarding thermal insulation" in F4 of the Building Regulations, in which paragraph (2) states that "the requirements of regulation F3 (2) relating to the average U value of perimeter walling *shall be deemed to be satisfied* if any one of the conditions prescribed in Rule 2 of Part IV of Schedule II is satisfied". This rule lays down, among other alternatives, that "perimeter walling shall be deemed to have a U value not exceeding 1.8 if...

(c) $\dfrac{AaUa + AbUb + AcUc}{Aa + Ab + Ac}$ (is equal to or less than) 1.8".

[The terms quoted being defined to facilitate calculation.]

This type of provision has the same effect of simplifying the task of complying: the designers and inspector are told precisely what has to be done. The difference is not that special instruments are needed, but that a certain amount of specialist knowledge is required to apply the rule.

Reservations

These characteristics of the method of "performance standards" give some indication of the nature of its possible disadvantages. It would seem that its use implies that a high level of technical competence is needed on the part of the designers and builders to meet the requirements, and also on the part of the administrators and enforcement officers. In addition, access is needed to costly testing facilities and other scientific resources in order to set up such a standard, and to maintain the information appropriate to its continued use.

While it may be considered as an ideal form of regulation, it can be seen that its adoption as the principal legislatory technique will depend upon the development of an adequate level of technology and a new kind of dialogue between the industry and the enforcing authorities. The tasks would be formidable and costly alike in terms of time and technical, scientific, administrative, and industrial effort. In the first place the law-makers would need to identify what aspects of performance in a building should be dealt with in the regulations in the interests of public health, safety, welfare, and convenience; then to decide what hazards there are, and so determine what levels of performance should be required to give adequate protection. In the second place, it would be necessary for systems of design to be devised that can be relied upon to embody the chosen standard of performance with predictable success in the completed project. Finally, it would be desirable to have adequate testing facilities, so that all appropriate steps can be taken to verify that the appropriate levels of performance can or are in fact being provided in normal practice.

Experience of work in the construction industry shows that the rate of progress of this kind of total industrial competence is closely related to the level of investment and the extent of the demand for its products. Consequently, it would be reasonable to suppose that the three variants of regulating method will continue in use in combinations which will inevitably change in balance towards an increasing use of the performance standard. Skilful administration can help to ensure that arrangements are made which will allow the process to evolve at a speed that is regulated by the needs of the community and by the development of industrial practice, in ways that will be shown in a separate chapter.

AN HISTORICAL REVIEW

To sum up it can be seen that each of the three regulating techniques at present in use in the UK has developed out of the prevailing social conditions and the changing methods adopted by the industry in response to the public's demands (see figure 15). The development has followed an historical sequence. Each technique has been suited to its own period, and the whole evolutionary process has been engendered as one *ad hoc* series by the communal and manufacturing environment. To enable a rational assessment to be made, it is

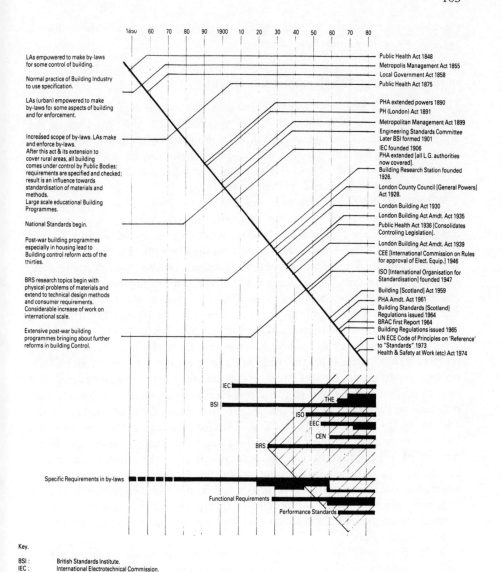

Figure 15 The historical development of regulating techniques

possible now to put the three methods into their proper place in the historical perspective, as the following summary sets out.

In the beginning: the specific requirement

First in the sequence was the specific requirement, which described what must be done without establishing why. This worked well at the time because the aims were obvious enough to be taken as implicit: buildings should be safe from collapse; and the dangers arising from their normal use, namely the health hazard due to the disposal of refuse and sewage, and the risk of fire from the use of solid fuel, should be kept under control.

With a craft-based industry using traditional materials, it was acceptable and effective to have specifications for materials and structures to mitigate these dangers, and for the builders simply to do what they were told without having any need to ask why. These specifications resulted from the Local Government Act of 1858 which empowered local authorities to make by-laws for specific purposes like the structure of walls for stability and fire protection; sewerage; and space, ventilation, and drainage. Other purposes, like the structure of foundations, roofs, and chimneys, were added by the Public Health Act of 1875 which became the ongoing basis for building control.

As a consequence of these Acts and their by-laws, the process of checking built construction against the rudimentary specifications enforced by law became customary. By the turn of the century, the manufacturers had developed the political will to come together to agree on how to standardize materials and methods in common use, because their experience had made the relevant facts familiar enough to them. The time was ripe for the creation of a national institute to promote industrial standards, and so to provide an official framework for the manufacturing consensus. It seemed a natural sequence of events that the industrialists should make the standards, because they were facilitating their own working-processes, while the consumers exercised very little influence beyond the remote one of having started the train of events by creating the legal criteria designed to achieve implied and elementary standards of health and safety.

When, two decades later, the first building research station was founded, its early studies were mainly concerned with the same familiar physical properties of materials and structures, but it gave to the specifications which had been admittedly founded on empirical knowledge a new form and the stamp of an authority based on objective judgements. These studies made information available about how best to solve the traditional problems of building using familiar materials, how the well-known methods worked, how they compared, and what alternatives there were. This engendered new attitudes and produced new information from scientific methods, and had the effect of encouraging a more objective approach to the making of regulations. The government department which was responsible for the preparation of the model by-laws was exposed to the influence of these ideas and, not having the direct burden of the enforcement of its own models, was probably more inclined to experiment with ways of expressing requirements. The introduction of a method based on functions became a possibility because it could now be assumed that information was available to show how such requirements were capable of being met. These ideas were in circulation at the time when, in 1935, the passing of the Public Health Act consolidated much of the legislation for building control and brought an interest in building by-laws to the forefront of those involved in public administration.

At this time the central government was able to prescribe a set of "model by-laws", and in doing so was taking a further step to standardize means by encouraging the many enforcing authorities to adopt standard criteria.

The building industry, in any case, was being much affected by the technological changes whose pace had been perceptibly increased by the impact of the 1914–1918 war, and so in this context the techniques of the specific requirement began to seem anachronistic. In the thirties the model by-laws acknowledged this with advice that stated: "the present time is seeing great changes in building methods and materials. *Local by-laws should be adjusted to keep pace with these...*". The same statement advocated reference being made to the British Standards Institution for its specifications of some familiar materials, and advised that consultation with the Research Station should be sought when "a material or method is so novel that there is neither a national specification nor general practice to serve as a guide".

As for this Research Board, now so prominent in the public's view, it was already advocating forms of regulation so far in advance of the ideas of legislators that—as it transpired—none would have the formal acknowledgement of the building control system's administrators until the first BRAC Report was issued and began to take effect three decades later. The Research Authority produced a report in 1936 (published by the DSIR in 1937) in which it pointed out that the tendency of by-law writers to "*specify particular forms of construction...usually based on traditional materials*" was "*confusing to the industry*" and was hindering new developments. It claimed in the same Report that the ideal would be for the by-laws to "state the *performance required, leaving open the methods by which the requisite standard is to be attained*". It made this recommendation as a practical suggesstion because the "scientific knowledge of building" had developed sufficiently to allow the performance required to be checked by scientific tests. Consequently, it seemed desirable that industry should be left free to devise new methods, and only when the stage had been reached for it to do so could it be claimed that full use was being made of the "*benefits to be obtained from scientific research*".

The emergence of the functional requirement

This was the time when the technique of the functional requirement became desirable. Legal instruments needed to allow more flexibility than was provided by the existing method of regulating by the description of established means. Some definition of the aims of the law must have seemed more appropriate. In the first edition of the model by-laws the traditional materials were covered by specific requirements, but "all other materials" were required to be "of a suitable nature and quality for the purpose" and "adequately mixed". Later editions were soon to claim that "the new bylaws are specifically designed to allow the utmost possible freedom in building methods provided the functional requirements are satisfied". Relying more and more on national standards to quote as examples, and on access to knowledge from research, the law-makers advising local authorities required that all materials must be "suitable", structures "capable of safely sustaining loads", and various aspects of performance "adequate".

The inherent disadvantages of the new system were not immediately obvious. Neither the designer or builder, nor the enforcing authority, were told what in law was suitable or adequate. Although guidance was given by the examples, it was for the enforcing officers to decide on what could be accepted. Consequently, there could be variations in ratio to *their* numbers, and this factor was not conducive to standardization.

The system depended on a higher level of technical competence than had been needed for the administration of the specific requirement type of by-law, and also on a widespread understanding of how requirements could be fulfilled in practice. Experience, now reinforced by research, provided this, but as long as the standards for products were defined mainly by producers, the factors of safety were likely to be influenced by *their* commercial stake in maintaining a high quantitative level of turn-over of the product; and as long as individual enforcement authorities were responsible for determining what was safe, the factors of safety were likely to be higher than strictly necessary, because it would be prudent to have wide margins of safety and make assurance doubly sure. It was not a combination of influences likely to achieve maximum efficiency and productivity.

The authors of the by-laws did not replace the specific with the functional requirement in all cases, but continued to use both methods. Where there was not a body of established experience, they backed up the functional requirement with "deemed-to-satisfy" guidance consisting of a catalogue of familiar specific requirements; where there was a consensus, they used the standards or codes of practice for the same purpose. These grew from the input of information from continuing research, atlhough their main intention was to encourage a standardization of products and methods in the construction industry.

A result was the proliferation of the documentation apparently needed to describe what was meant by the law of building control. But the system still had merits in the climate of technical change that prevailed. The statement in law of the "ends" in terms of function had the advantage of allowing *in theory* a desirable flexibility about what "means" could be used. A further benefit was that the system established a route for the transferance of knowledge from research to an application in general industrial practice. Although the expenditure on research was comparatively modest and promoted largely by industrial interests, the information produced could be directed to improving standard specifications and recommended practices, and because these were held up by the legal instruments as examples to be followed, the law had the effect of promoting the adoption of the findings of research.

While this route proceeded through channels controlled by the commercial interests of producers, it was subjected to economic constraints whose priorities were practicability and profitability, and while the main thrust of research was to the physical problems of materials and techniques, it could contribute theoretically to industrial efficiency; but the consumer—that is, the user of the built environment—could conclude that his interests were being neglected. It could be claimed in defence of the system as it had emerged that the consumer's needs were at least stated in law as objectives, no matter how vaguely; but as regards the means and the qualitative standards, the consumer was having to take what happened to be on offer. Improvements in standards did not come easily. In principle it would be difficult to justify an amendment to a by-law that called for a product to be "adequate or satisfactory" without implying that the condition previously accepted had been inadequate or unsatisfactory all along. Meanwhile, the multitudinous array of codes and standards used for guidance were changed piecemeal in answer to other claims and influences, causing a continuing problem of interpretation as to what could be accepted as compatible with the legal requirements.

The evolution of the performance standard

All these problems led to the evolution of the technique of the performance standard. It might have been that an increasing consciousness of social justice should lead naturally towards a system of legislative control that could deal more equitably with consumers' needs. These could be identified as qualitative levels of performance, and were enthusiastically advocated by the first Committee set up to advise the Minister empowered after 1961 to make regulations for national application at a time when once again the construction industry and its designers were in great demand, and were able to exercise considerable influence. The advantages of the new technique for regulating could readily be agreed. The method ensured that the law's objectives—that is, the consumers' needs—were precisely defined by the public as user of the built environment for the guidance of the designer, producers, and law-enforcers. These "ends" could be amended as standards might change, without difficulties about interpretation; and could be relaxed in particular cases where different standards became acceptable, and where improved standards were in demand.

The difficulties, too, were apparent. The successful adoption of the technique was more than ever conditioned by industrial skills and technical sophistication. The three main problems have already been mentioned. It was necessary in the case of each aspect of performance for which provision was to be made first to identify the appropriate standard; secondly to have in common use such practices of design and construction that could predictably embody the stated aims in the completed product; and thirdly to have testing facilities available so that the results could be confirmed on behalf of the consumer. Although the second problem could in theory be solved by an extension of the industry-oriented type of research, the first and third shifted the emphasis significantly from supplier to consumer, because it was seen to be essential that the public's influence must be that which should govern the statement of the standards, or the legal design criteria, and the process of testing for compliance. In stating performance requirements, it could be contended that society as consumer had in a hundred years of industrial development and legislation come full circle, from an implicit to an explicit statement of aims for its construction industry. In so doing it had come to determine the new goals which would guide the production of the built environment. The solution of the attendant problems lay increasingly with science. The burden of research, it seemed, must shift to consumer sponsorship. It would be needed on a hitherto unprecedented scale: in the "human sciences" to establish the user's standards; in the already well-developed applications of scientific study to materials and practices, to help establish predictable and systematic methods of design, and reliable tests.

The pattern was later to emerge in the national research programmes which showed a tendency towards user-orientation in the "development" work related to the public building programmes. The "rationalized" methods of increasing building productivity in the UK became strongly influenced by user-requirements, and these programmes provided a reasonable opportunity for adjusting national methods to fit the social change of emphasis.

But a particular truth had been re-emphasized and was to remain relevant, namely that the successful making and administration of building regulations depends on a well-balanced combination of theory and practice. It is no good prescribing standards of performance, excepting as theoretical targets for social and technical development, if there are no means of achieving them economically in practice. It is no good giving them the force of law if there are no reliable ways of ensuring compliance.

Enforcement

For any system of building control, when the public employs the process of the "common law" to ensure the enforcement of its aims, it is taking on all that is implied by the nature of a type of constraint that is backed by a penal code. As its name suggests, the common law applies equally to all persons: if it is to be obeyed by all, it must be understood by all. Some plain and perhaps familiar truths apply, and these can be usefully re-stated.

THE IMPLICATIONS OF COMMON LAW

Any requirement of the common law depends for its fulfilment on its popular acceptance and the willingness of everyone concerned to obey. Its enforcement is practicable only if the majority of citizens are law-abiding. This truism is readily illustrated by reference to the familiar rules applying to everyday functions of the community. Traffic regulations, like the requirements that all vehicles should carry lights after sunset, or the restriction of vehicle parking on double yellow lines, or the limitation of the speed of a vehicle to 70 miles per hour, are specific and widely understood. Yet if every road-user drove without lights after dark, parked in forbidden places, and exceeded the speed-limits, there could never be sufficient police patrolmen to ensure that the law was upheld. In short, enforcement would be impracticable. Such laws have, too, the powerful advantage of simplicity as befits a common demand. They are expressed in terms that are readily understood, so that the objective is very plain. There are no problems of interpretation, and even when instruments are needed to check whether the law is being complied with, as is the case for the speed-limit, these are in such common supply as to represent no real problem. It is perfectly clear to the public-at-large, the individual road-user, and the law-enforcement officer when the rules are being broken. Yet even when there is no doubt about meaning, the code would be unworkable without the public's willingness to obey.

ITS APPLICATION TO BUILDING ACTIVITIES

The same principles apply to the rules which a building control code may seek to apply, yet the complications are daunting by comparison. Buildings are complex industrial products. They are made up of materials, structures, and all the equipment that relates the services providing sanitation, energy, and environmental conditions suited to their use. It might be straightforward enough for the public to "lay down the law" by stating in broad, objective, and synoptic terms what it wants, namely that the structure should be safe from collapse or fire, and the building suitable for human occupation, without detriment to health and so on. Such aims will be readily understood by everyone as suits the universality of the popular demand for protection. The problems arise in translating these requirements into technical rules. Once this is attempted the legislators become involved in difficulties of definition and interpretation that can be seemingly overwhelming.

It should perhaps be admitted that the first option for the public is whether this step should be taken at all. The decision is concerned with the extent of the reliance the public is prepared to place on the expertise of those involved in the production of buildings. It would be a theoretically straightforward matter for the objective of health and safety to be expressed in simple terms of function or performance that everyone could understand, and leave the task of technical compliance to those professional specialists who will be designing and building the end-product. They can then establish their own guidance in terms suited to their skill, knowledge, and practice. This is a system not unknown in other fields of legal control, and even in the construction industry it has been used in the UK for the building of dams. If this system is to be adopted, it implies important qualifications about who may be regarded as an "expert". The theory would be that if the law is to apply to everyone as a potential building owner, then in turn that everyone should establish what specialists can be relied upon to produce the goods, and grant the privilege of licence accordingly.

The role of technical skill

The problem with this is that in the past the public has not been prepared to regard the production of a building as requiring necessarily any highly specialized knowledge or technical skill; that is, certainly not beyond the means of most people to acquire. Such a point of view may be explained by the information that the simple domestic structures happen to be the most numerous, and their construction is familiar to most people; but the term "building", as used in the legislation of building control, covers a wide range of product. It includes not only the small family house, but also the high-rise city-centre projects, industrial schemes, and the labyrinthine complexes—all types of building in fact. It is a strange and interesting feature of contemporary life, however, that even as these developments of advanced technology create a growing acceptance of the role of the professional skills, there exists a parallel growth of do-it-yourself facilities and an increasing availability of popular technical knowledge. Public interest has centred, too, on eradicating what many believe to be systems based on "privilege", like those which have established the professional institutions, with their codes of conduct and control of fees, in favour of the philosophies of the "open-market" which ostensibly favour the consumer.

Whatever developments may lie in store to affect the public's view of professional services, the present control system in use in the UK shows the influence of both popularist and professionalist views in a compromise that makes the legislators seem like prevaricators, whose shilly-shally serves nobody. The law itself starts with the simple statements in the Acts that are intended for everyone to understand, but it also makes regulations concerned with the definition of what is required in technical terms *that can be understood only by those with adequate specialist knowledge.*

This reliance on the expert technologist may seem grudgingly conceded, but it follows perhaps a natural and evolutionary course as may be expected to apply to the development of an industry of distant origins and long-established traditions. As we have seen, when regulations were first made they dealt with craft-based operations in widespread use. As buildings have become more diverse and equipped with highly-developed services, so the public, notwith-standing its own developing participation in technical affairs, has found itself acknowledging the role of the specialist more and more, and concerning itself increasingly with the training and qualifications of those involved in produc-tion and control.

The tensions are only too apparent in the existing forms of enforcement. Taking account of the need for the public (to whom the law applies) being willing to comply if enforcement is to be practicable in the first place, the need for clarity is even more important when the subject has such complexity. If it becomes difficult to know what the law requires, and equally difficult to recognize when it has been broken, the art of enforcement could become theoretically impossible, even when the community is well-disposed to the control and seeks to be law-abiding. The more the regulations are couched in technical terms and lay down their requirements in terms of functional or technical performance, the more difficult it may be to detect non-compliance. The inspector, by implication, will need special technical knowledge equal to that of the producer; and also some means of measuring performance or carrying out tests that are likely to require special instruments and expensive processes. The result takes the legislators several stages away from the simplicity of the language of the Act, with its appeal to everyman, to confront the new disadvantages. The expression of the law becomes technical and difficult; and the public is led to greater dependence on the expert to ensure that its requirements are understood and met.

Two versions of the same system of enforcement

In the light of the public's aim to control both large and small schemes alike, from the complexities of the macro project to the simplicity of domestic buildings, and in the light also of its hitherto unpretensious aim to achieve *basic safeguards,* the building control system in the UK has evolved two versions of a single system of enforcement. In order to identify these for more detailed discussion, it is best to see them in the perspective of a brief survey of the system as a whole, which can be simplified in the following way.

The community relies on the processes of its *central government* to create the system of control, to make the regulations, to oversee their application by making decisions on crucial issues, and to advise everyone involved with a view to smoothing out any operating difficulties. It expects these tasks to be a charge on the national exchequer, so that they can benefit from a scale of income that is logically commensurate with the responsibilities. It then relies on the due processes of its *local government* to give effect to the system by enforcing the regulations.

As a consequence, the task of enforcement has been subjected to the constraints of more modest budgets, which seems to indicate that in the mind of the public it has had a lower priority, or value. The arrangement has produced a varied pattern of enforcement. More money has been available to spend on surveillance in the districts of large conurbations, where control in any case has always had greater importance, and enforcement in such areas has been different in style and effectiveness from that practised in the smaller, less populous provinces. Traditionally enforcement has been a discretionary function of the public authorities, exercised in the service of the local community, and these principles remain, even though some important changes have been brought about by the reorganization of the local authorities, and the development of case law responding to consumer requirements.

Enforcement is governed by the same unwritten philosophy that applies in all the areas of jurisdiction. This requires that the public, having enacted its legislation and issued its regulations, *relies on its citizens to find out what the law is and to avoid breaking it.* In short, it leaves it to those who are concerned in building to do what the rules require, and in the general public interest it helps by ensuring that there is some checking of compliance through a local inspectorate.

It is at this local level of inspection that the two versions of enforcement have developed. The inspectorates do not have the powerful status of a formal police department, but rather function in an advisory capacity to their Councils; except in London. Nevertheless, it is the degree of authority employed that distinguishes the two types of enforcement. One method is authoritative: it operates through an inspectorate having direct legal powers and staffed by highly qualified surveyors whose control is exercised by the *inspection of the buildings on their sites;* the other is advisory, operating through an inspectorate whose officers have not been required to have any comparable level of qualification, and whose control consists basically in the *checking of plans.* In terms of the inspectorates involved, the former version has been more costly than the latter; but each has attracted criticism in respect of its ability to serve the needs of the modern community. The two methods are described in more detail in the paragraphs that follow.

THE LONDON VERSION

Of the main systems in operation for enforcing regulations made under the enabling Acts effective in the UK, the one which controls the inner London area is the longest standing and owes much to powerful and entrenched traditions. Perhaps because the hazards to the health and safety of the public are at their greatest in the great conurbations where there is a massive concentration of buildings, and also because the amount of construction work at any time tends to be greater, the regime has an aspect of unashamed authoritarianism. This springs from the customs of a construction industry whose particular forms of management have been firmly established by the long experience of labour-intensive operations. The regime exercises control over building in a direct, firm, and very personal way. Although the Council, as a publicly-elected body, has the function of controlling building, it places the responsibility for enforcement squarely on the shoulders of individuals appointed for that purpose. It is empowered to delegate in this way by the special Acts which relate to building in London.

The District Surveyors

These enforcement officers are known as District Surveyors, each of whom has an area of jurisdiction. They have a direct statutory authority. Their mode of appointment, qualifications, duties, and powers are all defined in the Acts of the central government in Parliament.

The London Building Acts give to the Council the authority to appoint "duly qualified persons to the office of district surveyor" to help it in the execution of the Acts and "any byelaws made in pursuance of those Acts". A number of administrative obligations are laid down by these Acts for the Council to follow, such as affecting the payment of salary and conditions of engagement, retirement compensation, the appointment of deputies, the provision of office accommodation, and the general directions which the Council is able to give to the district surveyors. But perhaps most important and unique are the provisions made for their qualification and the examination of candidates for office. Basically, any person wishing to qualify to hold the office of district surveyor must have a "certificate of proficiency" which is granted by a special Board, which is also set up by the provision of the Acts to conduct examinations for that purpose.

Their duties

The duties of the office are specified in three paragraphs which state in effect that all building works "shall be subject to the supervision of the district surveyor", who "shall...survey any building structure or work placed under his supervision *and shall cause every such provision to be duly observed*". Furthermore, if any district surveyor discovers that there is contravention of any of the Acts or by-laws which are "not within his competence to deal", this too must be reported to the Council.

The legal provisions or "design criteria" which the District Surveyor is required to enforce are contained, as has been shown previously, in both Acts and by-laws, in a way that differs from the national system where such requirements are confined to the building regulations alone. The London Building Acts themselves, *made by the central government*, set out requirements such as those dealing with open spaces, the construction of buildings, and means of escape (which in the national system are included in the regulations); and the by-laws, *made by the Council* under the Acts, deal principally with the safety of structures and materials. Except in regard to the rules governing open spaces and means of escape, the Acts cite the District Surveyor as the person whose judgement must be satisfied, as also do the by-laws throughout.

The Acts also state how the system of enforcement should work, in a degree of detail that is unusual and makes them different from other enabling Acts dealing with building control.

The control procedures

Indeed, the Acts and the by-laws together define what steps have to be taken by anyone wishing to build in the area affected by their jurisdiction, and by the controlling officers in carrying out their surveillance.

In the first place, when a "building or structure or work" is about to begin (or when it re-starts after a break of three months, or when the builder has been changed) the *builder* is required to "serve on the *district surveyor* a notice", which is known as a *"building* notice", and which is required to provide information as given in the Acts and the by-laws. This information must provide the name and address of the builder, the owner and the occupier of the site, and give the "situation, area, height, number of storeys and proposed use of the building" and its cubical extent. The "general" section of the by-laws requires that the notice should be accompanied by "plans and sections of sufficient detail to show the construction thereof and by copies of the design calculations" and particulars of the materials to be used and the work to be carried out. If the District Surveyor is not satisfied with the amount of detail submitted, he can call for more. The same section also states that "all work affected by any of the provisions of these by-laws shall be carried out to the satisfaction of the District Surveyor in a proper and workmanlike manner". In addition within 14 days of the completion of the work, the builder is required by the Acts to submit to the District Surveyor a statement of the cost, which is needed to help determine the fee payable to the enforcing authority. All this information, according to the Acts, is to be regarded as prime facie evidence of the nature and cost of the building "as against the builder or in his default, the owner or occupier...".

The District Surveyor, having received this building notice prior to the start of the work, examines the proposals, and if it appears from the information submitted that some provision of the Acts or by-laws will be contravened, he is required to serve on the builder or owner a "notice of objection" to the proposed work.

This particular provision does not apply to work which is proposed to be done to meet the requirements of means of escape in the case of fire, because these are dealt with in a separate part of the Acts. The requirements of that part entail the owner having to deposit at the County Hall, either before or at the same time as the building notice is submitted to the District Surveyor, another notice containing the same information but in addition two copies of the plans of the proposed building showing the means of escape. The Council in dealing with this separately is required to approve (subject to conditions if necessary) or refuse to accept the means of escape proposals within a given period and give notice accordingly, failing which the proposals are deemed to have been approved as they stand. Subsequently, after the completion of the building, the Council has to provide a certificate that the means of escape have been provided in accordance with the approved plans before the building can be occupied, and the procedure for doing so is again linked to a time limit.

As regards the controlling procedures which directly involve the District Surveyor, the serving of the building notice and any objections to its proposals are the steps that must be taken for checking compliance *before* the work is started. Further measures are applied to the control of the work in progress.

The District Surveyor's authority to inspect the work in progress is provided for in the Acts themselves, where it is stated that one of his duties is "to survey any building structure or work" and to do so "as often as may be necessary" to see that the rules are being observed "from time to time during the progress of the work". Further means are given in the by-laws, which call for other notices to be given shortly before work is done, enable tests to be made, and require work to be carried out to the District Surveyor's satisfaction.

During the progress of work on the site, if the District Surveyor finds that "anything is done in contravention of the provisions", or if he has not received a building notice and finds the work too far advanced for a check to be made, he is empowered to issue a "notice of irregularity" to have the work corrected within 48 hours, or to have any work that prevents an inspection being made to be undone or "laid open" to allow appropriate checks to be carried out.

This notice can also be served in respect of any building that has been erected or work completed without the requisite building notice having been issued in advance. In all cases it can be served on the builder in the first place, or on the owner or occupier as the case may be if for one reason or another its reference to the builder is not effective. *All these notices*, whether they are due before any work starts, or relate to work in progress, or completed work, *are supported by measures which define what legal steps can be taken by either party* to the enforcement process, and which can be seen as safeguards or penalties as the case may be.

In the first place, the Acts allow that any builder or owner who may be dissatisfied with a decision or requirement of the District Surveyor can apply to the council to resolve the question. The Council, in such event, "may reverse, affirm or amend" the District Surveyor's decision, and its own view is enforceable in the same way as the Surveyor's decision would have been, except that if the appellant is still aggrieved an appeal may then be made to the "tribunal of appeal".

There are two important qualifications affecting this process: the first being that a dissatisfied builder or owner is *not* able to apply to the Council for its determination "in the case of any provision that any work shall be carried out to the satisfaction of the District Surveyor in a proper and workmanlike manner"; and the second being that an appeal to the tribunal cannot be made about the Council's decision if the Council thinks that either the stability of the building or its protection from fire are being affected by the cause of the dispute.

As regards the "tribunal of appeal", the Acts describe in some detail its constitution, *modus operandi*, and powers. It is a panel comprised of six persons, one nominated by each of four professional institutions, and by the London Master Builders' Association, and the Secretary of State, whose representative presides at all meetings; it is served by appointed officers, and may obtain professional advice as it thinks fit; it is able to hear representations from the Council and other parties interested, in accordance with prescribed rules; and among other things it can administer oaths, receive evidence, and call for the production of documents or books. Most especially, it can state a case for the opinion of the High Court on any question of law, and any party to an appeal who questions its decision on any point of law can likewise ask for that case to be referred to the High Court for opinion. While the tribunal is to an extent a responsibility shared by the central government and the Metropolitan Council, its costs in terms of salaries, fees, establishment, and other expenses are defrayed by the Council. None the less, its decisions are ordained by Parliament by virtue of the Acts to be enforceable by the High Court, so that any order of the tribunal may be enforced "as if it had been an order of the Court".

Safeguards and penalties

These general provisions for appeals to the Council and thence to the tribunal may be seen as safeguards for both the builder (or owner as the case may be) on the one hand and the Council and the other, in regard to the operations of the District Surveyors in their role of enforcement officers. More specific arrangements are made in the Acts for dealing with the notices and to ensure compliance with the Acts and by-laws.

With regard to a "notice of objection", any person who is served with one but who is not satisfied with the decision of the District Surveyor in that respect is able to appeal to a court of summary jurisdiction within 14 days, and that court can by order affirm the objection or otherwise.

As to the notice of irregularity, if a person upon whom such a notice is served does not comply with it within the time prescribed, the District Surveyor is able to complain to a court of summary jurisdiction, and the court can make an order for the person to comply, in addition to the imposition of any other penalties that such courts can impose.

Further to this, and in a special part dealing with legal proceedings, the Acts declare that where a person has not obeyed an order made by a court of summary jurisdiction or a notice issued by the Council within the time-scale fixed, to remedy any contravention or to "remove" any building which is in contravention of the Acts and by-laws, the Council can, over and above any fines or other impositions due, complain to the court; and if its complaint is upheld, the court can authorize the Council to take direct action by entering the site and altering or demolishing the offending building or part, or removing the materials, and recovering all expenses incurred in doing so from the "person committing the offence".

Notwithstanding this formidable catalogue of prospective retribution, which the Acts of Parliament give on the macro scale to the task of enforcement in this area, the by-laws add, in micro scale, their own penalties in an introductory section dealing with general matters. This points out that any person who does not comply with the by-laws will have "committed an offence" and will be liable on summary conviction to a penalty of up to £50 and a daily penalty of up to £10.

The differences of the London system

All these instruments of authority add up to a form of control that is different in many ways from that employed in the other parts of the country. The main differences, which establish the essential characteristics of the system, are as follows. They are mainly to do with the status of the enforcement officer.

In London, the task of enforcing the by-laws and some of the technical requirements of the Acts themselves (which contain elements that are constructed as regulations for building), is delegated directly to the exectuive officers by the Acts of Parliament and by the Council. As a consequence these officers—the District Surveyors—have a *statutory* authority. Under the same statutes they are paid by the Council and are required to have special qualifications as determined by the Council in association with the professional institutions and other bodies of the construction industry, who represent those principally affected by the controls. As a result, the District Surveyors are perhaps unique among persons of their rank in the public service, having to qualify for admission to their status by taking examinations especially conducted for the purpose. Comparatively speaking, they are well-qualified and well-paid, and they hold a position endowed with unusual legal powers.

Although the law gives authority to their judgement and reliance is placed openly upon their opinion, the measures they enforce are designed to leave as little as possible to subjective interpretation. The by-laws deal exclusively with the strictly physical requirements of structure and materials, specifying what is required for stability and fire resistance. In so far as there are any provisions for public health, these exist only in the Acts and are expressed in specific terms of heights of rooms, dimensions of open spaces, and areas of windows. In principle, the instructions to builders as to precisely what has to be done are as direct in style as the powers for their enforcement.

Since it is necessary for each District Surveyor in his own area to satisfy himself that any building work complies with the Acts and by-laws, these documents ordain that plans, design calculations, and particulars of materials are submitted to him in advance of operations on the site, and give him powers to call for further information, which may include samples of materials and proof of their quality. In addition, notice has to be given to him before the start of various operations, so that he is able to inspect and call for tests as may seem to him to be necessary.

In all this paraphernalia of authority, the most significant element of the

District Surveyor's power is the requirement that all work must be carried out *"to the satisfaction of the District Surveyor in a proper and workmanlike manner"*. The strength of this provision is greatly reinforced by its exclusion from those matters which any dissatisfied builder or owner can refer to the Council for resolution when questioning any requirement of the District Surveyor. This means that in deciding what he might accept as satisfactory for compliance, he is shielded from effective criticism by those who are subjected to his decision.

In these terms, the judgement of the District Surveyor is the very substance of the law. If *he* is not satisfied, the *law* has not been complied with, and fundamentally there can be no scope for argument about interpretation or about what should be done. This has the effect, too, of reducing the need for recourse to the courts by the enforcing authority and of rendering appeals to them by building owners unprofitable, because all questions about whether or not the requirements of the regulations have been met have been pre-empted. A magistrate presiding at a court of summary jurisdiction and faced with the responsibilities of arriving at an authentic interpretation of the law would first seek to establish what the law comprised by calling the District Surveyor as an expert witness. If the by-laws require that the District Surveyor has to be satisfied with the work, and he states in the witness box that he is not, there is prima facie evidence that *the law* has not been obeyed.

Advantages

The system has some straightforward advantages for achieving objectives when these are limited and widely accepted. In sanctioning the control, the public is placing absolute reliance (with the basic aims of protecting its safety) upon selected individuals, whose terms of reference are clear and who are able to exercise a personal authority in a way that should promote efficiency and reduce delays by invoking prompt and unquestioning obedience. As an objective method, it has much in common with the familiar directives of military command. In theory, the public should get the kind of safety it wants without confusion or delay, provided that it can deploy enough of these enforcement officers to inspect all of the buildings under construction in the area at the time that inspections are needed. And the public should get the supply of buildings it wants provided that the prospective owners are not discouraged from creating their "fixed assets" by the rigour of the constraints.

By its very nature, the system concentrates on describing what must be done in terms of *means*, on the implied basis that the public's aims as law-givers are its own concern; but in framing its by-laws as specifications it is seeking to make them relatively easy for the construction industry to follow, since its executors work by reference to drawings and specifications. And by involving the professionals from the industry in the tribunals and the selection of inspectors it is seeking to promote their acceptance of the system and to improve its wider credibility. *The arrangement looks like a partnership between the "controlling" community and the "controlled" industry; and the community's resolve to*

see that the inspectorate is of high quality can be seen as complimentary to those who must submit to it.

The control system and traditional methods of project management

Indeed, as we have mentioned earlier, the control system reflects the traditional method of *managing projects* in the construction industry upon which it appears to have been modelled. The contract management techniques, evolved from experience or a particular operational situation, have worked well in their own context. The changes that were made in adapting the methods for the purpose of *managing enforcement* produced differences which are the weaknesses in the system.

The building owner's surveillance of a project is carried out by his professional agents: the architects, engineers, and quantity surveyors who supervise the work in progress. The architect exercises control through the authority given him by the building contract. Its terms provide the same kind of authority for him to see that work is carried out to his satisfaction on the particular project that is the subject of the contract, as the District Surveyor has for all projects under his jurisdiction. The difference is that the contractor has freely entered into the contract, and is himself committed to its objectives.

The architect's control is aimed at ensuring that the work is carried out in accordance with the drawings and specifications that formed the basis of the cost, so that the building owner gets the proper value for the money he has contracted to pay. These drawings and descriptions are the designers' technical instructions to the builder, framed to show him what he must do to embody the design in the finished building, which is the end-product and the whole purpose of the contract. The design itself has been completed at an earlier stage, having been drawn up to meet the owner's requirements for accommodation and expenditure. It is necessary for this to be agreed and fixed before work can begin on the final working drawings and specifications that will form the contractural documents. Any changes made after the design has been fixed will produce delay and extra costs, which increase in severity the later they are introduced. The highest cost penalties are caused by variations made after work on the contract has begun, for obvious reasons. These are: that on a large project there may be several hundred working drawings, detailed specifications and calculations, schedules of quantities of materials and operations, all of which have been used to work out the cost and to place orders; and that the contractor will have planned his work, with cash-flow projections, ordered materials, and deployed operatives, all in accordance with a programme to achieve completion within the period of the contract. At this stage, then, any changes, if practicable at all, would have costly repercussions. In this context the kind of authoritative control given by the contract is acceptable and appropriate: it is in everyone's interests to get the work carried out in accordance with the details, and finished on time.

The control of the District Surveyor is superimposed on this process with different ends in view, namely to see that the legal specifications are followed; and for this purpose his judgement has the overriding force of the common law, above and beyond the confines of the contractural authority.

It may be admitted in defence of this influence which is external to the normal relationships within contractural management, that the requirements that the law imposes are publicly available at all times, so the information exists to be taken into account when the design is drawn up. But the District Surveyor needs detailed information of the sort that only the working drawings and specifications can give, and he cannot begin his work of checking until the building notice is served. Already at this stage the pre-contract work is so far advanced that adjustments would impose delays and extra costs. Even so, he is obliged only to issue a notice of objection at this juncture if it appears that the law will be contravened; he has no obligation to approve, because the real object of his scrutiny is the condition of the building itself, so it is during the actual progress of the work on site that he will require changes to be made if he judges that the work is not satisfactory.

Disadvantages of a system of superimposed inspection

In short, the control of the District Surveyor can operate only when changes would produce delays and extra costs; and these penalties are at their greatest at the time when he has to carry out the inspections that are crucial to his function, which is during the contract period.

For the building owner there is, in theory, no way of avoiding the risks of incurring such cost penalties, because it is impossible in practice to find out what may satisfy the law as being proper and workmanlike, short of asking the District Surveyor to inspect during the progress of the work, and this is the time when the costs of change could be prohibitive. Strictly speaking, even if the designer can claim to have followed the legal specifications, the proof of compliance is in the execution, and it is the *District Surveyor* and not the designer *whose judgement is the law*, so the building owner can have no safe assurance of compliance, as he would have, in theory, *if he had been able to engage the District Surveyor to carry out the design and manage the contract*.

Any other arrangement than this hypothetical one must imply a doubling-up of supervisory effort, a loss of productivity, and a risk of higher costs.

Conclusions

All this points to the conclusion that the most efficient form of control would be obtained if the roles of designer and inspector were combined, because the crucial legal judgement would be applied from the beginning, and not brought into operation separately after the work had been carried out, when it could be too late. Ideal as this may be in terms of management, the public can make this type of solution impossible if it places reliance exclusively on the inspector to ensure that its requirements are met, as it does in London. By choosing *not* to place this reliance on the designer, the public is exposing the building owner to the risk of cost penalties. The level of this risk can be reasonable if the scale of investment is modest, and the skills used in building are of a traditional kind. But when the scale of operation increases, the cost hazard rapidly becomes less acceptable. When buildings become increasingly complex, using highly developed materials and equipment, and the work of the builder is more of a management role in an industrial process whose economics are governed by influences beyond the scope of any one particular project, the cost penalties can become too great to be acceptable hazards. At this scale, too, the building owner is likely to be the public client, or the publicly-owned company, so the public's interest in safeguarding itself can come round full circle. In seeking to get safe buildings in a way that puts the building owner at risk, the community is placing itself at risk, and to the increasingly onerous penalties that its scale of operation entails. In such event, a shrewd public can be expected to devise surer ways of protecting itself.

Questions of scale

The efficacy of a system of enforcement that involves the exercise of such a personal authority, then, is related to the scale of the activity it seeks to control. The closer the District Surveyor's sphere of operation is in scale to the contractural supervisory situation upon which the system is modelled, the more efficient the control is likely to be. The more involved the inspector can be in the design stages and the subsequent development of the scheme, the less likely are any drastic changes to be required at the later stages of approval. In this respect, too, it is helpful that the inspector should be as well qualified as the professional designer needs to be, and it is a point in favour of the system applying in inner London that the district surveyors should have the high level of qualifications that the selection process there ensures.

In this respect it is significant that the system operates within the central area of the London conurbation. In this situation the concept of one highly competent inspector exercising control in a compact area, with projects in easy reach, and having close relationships with the designers and managers, is a suitably practical proposition. One person like this can know enough about what is going on in his area to have effective influence. If the area is too large, or there are too many buildings under construction to supervise, the surveyor's department will grow and at the working level of control the inspector will be less well equipped for the task. Such a proliferation of assistants can lead to the development of a bureaucracy of the worst kind, comprising pedantic officials imposing petty restrictions with the powerful authority of the common law. This leads quickly to all of the crippling faults. The designer and builders whose work is affected will soon become resentful, and in self-defence will tend to rely rather deliberately on the inspectors on the basis that the law does, after all, require them to be satisfied. Such a "let-him-get-on-with-it" attitude will result in a deterioration of efficiency affecting the management of the scheme as a whole, producing delays and higher costs on the projects and more work for the inspectors. It also has the curious faculty of self-perpetuation. Inspectors placed in this position will become firmly convinced that the builders can never be relied upon to get things right, and will always be able to provide evidence to show that their own services are indispensable. A classic malaise of bureaucratic management will become evident in their exercise of authority without financial responsibility.

The growth of a powerful and self-righteous inspectorate in this way, enforcing fixed technical specifications, is an in-built barrier to technological development, and can soon do more harm than good to the community it is supposed to serve.

Is the system suitable for wider use?

It would seem then that this kind of enforcement has some obvious disadvantages to discourage its use on a national scale. The main drawbacks are to do with economics. Any national industry engaged in construction has at all times a need for higher productivity. When it is experiencing a period of peak demand it will be stretching its resources to produce more; when it is faced with a recession it will be competing with the demands on a reduced money-supply and struggling to reduce costs. As a consequence, it has a permanent interest in reviewing its methods and introducing change where necessary. It takes account of new industrial equipment and the related new methods of working, and, especially when demand outstrips the supply of familiar materials, it will experiment with the use of new materials. If the work of such an industry comes under the personal surveillance of different inspectors throughout the country, who would be exercising their own subjective judgement at the time when the cost of any changes needed is at its highest, its ability to achieve higher productivity would be obstructed. What may satisfy one person might not necessarily satisfy another, and there would be a high risk of requirements varying from one person and one area to another in unpredictable ways. This would discourage the kind of standardization that would serve the interests of economy, and inhibit the development of industrial techniques aimed at bulk supply, unless some overriding mechanism for approvals could be brought into operation.

When inspection is applied to the work on site and to the end-product, it needs precise terms of reference against which to check, which implies that by-laws should specify what materials must consist of, and how they must be used.

We have seen how such specifications have the effect of frustrating new industrial practices, and how the District Surveyor's ability to grant waivers may be claimed as a way of dealing with these problems. But this again means that dependence has to be placed on personal judgements in a way that is outdated in times of scientific assessments. Furthermore, the financial consequences of a mistake due to "human error" are out of scale with this level of judgement. The high penalty of failures in the modern built environment is perhaps the ultimate objection to the continued use of the central and personalized control system on any wide scale in a highly developed community, especially as the severe financial burdens threaten the public in its role as building owner and building inspector alike.

The effect of the consumers' interests

It seems unlikely that a system like this can survive in the changed climate of opinion about the protection of the public in a consumer-oriented community. Its very existence as a viable control seems to have been rooted in the nature of the duties laid on the public authorities in the UK. As we have seen, the enforcement of regulations or by-laws is a statutory duty placed on local authorities, but their powers have always been *discretionary*. In the traditional practice of this function if an authority made a mistake in carrying out its statutory duties, it was well protected from actions concerned with private interests by the absence of any contract between itself and the aggrieved owner. This avoidance of liability due to the absence of any individual relationship in law is of critical importance to an enforcement system which involves a local authority delegating its responsibilities to individual inspectors, or allowing those inspectors to be held directly responsible in law for their duties, as is the case in London. The responsibility for each District Surveyor to be satisfied is virtually absolute. Without the traditional immunity from prosecution for compensation in the event of his making a mistake, it would not be practical for a salaried official to undertake the duties and expose himself to such liabilities.

Changes in the law which can be brought about by the public's attitudes to consumers' rights can remove this immunity. In the UK judgements of law during the seventies introduced a new principle which is, in effect, that a law-enforcement authority may be sued, if the law is broken, by anyone suffering consequential damage. This places penalties for faulty enforcement on anyone involved in the responsibilities of enforcement, adding new problems to the many technical difficulties of trying to see that the law is being complied with. The more power is vested in the individual inspector, and the more personal his authority, then the greater is his vulnerability. As long as such trends continue, any control system that makes the task of enforcement a personal matter will be creating duties that are themselves too hazardous for any prudent person to perform. It seems likely that a reasonable person involved in inspection will carry out his duties with ever-growing caution, giving approvals or expressing opinions with increasing reluctance, and so qualifying his views as to make enforcement too protracted and expensive to be acceptable.

THE NATIONAL VERSION

A more familiar system of control than that applying in inner London is in use throughout all other parts of England, Wales, and Scotland. The Scottish arrangements have some similarity to methods used in London, as will be seen, but in most major respects are in accord with the operations as practised in the rest of the UK. The use of authority may seem moderate by comparison with the regimes of the District Surveyors. It can be said that the public generally seems to equivocate about where it should place reliance, and appears to depend on the industry and inspectorate alike to see that the law is obeyed, as though it expected better results to come from compromise and mediation rather than from any semblance of dictat.

As regards equipping the inspectorates with power or qualifications, the system seems to shy away from extremes, even though this may give its critics good cause to claim that its resulting characteristic is mediocrity.

The reliance on local authorities

In these regions the enforcement of the national building regulations is a statutory duty of the local authorities: a responsibility placed on them by the enabling Acts, as it is in London. These authorities have discretionary powers, which means among other things that they are able to decide how much of their income should be allocated to enforcement, and how it will be done. The law requires that plans and other particulars should be deposited with them by any person intending to build, and they have a statutory duty to *pass or reject* such submissions. However, unlike London, they have no duty to inspect the work in progress, or the completed building, though it is within their discretion to do so, and to this end the law requires notice to be given to them of the start and completion of various stages of the work. As a consequence of their obligations imposed by statute, they need to ensure that the resources they deploy are equal to the task of dealing with the plans, but it is for them to decide the amount of any inspection of the work.

The special nature of the system lies in the way the responsibility is borne directly by the Councils themselves (or the corresponding "buildings authorities" in Scotland), who are the elected members of the community, and *not by officials* like the District Surveyors of the London Building Acts. These bodies employ inspectors or technical officers, but as far as the law is concerned they are only there to advise and assist. Their building inspectors do not have any statutory powers or responsibilities. They provide a familiar service, and one which the public sees as a traditional function of local authorities, but the law gives them no status like the London Acts give to the District Surveyors. The regulations they enforce do not stipulate that they must be satisfied with the work or the workmanship, so that their opinion is not the law. The limit of their legal standing would be their appearance at the calling of a magistrate in a court of summary jurisdiction to give evidence as an expert witness if their

Council had taken action against some building owner for contraventions of the regulations, but in this they would have no legal precedence over other experts called by the defence. Their views, in short, can be challenged and argued accordingly, and their strength tends to rest on the premise that it is less inconvenient for a building owner to do what they ask, than to oppose them.

The building inspectors have had a role in the affairs of local authorities since before the time when regulations were made by the central government, having been engaged in the enforcement of the local authorities' own by-laws, in the days when the control was less ambitious and dealt only with comparatively limited problems of structure and fire. Their service in those times had been affected by the very modest size of some local authorities, and of their budgets. No special qualifications were ever laid down for membership of the staffs engaged in the service, and this had a predictable effect on the nature of recruitment to it. These disadvantages have persisted into the present time, not much relieved by the reorganization of local government when the duties were allowed to pass to the smaller authorities in the new hierarchy of local government. Their modest inspectorates now have the task of enforcing the regulations of the central government on behalf of their employing Councils, as a means of controlling the work of an industry whose technology can now be highly sophisticated.

Their duties

It has been shown that these duties are described in the Public Health Act 1936, Part 1, Section 1(1), and in Section 4(3) of the 1961 Act, where it is stated that "it shall be the function of every local authority to enforce building regulations in their district". Where these provisions apply in England and Wales, the main authority for the procedures used remains in Sections 61, 64, and 65 of the earlier Act.

The control procedures of the Acts

Section 61 establishes that by-laws made for regulating buildings *"may"* call for "the giving of notices and the deposit of plans, sections, specifications and written particulars; and the inspection of work; the testing of drains and sewers, and the taking by the local authority of samples of materials to be used in the construction of buildings, or in the execution of other works". Section 64 stipulates that a local authority, having received these plans when lodged for this purpose, *"shall...pass the plans* unless they either are defective, or show that the proposed work would contravene any of those by-laws, and, if the plans are defective or show that the proposed work would contravene any of those by-laws, they shall *reject the plans"*. According to the same section, this must be done within a time limit, normally one month, but in some respects dependent on the time-scale of the authority's own meetings, when notice must be given to the applicant whether or not the plans have been passed. A "notice of rejection" must inform the applicant of the defects that have caused the authority so to decide, and a "notice that plans have been passed" must be qualified by the statement that it represents approval "only for the purposes of the requirements of the by-laws" and, of course, of the Act itself in so far as its sections are relevant.

Section 64 also provides that if any question arises "as to whether the plans are defective or whether the proposed work would contravene the by-laws" between the authority and the applicant, it may be referred by the latter to a court of summary jurisdiction for determination.

Penalties

The penalties for non-compliance with the by-laws, which give the local authority some legal strength to go about its enforcement, are contained in Section 65. This states first that if any work contravenes the by-laws, the enforcing authority "without prejudice to their right to take proceedings for a fine" can make *the owner* remove it or otherwise carry out alterations to see that it does comply.

Furthermore, if work has been carried out without the prior deposit of plans, or has been executed notwithstanding that the plans have been rejected, the authority may require that it is removed, or give the owner the option of removing it, or otherwise complying with the conditions the authority would have made for passing the plans. In each of these cases the authority must give notice of its requirement, and the person receiving the notice must comply within 28 days (unless he can obtain an allowance for a longer period from a court of summary jurisdiction), failing which, the "authority may pull down or remove the work in question, or effect such alterations therein as they deem necessary, and may recover from him the expenses reasonably incurred by them in so doing". The section includes a safeguard prohibiting action of this kind from being taken after the expiration of 12 months from the date of the completion of the work. It also makes the important provision that the enforcing authority, or the Attorney-General, *or any other person*, has the right "to apply for an injunction for the removal or alteration of any work on the grounds that it contravenes" the law, even if the deposited plans had been passed by the authority, or it had not given notice of its rejection within the prescribed period, in which cases the court could order the authority "to pay the owner of the work such compensation as the court thinks just".

Safeguards

As to safeguards dealing with the right to appeal, Section 67 allows that if there is a dispute between the authority and the owner ("a person who has executed, or proposes to execute, any work") about the application of the by-laws to the work, or about whether the plans or the work itself are in conformity with the by-laws, the question can be referred to the Minister for determination *provided that the application is made jointly by that person and the authority*. The Minister's decision on such applications is final, and he is able to refer any question of law which may arise for the opinion of the High Court.

Another important provision for enforcement is made separately in the Act in Section 63 which enables an enforcing authority, with the consent of the Minister, to relax or dispense with the requirements of any by-law if its operation "would be unreasonable in relation to any particular case".

The 1961 amendment Act did not change these powers relating to enforcement in any substantial way, except that it replaced Section 63 with a provision for the Minister to relax or dispense with any requirement of the building regulations, and to do so as he may think fit on an application made by a local authority or other applicant, so that it was no longer necessary for such applications to be made jointly.

Improvements

The Health and Safety at Work Act 1974 again did not alter the generality of these provisions, but used the earlier Acts as a base upon which it added measures, some of which would affect enforcement with a view to improvement by making the process more flexible.

It is important to note that these new provisions did not come into operation at the date of the Act. It provided for the Secretary of State to appoint when the various subsections might come into force, by orders made by statutory instruments. The reforming measures also gave the Secretary of State enabling powers for the making of new building regulations which would themselves contain the new propositions, so that none of the changes would become operative without an appropriate commencement order, or without the making of the relevant building regulations as the case may be. In either case this would involve the process of making a statutory instrument and laying it before Parliament. Owing to economic constraints during the decade after the date of the Act, the implementation of its Parts was much delayed, and by the end of the seventies only two commencement orders had been made. The Secretary of State had used the authority given him to make two "type relaxations"; under one of the sections of the Act, to amend the regulations (in 1978) for the purpose of conserving fuel and power; and to begin work on introducing some of the measures aimed at more flexible enforcement procedures.

These new powers as contained in the Act are nevertheless referred to here whether they are yet effective or not, because they demonstrate the central government's interest in improving its system of controlling building by rationalization, and its intention to extend and update it acordingly. The new Act itself provides for the relevant parts of the 1936 and 1961 Acts, together with its own provisions, to "be construed as one". The reforming measures give an indication of the ways in which the previous measures have not been working well in practice, so that for the purpose of establishing principles the three taken together provide the most up-to-date blueprint for this particular style of enforcement.

Among the more important of the new measures were those which gave the Secretary of State power to make regulations to allow local authorities to consult with "any prescribed person" before taking action in connection with regulations (that is, they could take advice from experts); to accept certificates that requirements of the regulations had been met, as evidence of compliance, from "persons of any class or description prescribed... or... a person nominated in writing by the Secretary of State;" to charge fees for their functions relating to building regulations; to make "a prescribed person or class of persons responsible (instead of local authorities) for performing prescribed functions of local authorities under, or in connection with, the building regulations...". In plain language, this might result, for example, in an enforcing authority accepting certificates of compliance from chosen persons instead of carrying out inspections itself; or relying on someone (as a District Surveyor is relied upon) to carry out its work of passing plans and inspection, and making all necessary arrangements to defray the costs by charging fees.

In dealing with the deposit of plans, the Act introduced greater flexibility. It allowed a local authority to pass *by stages* plans deposited with them in accordance with the regulations, *or to pass them provisionally* (that is to say, subject to modifications that they might think necessary to remedy a defect or avoid contravention). It also allowed that building regulations might impose *continuing requirements* on owners (for example, to see that lifts were kept in good condition) as the Secretary of State might consider appropriate. Furthermore, it provided for the Secretary of State to dispense with or relax requirements "in relation to any particular *type of building matter*" (either conditionally or subject to specified conditions); or "to *approve* any particular *type of building matter as complying,* either generally or in any class of case", and to issue a certificate to that effect; and it allowed for the regulations to prescribe a fee to be paid to the Secretary of State on so doing.

The power of local authorities to require or carry out tests for conformity with the building regulations was strengthened. In addition to the existing ability to test subsoil and drains, it was made possible for them to call for tests on any material, component, or combination of components "in the building construction", or "any *service* fitting or component" so that the mechanical and electrical services could be properly dealt with. In each case the test could be carried out on anything which "has been, is being, or is proposed to be provided".

Additional provision for appeals were included, giving the Secretary of State discretion to allow an appellant and a local authority to be heard by a person he might appoint, in certain cases, and to give directions for giving effect to his determination. In these cases, and in reference to the Secretary of State's own decisions on certain issues specified, the Act made provision for further appeal to be made to the High Court "against the decision on a point of law".

On the other side of the enforcement process the Act increased the available penalties by imposing a "fine not exceeding £400 and...a further fine not exceeding £50 for each day on which the offence continues..." for contraventions of certain particular requirements.

The control provisions in the regulations

These three Acts, then, taken together, are the central terms of reference for authorities in England and Wales to enforce regulations. The building regulations contain additional instructions affecting the mode of enforcement, principally in the procedural sections describing what must be done in the giving of notice and the depositing of plans. These provisions require that anyone who intends to erect, alter, extend, or make any material change of use of a building, or *install* any fitting in connection with a building" must give notice and deposit particulars in accordance with certain rules which are given in a schedule. These rules specify what drawings and other documentation are required by the enforcing authority for the erection of buildings, alterations, and extensions and for "works and fittings". The information, which is required "as necessary to establish whether they comply with all such requirements of these regulations" is comprehensive. Apart from details of the size and position of the building, its site, its materials, mode of drainage, and water supply, other requirements are included with special reference to fire protection, means of escape, structural stability, sanitary equipment, and the installation of fittings. In certain cases the giving of notice and the deposit of plans relating to the installation of a fitting is excluded, and among these is the installation of certain kinds of gas appliance by an Area Gas Board.

The same section of the regulations also gives the requirements for the notices to be given in connection with the "commencement and completion of certain stages of the work". Apart from the notice of 24 hours for such traditional parts as excavations, foundations, damp-courses, and drains, and the 7 days' notice after the completion of drains and sewers, the builder is required to give the local authority notice 7 days after the completion of the erection, alteration, or extension of the building and also after "the execution of works or the installation of fittings in connection with a building".

HOW ENFORCEMENT WORKS IN SCOTLAND

Building control in Scotland is exercised under separate Acts and Regulations particular to that country. The system differs in ways that are due to the practice of Scottish law and jurisprudence, and the scale of operations being dealt with. As mentioned previously, the central enabling control is the Building (Scotland) Act of 1959, under which regulations are made not only to control buildings (by the Building Standards (Scotland) Regulations which are equivalent to the Building Regulations in England and Wales), but also to control *operations, procedures, and the forms* to be used in the general administration of the system (by the Building Operations (Scotland) Regulations, the

Building (Scotland) Act 1959 (Procedure) Regulations, and the Building (Forms) (Scotland) Regulations). In this way the form of enforcement is dealt with clearly, and is shown to be in all matters of principle similar to the arrangements described for England and Wales. In fact, the two systems appear to have influenced each other in the sense that the administrators in each case, when faced with reforming or updating their legislation, have had a parallel model to use in formulating new requirements. The modernization of the machinery for building control in the second half of the twentieth century was effected first in Scotland with the 1959 Act, so that the administrators in England and Wales had this Act and the Regulations made under it before them as examples when working on the 1961 Amendment Act and the first set of building regulations made in consequence of it in 1965. Similarly, the Health and Safety at Work Act of 1974 drew on the experience of both systems, and the schedule of amendments in it of the Scottish Act of 1959 were designed to bring the two control procedures into full parallel. The brevity of that schedule is an indication of how much of the changes to the other system owed to the practices already adopted in Scotland.

Reliance upon a "building authority"

In Scotland, in place of the local authorities of England and Wales, the building control system is enforced by a "buildings authority" for each burgh or county. This authority may be the "dean of guild court of the burgh", or for other formations of local government a group of "not less than three persons appointed by the local authority from among their number". The procedure for administration of all of these authorities is uniform throughout the country because it follows the appropriate *regulations for procedure*. Among these are requirements that meetings of buildings authorities must be held in public, that parties be heard before it in person, and that assessors may be appointed where special knowledge is called for.

The inspectorate

Another section of the enabling Act enables a local authority in connection with the buildings authority to appoint a "master of works" and pay him a salary. The duties of such officials are laid down in the Act as:

to report to the buildings authority upon all plans, specifications and other information lodged with applications to the buildings authority, to see that the orders made...are duly carried into execution, from time to time to inspect the works being carried out in pursuance of any warrant granted by the buildings authority and to report to the buildings authority any breach of the conditions to which the warrant is subject; and also to peform any other duties which he may be required by the local authority to perform.

The master of works must not have any direct connection with or interest in any part of the builing trade in his area, or give assistance or receive fees in connection with his work, and he must be "qualified in such manner as may be prescribed by the Secretary of State after consultation with such bodies as appear to him to be representative of the interests concerned...".

These requirements are reminiscent of the parts of the London Building Act relating to the service of the District Surveyors, although the masters of works created by them do not have the same unequivocal legal authority of those officers. Their responsibilities are similar to those of the building inspectors employed by the enforcing authorities in England and Wales, the difference being that they have the status given them by the Act itself, and that steps are taken to make qualifications a legal necessity, albeit with standards at the discretion of a Secretary of State.

The procedures of the Acts

In place of the "giving of notice and the deposit of plans" required by any person intending to build in England or Wales, the Scottish Act makes it an offence for anyone to "conduct any operations of the construction or demolition of a building", or "change the use of any building" (in a strictly technical—not a town planning—sense) without a *warrant* having first been obtained for that purpose. Applications for such warrants are made on forms prescribed by the relevant statutory regulations. The information needed by the buildings authorities is similar to that required elsewhere at the same stage of the control proceedings, but some attention is given in Scottish practice to the applicant having to deal with objections to his proposals from neighbouring proprietors.

A building authority is required by the Act to approve any application for a warrant provided they are satisfied that there is nothing in the plans to indicate that the building would not conform to the Regulations when completed. If the application is rejected, reasons must be given, but otherwise the authority is obliged to return the drawings duly certified for warrant, and such a warrant will remain valid for three years.

There are two categories of warrant, one relating to minor works and the other to works whose cubic capacity is in excess of 4000 cubic feet (113.20 cubic metres), to which different procedures apply. Applications for a warrant for minor works are dealt with by the master of works or the clerk to the buildings authority without formal reference to the buildings authority itself, although in the event of a refusal the applicant can insist that the application is placed before the authority.

All warrants contain a requirement that the appropriate building regulation must be complied with. In order to enable inspections to take place for this purpose, the *procedure regulations* call for the buildings authority to be notified of the dates on which work is started, and the master of works is able to "enter the premises at all reasonable times for the specified purposes of inspection", and otherwise to carry out tests or investigate matters concerning the works.

If he is not satisfied that the conditions of the warrant are being met, or where work is proceeding without a warrant, the master of works is empowered to issue a *notice* on the owner requiring him to show cause why he should not be required to put things right or remove the building; if he fails to do so, the buildings authority can take steps to execute the operation required. In this respect the force of the requirement is the same as applies in England and Wales, and in taking the necessary action the enforcing authority is able to charge its expenses to the offending owner.

After the construction of a building has been completed it cannot be used or occupied until a *certificate of completion* has been issued by the buildings authority concerned. It is necessary for the owners (that is, "any person having an interest to do so") to apply for this under the relevant rule. The certificate must be granted by the authority but only if it is satisfied that the building complies with the conditions of its warrant. So far as electrical installations are concerned, the authority is required, under the Act, to obtain a certificate "by the person who installed the installation, certifying that the installation complies" (an amendment in the 1974 Act extends this to other types of installation—that is, not electrical installations alone).

The Act also enables the buildings authority to delegate its function in this respect to (among others) the master of works, who is empowered to issue a notice with the same force as that described above if it appears to him that the building (in the words of the Act) "has been...constructed...in contravention of the conditions on which a warrant was obtained". In short, if the building is not judged to be in compliance, the owner can be forced to alter it as necessary, or to remove it, as the case may be, on pain of the enforcing authority doing what he has failed to do, and the owner is not able to use the premises at all until he has been granted the certificate of completion.

Safeguards and penalties

The Act makes provision for any aggrieved person to appeal to the Sheriff against any refusal by a buildings authority to grant a warrant or a certificate of completion, or against orders of one sort or another requiring buildings to be brought up to standard, or removed, etc., or against "charging orders" (by which expenses are recovered). In such a case the Sheriff, who may be advised as need be by technical assessors, may quash or confirm the decision of the authority concerned, or direct the substitution of some other decision. The procedure on an appeal of this kind is governed by an Act made by the Court of Session. The Sheriff's decision is final and binding on all parties, subject to references on questions of law being made by stated case to the Court of Session.

The Act also specifies penalties for offences in terms of fines, and provides for fees being levied by the enforcing authorities, empowering the Secretary of State to prescribe an appropriate scale of fees.

Comparative summary

To sum up, it can be seen that in respect of enforcement the Scottish provisions reflect aspects of both of the other systems of control in operation in the UK., Scottish enforcement practice is like the London system so far as it demands inspection of work in progress, requires the issue of a certificate of completion thereby making necessary the *approval or rejection of the completed building,* and provides for the qualification and appointment of an inspector, who it describes as the "master of works". It is like the system in England and Wales, and unlike the London system, in so far that it makes *elected members,* comprising buildings authorities, directly responsible for the jurisdiction and functions of the Act, and while it allows them to delegate some of their functions to an employed official, it provides that person with criteria in the form of building regulations that *do not make his opinion the law*. His status in regard to the interpretation of those regulations is, in strictly legal terms, neither more nor less than that of any other witness of similar qualifications. In this respect the powers of the masters of works are like those of the building inspectors in the district councils of England and Wales. In these ways the enforcement practices in Scotland, England, and Wales conform to the same principles and can be taken together as forming one example of a particular mode of surveillance.

THE NEW VULNERABILITIES OF ENFORCEMENT AUTHORITIES

It has been shown previously how this method of depending upon local authorities had the traditional advantage of shielding the inspectorates from legal actions concerned with private interests, due to the discretionary powers used and the absence of any individual relationships in the law of liability; and how this immunity from actions has been eroded by the effects of judgements in court which have favoured the rights of consumers.

In this respect the building inspectors of the UK control system have become particularly vulnerable, and their exposure to the risk of actions is a peculiar consequence of the way the practice of this control has developed historically.

When local authorities were responsible for enforcing their own by-laws, the requirements were minimal, being for the most part related to low cost housing, and were expressed in specific terms which made checking for compliance, inasmuch as it was needed at all, reasonably straightforward. The service in those times had been run on low budgets and no special qualifications had been thought necessary for its staffing, except in inner London, where city-centre building had more complexity. The low-priority, low-budget tradition became entrenched in practice, and persisted into an era when the regulations were transformed with national intruments for dealing with new aspects of the performance of buildings, making demands on new professional skills. A gap developed between the level of technical knowledge needed for the design of buildings and the traditional level of knowledge deployed in the enforcement services and soon became too great to enable inspectors to deal with the interpretative demands made on them by the new regulating techniques favoured by the national law-makers. This led the system as a whole to run into very serious problems affecting its acceptability in the eyes of the construction industry, even though the major part of the work of enforcement in practice still consisted of inspectors dealing with large numbers of applications relating to small works.

THE IMPLICATIONS OF ENFORCEMENT: A SYNOPTIC VIEW OF THE SYSTEM

To understand these problems fully, it is useful to take a synoptic view of the whole process of building control as exemplified by this form of enforcement which reflects a characteristic approach to the use of authority.

What the public expects

In this view, the system is one in which the public, through its democratic process, makes laws to control buildings for its own protection in regard to matters of crucial general interest, and in which it is held to be self-evident *that it is for its individual citizens to obey those laws*. As the public is itself made up of these individuals, *compulsion* is not seen as a primary factor in the encouragement of compliance, as it would be in theory if the laws were dictated by an authority not founded on public participation and consent. The laws are made, then, in the belief that they are there to be obeyed regardless of whether an inspectorate exists to enforce them. The regulations describe what is required of buildings, and all buildings must be constructed to comply: if they do not there are penalties for their owners involving financial disbenefits and legal retributions.

What it does to help

In the light of all this, the public also employs people to help ensure compliance, primarily with the objective of promoting its own safety, but also to assist or encourage the individual to conform, by advising him if he is not doing so, and only taking steps in compulsion after he has shown that the advice has not been heeded. The pattern of enforcement adopted for this purpose is a procedure that requires the individual wishing to build to display his intention, so that the question of whether he is likely to comply or not can be determined in advance. The building itself when completed may also be examined, but, in any case, whatever may be done in the process of checking intentions or inspecting work, the building must finally *exist in compliance*, and it is the responsibility of the owner, in law, to see that it does.

Benefits and impositions

The assistance which the public provides for the individual in this way is a benefit to him, but its value is reduced by the degree of loss and inconvenience that the constraints place on him, due not only to the standards imposed by the law, but also to the method of control itself. If the standards are higher than he would adopt for his own requirements, and if in providing them he has to submit to irksome procedures, protracted inspections, disrupted programmes of work, delays, and extra fee payments, he may find that the benefits are all cancelled out by the counterbalancing disadvantages. In such circumstances the individual building owner becomes resentful about the control system, to the ultimate detriment of its efficiency.

The condition of negative balance is reached when the apparatus of control is not aptly suited to the true objectives of the public. A number of disadvantages, always endemic in any form of restriction, are readily identified in the system as described. The system requires that checks will be made first on the "plans, sections specification and written particulars" which must be deposited before any work starts on any building, and secondly, though in varying degrees, either on the work in progress or on the completed building, depending on the area of jurisdiction, and subject to the discretion of the enforcing authority.

What is required of inspectorates

The first requirement of any inspectorate charged with such duties must be that the number of inspectors must be equal to the demand for inspections made on each project at the requisite time. The extent of this work-load is governed by the building programme in operation, which reflects the level of demand being made on the construction industry, and determines the *number of projects* in need of inspection, and the amount of checking and testing that needs to be done in each case, which depends on the *number of standards* governing various aspects of the performance of buildings laid down in the regulations and on the degree of complexity of each building and its equipment.

The problems

(1) Fluctuating work-loads

In each case the determining factors are outside the control of the enforcing authority, so its ability to achieve and maintain a proper match between staff and work-load is rendered too difficult for any real prospect of success. A well-known characteristic of the construction industry is that it has to contend with remarkable fluctuations of demand, due not only to the natural variations of market forces but also and primarily to the economic policies of governments who find the industry especially suitable for the "stop–go" controls of demand management. If local authorites appoint staff for periods of peak demands, they will be over-staffed for an equal proportion of the time when recessions cut back the industry's output; and if they do not, they will cause delays at the very time when the maintenance of high productivity is essential. As to the number of standards to be checked, it is the central government that controls the scope of the regulations and that will introduce new measures according to changing circumstances, as when the conservation of fuel becomes a national priority, or improved standards of safety are called for in response to some well-publicized disaster. Even if an enforcing authority were able to predict these fluctuations, the tradition for low budgets to prevail in its assessments of expenditure for building control would be likely always to prevent it from establishing an optimum deployment of services at all times.

(2) Multi-professional competence

For similar reasons these enforcing authorities are always likely to fall short in this deployment of an adequate level of technical competence, which is the second fundamental requirement for efficient enforcement. As we have seen, inspectors must have a technical proficiency for the effective performance of their duties, and this implies their having a level of qualifications and experience commensurate with that of the designers and managers of the construction industry who most submit to their inspection. In general, however, local authorities created their inspectorates when qualifications of this kind were not considered to be necessary, and this traditional attitude, taken together with their inclination for minimal spending, has always had an adverse effect on recruitment and quality.

Again, even if there existed a willingness to spend at levels which might secure the appointment of an aptly qualified staff, there would be little prospect of the balance of skills in the inspectorate team being kept in conformity with the nature of the work-load at any particular time, because the types of product that make up the output of the construction industry are as variable as the quantities it deals with. Its work includes houses, hospitals, factories, abbattoirs, leisure centres—diverse projects requiring many different skills and specialist knowledge, and it would be uneconomical for an enforcing authority to maintain personnel of such differing professional disciplines at all times. Some acknowledgement of this problem by the central government has been indicated in the provisions in the Act of 1974, in which authorities have been allowed to accept certificates as evidence of compliance from prescribed persons so that, by this means, specialists might be called upon, as already had been the case in Scotland with the similar provisions for electrical installations.

(3) Bureaucratic procedures

A third problem bringing disadvantages is the need for standard procedures to be adopted by the enforcing authority and applied regardless of the variable circumstances, because the law ordains such disciplines. The procedural "trigger mechanism"" for getting the process of inspection to begin is the requirement for the deposit of plans with the giving of notice of an intention to build by the prospective building's owner. The information required at that time can only be provided when the work of designing and detailing has reached an advanced stage, by which time it is too late for any alterations to be made conveniently. Similarly, when inspections are required for the issue of certificates of completion, it is already too late for the finished construction to be altered without incurring delays and extra costs. These systematic procedures have the effect of making the task of inspection unavoidably burdensome to the owner if the inspector finds something that he considers to be at fault. Such a method of ensuring compliance is clearly contrary to the interests of everyone concerned and a constant obstacle to efficiency and economy.

It puts the inspector in a position where he cannot avoid the dificulties unless he himself disregards the rules, and tries to have consultations with prospective owners at earlier stages of the work on their projects. Again the measures in the 1974 Act seem to have taken this into account in allowing plans to be passed by stages, and also provisionally. By such means it would be possible for an inspector to check drawings during earlier stages of preparation, and to inspect some details (such as foundations) before others (such as electrical installations), and give approval, if necessary, with conditions attached, all in phases that are more in keeping with the general programme of work on the project. All this however depends very much on the inspector's own approach to the work, the time at his disposal, and his willingness to take action that may put his own department at risk under the new punitive court rulings on liability.

A further disadvantage is the implication that each scheme must be dealt with separately and treated, for the purposes of the law, as a unique product. It is, of course, true that each building must be built in compliance, and therefore requires attention separately, but when the construction industry is coping with large building programmes at times of peak demand, it is likely to want to employ techniques of mass-production, perhaps involving repetitive prefabrication, which otherwise might qualify for batch inspection or other processes of quality control. These methods have not been available to building inspectorates, so that inspectors have not been able to improve their service to meet the increased pace of supply when the industry has been under such pressures, and so have not been able to play their part in helping to improve national productivity. The central government has taken a step to ease this situation by granting to the Secretary of State the power to relax or dispense with requirements relating to types of "building matter"; and, if he thinks fit, to publish notice of his decision. Under this arrangement it would be possible for a type of construction or component used in building to be accepted without subsequent checking, and for its "immunity" from the regulations to be advertised for the benefit of users and inspectors alike.

The effect of such disadvantages

These disadvantages have a pernicious character because they are built into the framework of the control system itself. They prevent its operators from achieving a fully satisfactory effect, no matter how much they are prepared to try. They induce others involved in the management of the construction industry to regard inspection by enforcement authorities for building control as a blight on its efficiency. When inspectorates become unpopular in this way a gap is opened between the controllers and the industry that can lead to irreconcilable division, and to the ultimate failure of the system of control to function as a true protector of the public interests, as its creators would intend. The problems then entailed can be self-perpetuating, with the industry placing more and more reliance on the inspectors to get things right; and the inspectors becoming isolated and forming their own institutions in which their communal attention is centred on themselves, and how best to develop and prosper their separate policing skills.

The introduction of a scheme for fees to be charged by the inspectorates for their work, and levied on the building owners, does not help to bring the two sides together. In theory, fees for any service are charged and paid by parties who have freely entered into a contract, and it is a principle of fair trading that there are options to that chosen course of action. By such normal standards it is difficult to justify fees being charged for actions made obligatory by law. The regulations in principle are made by the public for the protection of the public's interests, and the tradition that the enforcement services are a public duty laid on local authorities seems fitting. Since fees charged for the inspections for enforcement are additional to those already being paid by building owners for expert advice, the charges have an inflationary effect on the industry's costs, especially as one of the purposes of the expert advice is to produce a satisfactory building in the first place. For the mass of minor works applicants the situation can be especially disadvantageous. Such owners tend to avoid the advice of accredited experts on the grounds of cost, and employ instead some drafting service to prepare whatever plans are needed for deposit. If such owners are then charged for the inspection of plans which are unlikely to be entirely adequate, they will find themselves spending more for what, taken as a whole, is an unsatisfactory process, and which by virtue of its procedural limitations can never be properly suited to an efficient production service.

The greatest disadvantage of all under which a control system can attempt to function is that caused by the exposure of inspectors or enforcing authorities to private actions to recover damages for buildings that have proved to be faulty. The charging of fees can lead to mistaken assumptions that such actions can be justified, but their effect can be almost totally disrupting for the industry. The causal sequence begins with the unfortunate status of the inspectorate having authority, *without responsibility or accountability*, to the individual building owner. The inspector owes allegiance to the enforcing authority, *not* to the owner who pays the fee. If the inspector is made liable to heavy financial penalties for his actions, he has no direct incentive to consider the effect of his decision on the owner's costs. The incentives work in the opposite direction, giving the inspector the most powerful reasons to exact the highest standards and doubly-secure safeguards, regardless of other factors or priorities; or else to avoid taking decisions; especially any which might be taken to indicate approval. No enforcing authority faced with the unending liabilities attaching to all of the buildings in its area could be expected to sanction any other service than that governed by painstaking caution; and no industry, faced with such delays and cost-burdens being applied (as we have seen, by the nature of the system) at the later stages of the production process, could be expected to achieve true efficiency or provide the best value for money.

Such damages to the function of the control system may seem to be exaggerated, but they must be judged on a proper assessment of what an inspector is being asked to do. If the law requires that all work must be carried out to his satisfaction, his liability is seemingly absolute, and the financial hazards entirely out of proportion to his means. If regulations are cast in a functional mould, and require for example, that a structure must "safely sustain and transmit" all loads "without such deflection or deformation as will impair the stability of, or cause damage to, the whole or any part of the building", then a judgement is called for in deciding whether or not the requirement has been complied with; so that if an inspection has been made, and approval given, the enforcing authority is accordingly liable for any consequences of failure.

Functional requirements call for judgements in many different fields of speciality, so if inspectors have been appointed without matching qualifications, then too much is being asked of their judgement, and their reluctance to offer an opinion is entirely justified. This does not contribute to efficient enforcement.

Problems of change

Clearly, radical changes are needed to ensure that the public gets the kind of enforcement it is entitled to expect. These are difficult to bring about: indeed, the very nature of the control system tends to prevent any widespread acknowledgement of the need for change because the elected members of central and local government are inclined to rely upon the officers involved in the administration of the existing system for their knowledge of the system; therefore their understanding of its problems may be handicapped. For example, the department of central government concerned with building control may keep a dossier on the appeals and decisions referred to the Secretary of State, with a view to revealing which regulations present the most difficulties in practice. Those which give rise to the greatest number of disputes must be the first candidates for amendment. Consequently, the

Minister's advisory committee may have its time taken up with proposals for amendments based apparently on impeccable statistical evidence of the short-comings that are to be eradicated. But this procedure is unlikely ever to reveal that entirely different and more comprehensive reforms (like replacing a specific requirement with a performance standard) could make the measure itself unnecessary, sweeping away not only the disputes about its detail but also the root of the problem. Similarly, the inspectors, finding themselves increasingly under pressure to make decisions and issue certificates, will always produce persuasive justification for their own role as the central and indispensable factor for enforcement, and one which is always in need of strengthening.

OTHER METHODS OF ENFORCEMENT

Apart from these methods of enforcing building regulations and by-laws made directly for the purpose of building control, there are other methods in use for applying other types of constraint, which reveal that other options exist for the building control legislators. These other ways of practising enforcement are also used to control some aspect or other building, though with different objectives in view.

The control of special building types

First there are the regulations made by the Ministries of central government, with responsibilities for particular functions like education, health, and living accommodation (as referred to previously), to control the special types of buildings, such as schools, hospitals, and houses. These regulations are *administered* in similar ways to those used for the national building control in the sense that the rules are made by the central government covering educational policy and building, but are put into effect by the local authorities who have the executive responsibilities in their areas. Enforcement is not so much by legal sanction as by the Secretary of State of the relevant department of central government denying finance to those not complying. The building owners are the local authorities themselves, who obtain their funds for the buildings largely from the central government, so the relationships between the executive bodies are different in this sphere of control. The buildings affected by these arrangements must nevertheless be constructed to comply with the standards applied to all buildings by the national building regulations: the special provisions are additional and have different objectives.

Setting aside these differences, these methods of enforcement were of course much in evidence during the times when there was extensive capital spending on the large-scale building programmes. Among the more familiar, if not the more successful, was the method used by the national Department for Education in its control over the building of schools. The local authorities, as building owners, employed professional consultants and designers as their agents to manage their programmes; that is, to design and supervise the contracts for building the schools.

The central government department also employed professional advisers of the same skills and disciplines to inspect and improve the drawings and other particulars submitted to them. This made it possible for procedures to be developed to enable consultations to take place during all the critical stages of the schemes' development, and for these to include informal as well as official reference. The key to the effectiveness of the system was that the "inspectors" in the department of the central government were themselves part of a team who carried out experimental building projects to explore problems and demonstrate solutions, so that the rules that were enforced were based on experience gained from direct involvement, as well as from the surveillance of the generality of work on the national programmes. This meant that the "inspectorate" was highly specialized, and in may ways functioned as a central depository of knowledge gained from all the current experience of the type of building it sought to influence. It was able to publish technical advice, organize conferences, promote symposia, and generally play a leading part in establishing how best to achieve the common objectives of the department's own regulations.

Other departments sought to influence their building programmes in similar ways and with comparable degrees of success. Although such methods of enforcement were the outcome of the particular circumstances surrounding the demands for special types of buildings in the public sector of the economy, they have a value for the student of building control methodology. They showed that it was possible to achieve a different relationship of *collaboration* between the "controllers" and the "controlled" with beneficial results for the public's interest in getting good value for money in the end-product. *They demonstrated too that there was much to be gained in the establishment of a directorate of high quality as the focal-point of the control system, which could acquire and maintain a high acceptability in its specialized field, and so guide as well as control the work to which the regulations applied.*

Statutory suppliers

A second example of other controlling methods is to be found in the methods used by the statutory suppliers, who provide electricity, gas, and other services, and who are also accustomed to making regulations as safeguards in connection with the installations constructed to receive and use their supplies.

These regulations are made and enforced by the suppliers withholding the supply of their service until compliance is confirmed by their own inspectors. The method seems to involve practices that are antithetical to those described above. The regulations themselves are familiar to their authors but otherwise obscure and written in a way that seems to make no concessions to the user's comprehension. The model water by-laws, for example, which were made by the central government Department for the guidance of the former waterboard authorities, might be included among the most baffling essays in legal phraseology ever composed. The inspectors who enforce these requirements are employed by the suppliers. There seems little apparent effort made to develop any communcation between the controllers and the owners of the installations or their professional agents, who must comply; nor any sustained attempt to disseminate information for guidance or to promote a wider understanding of the aims of the controllers. By comparison, this control system seems to be a closed technical world, in which the controllers operate from a protected base. The system works on a form of "dictat", and any person wanting a supply simply complies with the advice of the inspectors, so it is difficult to assess the efficiency of the control and to draw any conclusions about its usefulness as a model. In principle, systems of this kind which in practice apply specialized and, therefore, somewhat obscure criteria under a control that may seem immune from influence, are not likely to survive in such form in the new climate of opinion that favours more consumer protection. The high penalties for failure, the consequential need for indemnity, and the interest in cost-effectiveness that apply in the wider field will all affect the inspector and consumer alike; and in this general context the need for methods to be predictable and widely acceptable is of paramount importance to their survival in use.

POSSIBLE IMPROVEMENTS

Old methods and new situations

The systems of enforcement described in this chapter have evolved during long periods of bureaucratic experience. Methods were devised in times to meet the circumstances which then prevailed, and each has tended to survive beyond its era of usefulness, to be inherited by later users facing new conditions. Modifications made to meet problems as they have arisen have been collected into the canon, and the various administrative habits have been nurtured in practice by succeeding generations of legislators. In London, particularly, the problems of enforcement have had a powerful influence on the development of the system as a whole.

In recent decades there has been a great expansion of knowledge about user requirements, and about what the public needs to do to take care of its health and safety in the face of newly recognized dangers, as well as those that have become familiar. At the same time, industrial development has promoted new ways of providing for these needs. Yet when the framework of local government was reorganized during this period, no special steps were taken to try to match the new inspectorates with the changing and far-reaching demands affecting the control system in the modern world. On the contrary, the task of enforcement seemed to be treated as one of the local duties to be assigned to the new district councils, who were the most modest in size of the authorities then created. As a consequence, the public found itself having to rely on the new staffs, recruited before any recommendations had been made about the qualifications and training needed for such responsibilities, at the very time when the legal changes were becoming effective, and the financial burdens of any failures (which might be undetected by surveillance) were increasing.

In spite of the obvious need for more radical reform, it is rarely possible in practice for anyone to have the opportunity to design a control system comprehensively to suit the prevailing needs. But it is possible as an interesting theoretical exercise to assess the existing methods of enforcement objectively and to postulate how a new structure of management for controlling building could be set up, taking account of the past experience of the public's administration and of the nature of the construction industry. What is needed in the productivity-conscious world of today is a way of ensuring that the public gets the standards of safety it needs, with the least disruption to the flow of the work being controlled, and with the minimal additions to the normal costs of production.

What good are the existing systems?

At the outset of any review of the performance of the systems of *enforcement* it would have to be admitted that there are difficulties in establishing how effective they are, or whether indeed the degree of safety achieved by the construction industry would be the same without them. As the construction industry's professional institutions have not been loathe to point out, during the post-war decades when there were large-scale building programmes in progress, half of the total national output was being financed by public spending. This meant that a significant portion of construction was being carried out without the involvement of the building control enforcement inspectorates at all. The work had to comply with the requirements of the regulations, but did not come under any formal surveillance by the local enforcement authorities. Yet there is no evidence of the half-portion of the national output of buildings that escaped the formal control system being less safe or having lower standards than the half that was governed by the control procedures. The two most published failures during this period were the Ronan Point disaster, and the collapse of structural-concrete members made with high alumina cement. In the case of Ronan Point, the Minister's inquiry showed that the structural regulations had *not* been contravened, and that the project had been dealt with, as it happened, by the local enforcement authority. In the case of the deterioration of concrete, the use of high alumina cement had not been confined to public sector projects.

There *is* evidence, on the other hand, of the high standards of value for money achieved in the public sector over a comprehensive range of building types: for example for the education, health, defence, and housing programmes.

The reasons for this have often been expounded by prominent members of the construction industry. The public building programmes were carried out under the surveillance of the architect, engineers, and quantity surveyors who form the normal design-management structures of the industry, and for the most part executed by reputable builders under standard forms of contract. The professional designers are bound by their own terms of appointment or conditions of engagement, and have a duty to their clients to ensure that their buildings comply with legal requirements and have clear responsibilities in this respect, for which they are covered by their professional indemnities. The builders are working under a contract the conditions of which require them to ensure that the building does not contravene the law.

In short, the normal duties of those involved in the construction processes include ensuring that regulations are complied with. The professional status of the persons concerned is bound up with the proper discharge of those duties.

In the light of these facts, the public may well ask what had been gained by its expenditure on the enforcement procedures applied to the private sector, and whether the spending had really been necessary at all.

In defence of the control system it may be argued that a major part of the work in the inspectorates was involved with the large number of *small schemes* carried out without professional advice or standard forms of contract, so that the control system at least provided a safeguard for those minor works. Against this would be the contention that such schemes are for the most part so modest in scale that they do not represent any danger worthy of public precautions. Such arguments, however, need to be enlightened by reference to statistics that are not readily available in any form that would provide useful evidence for assessment.

A similarly disparaging comparison can be made concerning the system of control by the District Surveyors of inner London. The capital is a large conurbation in which only the inner boroughs come under the jurisdiction of this system. The remaining outer boroughs employ the national system of enforcing the building regulations with the help of their own inspectors. Yet there is no evidence that the properties in one area are more safe than in the other, nor that there are more building failures in the outer boroughs. If it is true that there is no difference in these standards of safety, the public may well ask what is achieved by the uniquely authoritarian and more costly arrangements of the regime in central London.

Such doubts need to be taken into account in any considerations aimed at introducing reforms on a comprehensive scale to the enforcement system. To give them expression may seem contentious, especially to those persons who are involved in the public service in the present arrangements, but the purpose of mentioning them is not to exacerbate any existing controversies or bureaucratic rivalries. Rather, it is to show that however conscientiously they may be applied, the existing practices cannot be regarded as proven as essential to the maintenance of the existing standards of safety; so that, on these grounds, the present level of spending on building enforcement may be open to question.

There can be no doubt that the amount of public expenditure on enforcement will continue to rise if the legislators continue to favour the use of the functional requirement as a regulating technique, and the legal penalties for failure go on increasing. We have seen that there are direct pressures resulting from this type of regulation. The inspectors are required to make technical judgements about safety, and will be faced with making calculations to prove that the design theories used by the designers are satisfactory, and inspecting to ensure that the complex requirements of the manuals are being embodied in the structure. A predictable consequence would be an expenditure of time and effort far beyond the limits hitherto considered appropriate for enforcement.

What the public needs, however, is a safe-and-sure method of achieving its protection without undue direct cost and without additional cost burdens being imposed on the *production* of its buildings.

How best to ensure that a building complies with regulations.

In order to ensure that a building complies with all aspects of the regulations it would be necessary to bring to the task of inspection the right *quality* of judgement, and the right *type* of professional or technical skill, at the *correct time* during the progress of the work of producing it. If the assessment is apposite, and the timing is right, the standards are most likely to be achieved without delays and extra costs. Furthermore, the task needs to be carried out in a climate of opinion which accepts the public's concern for its interests. In this regard the co-operation of the construction industry (using this term to include its professional designers and advisers) is valuable in getting the best results. Its members need to be able to respect the public's representatives and to feel that the work of enforcement is helpful and not a hindrance to efficiency and detrimental to productivity.

The work of enforcement concerns not one building but a continuing programme of projects of varied size and differing types, and, in a free community, tending to occur at random times which are outside the influence of the inspecting authority. No inspectorate could be expected to have within the bounds of an efficient and economic service the proper array of skills at the right level of qualification at all times, and for all projects. Yet it would be failing in its task if it did not bring these resources to bear on each building as the need arose. This is the classic situation for using private consultants or advisers as an occasion demands, instead of maintaining a permanent establishment of many skills.

The case for a collaborative control

The projects are all produced by the construction industry, however, and it is part of its system of working that the teaming-up of these professional skills must always match the requirements of each scheme. No truly economical project can be produced without its quota of skills of design and management.

In the normal course of practical events, therefore, every project coming before the scrutiny of an enforcement inspectorate is already equipped with its technical and financial pilots. Those owners who attempt to build without proper advice, in the false hope of spending less money, will in effect be using the public's inspectorate to get things right, and will be involved in a wasteful process of trial and error.

As mentioned previously, the consultancy and the contractual production teams are already responsible to their clients, the building owners, for seeing that the projects are built in compliance with the regulations, so theirs are the skills, deployed for the purpose of each job, that ought in theory to be used by the public to provide guarantees that its requirements, too, have been met. In the logic of this theme it would be for the public to pay a fee for this service, and so establish a bona fide contractual relationship to get what it wants. By this means the function of the designer and the inspector would be combined to establish what is theoretically an ideal condition for effective and efficient conformity with the law.

Arrangements of this kind are not new, but have been in use in various forms for a long time: sometimes informally, but more recently by formal contracts. In the days when local authorities made their own by-laws, some would ask the professional consultants residing in their area to sign certificates that work had been carried out in compliance with the by-laws, and had accepted these certificates as substitutes for confirmation by their own building inspector. More recently, authorities have employed independent specialists to check the calculations for structures submitted for approval by the engineer-designers. The custom has been given official recognition in the provision of the 1974 Act that regulations could be made to authorize enforcing authorities to accept such certificates as evidence of compliance, provided that they were signed by persons approved for that purpose by the Secretary of State.

New enforcing methods

This would indicate, then, that a reasonable basis for an enforcement system would be one that is based upon the professional skills of the industry itself. Such a system could follow the principles of the existing arrangements, operating within the familiar procedural framework, but using enforcement authorities functioning at the regional level.

Each authority would have an area of jurisdiction large enough to enable it to maintain an effective service of high quality, which would indicate a size equal to that of an existing county. It would need a close liaison, on the one hand, with the department of central government concerned with making regulations, and on the other, with the local representatives of the building industry and its professional institutions. It would also require contacts with the fire authorities in central and local government. Its links with the public in charge of the system would be through the normal channels of the electorate, locally and nationally. It would employ a high-ranking executive officer, at least of the status of the present chief officers in the County Councils, and a small but highly qualified staff, whose duties would be like those of the existing enforcement authorities, involving discretionary powers and the duties relevant to the enabling Acts.

The main difference from the present system would be that the "field work" of enforcement, consisting of the checking of plans and the inspection of work, previously carried out by the employees of the local authorities, would be performed by the professional consultants and other qualified persons of the industry. These would be duly accredited by the Secretary of State responsible for building legislation, and it would also be the duty of the professional institutions in collaboration with the government to ensure that the qualifications needed for professional practice should include provisions for candidates wishing to qualify for their registration for such building-control work in their discipline.

The implications of this kind of system, especially in regard to the various aspects of responsibility for enforcement, will be dealt with in more detail in a later chapter. The basic power to enforce the regulations would still reside in the executive local authorities, as prescribed by the Acts, together with the ability to grant relaxations, deal with appeals, and otherwise discharge the duties required of them. A main task for the new authorities, however, would be to function as a focus for all matters relating to the regulations in its area, and to provide surveillance and leadership of the *system* to that end.

Of course, these are broad outlines only of how enforcement might work efficiently and without undue cost. The general concept is that the public would rely technically on the skills of the industry to see that its legal requirements were met, but would maintain a highly-trained elite service in each region as a monitor of efficiency, and as an enlightened adviser on the effectiveness of the system as a whole.

CHAPTER FIVE

Standards, codes, and assessments

THE MEANING OF STANDARDS

In addition to the regulations that have the backing of law, most countries in Europe have national standards and codes of practice relating to the construction industry, which are published as documents giving detailed prescriptions and advice and which are frequently referred to by the legal provisions for building control.

Standards vary in status from country to country, but invariably do not originate as legislation. For the most part they represent a consensus of the views of those with interests in the industry, although they are produced in a co-ordinated way that involves governmental interests too, and so have an authoritative standing. As regards subject-matter, they deal variously with materials, methods of manufacture or construction, and procedures. For general purposes the word "code" is synonymous with "standard", though in some countries it is more related to the work of establishing what is good practice, and owes more to the professional sector or the industry attempting to establish principles and to propogate established theories, or to lay down rules of behaviour.

It seems that a good deal of misunderstanding and confusion can arise with regard to the role and the meaning of standards in the hierarchy of control instruments. This is due in no small measure to the ambiguities that seem always to have affected those two aspects of standards: what they are intended to do in themselves, and what their status is in legal terms.

As regards meaning, the word "standards" in this context can have a dual purpose: to denote *typification* on the one hand, or a degree of *quality* on the other. Among the many meanings ascribed to the word in the *Oxford Dictionary*, the two most relevant to its use in the sense which relates to building activities are: (a) that it is an "authorized exemplar of a unit of measure", that is "a normal *uniform* size or amount; a prescribed minimum size or amount"; or (b) that it is an "authoritative or recognized exemplar of correctness, perfection, or some definite degree of any *quality*"; and the verb derived from it—*to standardize*—is given as meaning "to bring to a standard or uniform size, strength, form of construction, proportion of ingredients or the like". This latter meaning probably reflects accurately enough the original purpose of those who set about preparing the original "standards" for industry in the first place: they were responding to the need to reduce varieties of products being made for similar applications, like nuts and bolts, and so to cut out the wastage of materials, time, and money in the interests of general efficiency.

This clearly could not be done for the construction industry (nor for any other industry) without acknowledging the implied need for an assessment to be made of the appropriate quality for the product being standardized. For example, it would "go without saying" in the construction industry that structures must be safe, so that the need for safety would be a guiding principle. In consequence, products would need to have stability or reliability, and this would imply a "level of correctness" or quality, and lead the standard-makers to assumptions about what the *quality* for the standard would need to be.

The idea that there should be standardization for the purpose of economic production probably came first, and in following this task through the original makers of standards would have had little guidance about degrees of safety, or any other aspects of performance for the article being specified. At that time, neither the public using the products, nor the construction industries, had begun to think in terms of setting qualitative standards for *performance* as a means of serving the interests of safety and health. This problem of co-ordinating public's or "consumer's" needs with the needs of industry remains largely unresolved, even in present times when use-requirements have become more widely recognized as being capable of definition by the customer. It is still true of most countries that consumer needs, which *should* represent the aims of the construction industry, and which set it the problems to be solved, have never been adequately codified before the industry attempts to standardize its answers in terms of products and practices.

The ambiguities are in some respects reflected in the laws made for building control. These can be made either with the objectives of public health and safety, or with the additional aims of achieving good value for money in buildings. Most enacted laws have the first objective in view, but the second is in all minds as desirable, and functions in the background as an unwritten law. This seems everywhere apparent in the use which is made of the standards and codes by the formal legal provisions of building control from country to country.

In using standards to represent the more detailed requirements of the law, the control systems encounter the problems of approval. It is one problem to decide how to accept products that are purported to be made in accordance with a standard, or methods that follow an accepted rule of procedure, and another to deal with new materials, components, or techniques that have not yet entered the canons of the "norm". Alongside the continuing preparation and updating of standards, then, control systems usually have some way of making assessments, or methods of approval, which also vary in status from one country to another.

STANDARDS IN EUROPE

Scandinavia

In the countries of Scandinavia the pattern of building control is similar to that used in the UK, consisting of national building laws authorizing the central government to administer the system and to make regulations; subordinate provisions which take the form of regulations applied nationally; and enforcement by local authorities. The regulations, which are intended to govern the "design, construction, and execution of buildings" are made not only in the interests of "safety, fire protection and health—including insulation against cold and heat, noise, damp and odours", and the "design and operation of sanitary and technical installations", but also to encourage good quality in building, efficient management, and technological development by such means as the application of information from research and the adoption of requisite levels of standardization in materials, components, and fittings.

In Denmark the national standards are, in effect, prepared by the Danish Association of Engineers (the DIF). This is a professional organization having a high standing, and which through its members as well as by formal means, has close working relations with the building research institute, the technical universities, and the staff of local government departments involved in building control. The DIF sets up committees who prepare the codes or "norms" and these are adopted and published as Danish Standards (DS). Extensive reference is made to these in the national building regulations, and in certain subjects, like structural design and thermal insulation (which are basic objectives of the primary legislation), the adopted DIF Codes are the main instruments of the control system.

In Sweden, codes of practice are also prepared by other bodies like the Committee for Structural Design in Steel, and the Concrete Committee, dealing, for example, with structural steelwork and concrete, but the national regulations (Svensk Byggnorm 67: SBN 67), which are prepared by the Board of Urban Planning (SPV) (or such other department of central government as may be designated from time to time), are themselves regarded as a code, as implied by the title which translates as the "Swedish Building Code". The codes produced separately are, where appropriate, re-issued as supplements to the SBN 67. The Swedish Standards Institute (SIS) does not play any central role as regards the technical aspects of building control, though reference is made to various standard methods of description. There are again strong formal and informal connections between the department responsible for the national code, the research institute, and the technical universities.

In Norway, where the building law places responsibility on a central government department to make and administer the national regulations, these are prepared on the advice of the Norwegian Council for Building Standardization, and the Norwegian Building Research Institute, since there is no practical distinction between the legal provisions and the standards.

In all three countries there is a General Approvals Scheme which operates as an integral part of the central system for the administration and monitoring of the national building regulations. Products, designs, and building systems are subject to a General Approval certificate, for which application can be made by the industrialist (or others concerned with supply), to the central building-regulation authority. The drawings, specifications, and test data are examined and if necessary other checks made either by the central authority (as in Sweden), or by the research institute acting as its agent (as in Norway and Denmark), and a certificate is issued on a standard format, giving such information as the period of its validity, the conditions of its use, and the regulations that can be considered to be satisfied. This approval gives the subject of the certificate a status of being deemed-to-satisfy the specified requirements of the national regulations, and all the local enforcement authorities are notified accordingly.

In this way the standards and codes, together with the certificates of General Approval, are closely related to the building control system in Scandinavia, and are in many respects indistinguishable from it. The certificates of approval are passports to the acceptance of a product or system as meeting the requirements of the regulations; and by virtue of their terms of reference, the building regulations also function in the role of standards, being either issued as codes, or else lending their authority to other codes made separately but in full recognition of the status that will be conferred upon them.

West Germany

In the German Federal Republic the member States, or *Länder*, being self-governing, enact building legislation in the form of ordinances (*Bauordnungen*) which are guided by a national model (*Musterbauordnung*) drafted by a federal committee. Other orders ensure that the ordinances are implemented, and a national scheme for the approval of new materials and components and for quality control together complete an archetypal form of building control.

Other legislation affects building by regulating land-use, values, acquisition, dealing with large-scale development planning, and providing general rules for industrial safety and the installation of plant and equipment; but these apart, the *Bauordnungen* comprise the regulations for building. They deal with the construction, demolition, and the use of buildings in respect of the needs of health, safety, and general amenity; identify the tasks of the various building authorities; set out the procedures for inspection and control; and cover aspects of planning that relate to individual buildings, such as building lines, heights, spaces, orientations, and access. Their technical provisions, however, are given in general terms, to avoid the need for the State parliaments being involved in making frequent amendments to keep pace with technical and procedural changes. Crucial to the functioning of the control system is the requirement that *construction must be "in accordance with the accepted rules of building"*, a provision that is implemented by reference to the national standards and by the measures governing approval and inspection.

The standards are produced by a national standards organization, known as the DNA (*Deutscher Normenausschuss*) which functions as an independent institution. It has a permanent secretariat which co-ordinates the work of commissions or committees made up of representatives of the government, industry, professions, universities, and technical colleges who act in an honorary capacity. Standards of all kinds are drafted, issued for comment, finalized, and published, and then kept up to date by an organized process of revision. When finally promulgated, these are known as the DIN standards. The institute is funded by contributions from the government and industry, and from the income earned by its own activities such as that received for the sales of its publications. In all these aspects the organization bears a close resemblance to the British Standards Institution.

Within this organization the whole of the work relating to the construction industry for the purpose of promoting standardization—covering materials, dimensions and tolerances, methods of execution, and methods of testing—is the responsibility of a Commission on Building (*Fachnormenausschuss Bauwesen*) which carries out its work through many sub-commissions and working committees.

One of these produces the standards for building methods affecting health, safety, quality, and durability, which together form a comprehensive set of rules or codes dealing with subjects like structural stability, loading, fire protection, sound and thermal insulation, damp exclusion, and workmanship.

These standards are designed to set out the requirements for each topic, and then to describe the ways in which these can be met. They are known as the *einheitliche technische Baubestimmungen*, or ETB; that is to say, the "uniform technical building rules" or criteria for the control authorities in their tasks of inspecting and approving work. Other powers also enable the building control ministries to make standards compulsory by the issue of legal orders.

In a similar way the DIN Standards dealing with materials are adopted by the States' building ministries as the "technical building rules" for the purpose of building control, and another set of standards deals with tendering and contractural procedures.

Other standards, produced separately by independent bodies like the German Association of Engineers, can also be adopted. These often deal with new types of practice or testing not yet covered by the DNA, and are in time overtaken by confirmatory work to become issued as DIN standards.

This system ensures that the standards issued by the central national standards organization are either given direct mandatory status, or referred to as being deemed to satisfy the requirements of the law in each state. Enforcement is carried through by means of complex bureaucracy which is operated by a large and highly qualified staff. In consequence the guidance given to the construction industry is uniform in character and represents a powerful influence for the achievement of standardization in all aspects of building activities.

The control of building is extended very firmly into the sphere of practice by the methods adopted for approvals, quality control, and testing. Any material or component used must be shown to conform with the "technical building rules" (the standards), and those which are acceptable are listed by the control authorities, but their use is only permitted if they have been manufactured in a plant which is properly subjected to the arrangements for quality control. The task of organizing quality control in industry is co-ordinated and administered by another commission of the DNA, namely the national standards authority.

Manufacturers participate in quality control *either* by belonging to an association for the relevant product group (for well-established materials) which carries out quality control for its members using agreed standards and test procedures, and issuing certificates; *or* by getting one of the officially recognized testing stations to check and certify a product under contract (for new materials). All test methods must be approved, and for the most part are covered by the DIN standards. The central institute which co-ordinates the technical work of assessment is able to issue general approvals which are valid throughout the Republic. These are issued to include the properties and use of each product.

Materials and methods that are too new to have been included in a DIN standard need to be given official sanction before they can be used, and such approval can be obtained either from the State government for a specific application, or from the central body which can award a certificate for the product's general use. There are procedures for these purposes. The test certificates have a standard format of contents which give full details of the specification, results of test, conditions of use, and the period for which the certificate remains valid, which does not extend beyond 5 years.

Checks are made by the various testing stations who carry out assessments for the purposes of inspection by the enforcement authorities and for quality control. Some of these laboratories are government institutes—there is a federal testing station and several others run by the State governments—and others are independent, and where recognized, carry out work under contract for the enforcement authorities. Many are at universities and other educational establishments, and specialize in different subjects, like fire, structures, and the physics of sound.

From this it can be seen that building control depends very much on the existence of scientific methods of testing, the application of research activities, and the use of information derived from these in practice. (This work of assessing and approving new products began in parts of Germany in the early years of this century, and by the twenties several States had set up special committees for the work. This led to the establishment of a national procedure in 1937. The States took over responsibility for approvals after the war and by 1951 had agreed a system of collaboration, leading to the present situation.)

The whole apparatus of building control functions as a comprehensive system which, by its criteria, procedures, and processes of certification and approval, promotes standardization affecting both *products* and *methods;* and the degree of commitment to it is related to the flow of responsibility in the event of failure. The State enforcement authorities, in discharging their legal duties and granting building permits and approval certificates, assume the primary responsibility for the buildings conforming with the law, and consequently for their safety. They may transfer a share of responsibility by arranging contracts with consultants or others for checks and tests, *but the burden of responsibility is theirs,* and the whole official framework of control seems to have been designed to make the bearing of it a viable proposition.

Switzerland

By contrast, in Switzerland these responsibilities rest on the professional consultants—the individual architects and engineers; and there exists no national standards organization, nor any official scheme for certification and approval. The responsibilities are imposed on the architects and engineers by law, and consist of the usual liabilities under civil law in respect of contractual duties and the compensation of injured parties in the event of failure, together with an additional obligation under the criminal law to comply with the *"recognized rules of building"*. Any negligent disregarding of these rules is punishable by imprisonment or fines; *but the law does not include any definition of what the rules are,* leaving this to be determined by legal precedent. Neither does it require that the consultants should be insured under some approved scheme of professional indemnity. In this way the Swiss system has the salient features of both the German and the French methods of control, but without the safeguards that those countries deem essential in each case. In Germany, the idea that buildings must, by law, comply with recognized rules goes along with the notion that these rules should be thoroughly detailed, and also that the checking should be officially supervised; in France, the legislation that makes architects and engineers responsible for their buildings goes along with an insistence that they should be suitably insured.

The "standards" in Switzerland are produced by various professional, technical, and industrial organizations each covering its own specialized subjects. Perhaps the most important, and those having the widest recognition, are the standards produced by the Swiss Association of Engineers and Architects (SIA), which have acquired a national status as "recognized rules for building" partly through legal citations. Standards are also established as being acceptable through their use in government contracts, or their nomination by authorities as conditions for the granting of subsidies; for example, as is the case for educational building and other programmes sponsored by public-sector funds.

Among the many organizations concerned with preparing standards, the following are the most prominent.

The *Swiss Association of Engineers and Architects* prepares standards or "norms" for materials and structural design, which are generally adopted as the "rules" for structural stability. The Association, additionally, publishes codes of practice for various building techniques. These standards are prepared in the same way as national institutes in other countries go about their work to provide their national standards. The Association sets up committees on which all interests are represented, including those of the government and the local enforcement authorities, the universities, contractors, and suppliers. The committee prepares a draft for circulation, and after receiving comments prepares the standard in its final form. Once adopted by the Association, the advice contained in the standard becomes binding for all the members.

The insurance companies produce rules dealing with safety measures of different kinds. The *Swiss Accident Insurance Association* (SUVA) is a state-owned body whih produces safety requirements connected with the obligation that industrial workers must be covered by insurance. Furthermore, the *Association of Cantonal Fire Insurance Offices* issues instructions about fire protection and measures for fire-fighting. These, and others like them, are cited in the orders issued by various local government departments dealing with building control in their own areas.

The *Swiss Association of Electrical Engineers* (SEV) and the *Swiss Assocation of Gas and Water Engineers* (SVGW) are among the specialists who publish rules which govern the work of their members, for which they issue certificates of compliance. These may be given an authoritative status in some places by being cited by the controlling authorities for use in connection with the relevant type of installation.

Another organization, the CRB (*Centre for Building Rationalization*) has been concerned with preparing standards with a view to co-ordinating dimensions and tolerances, and also the documents used in building and in accounting for building costs.

In addition to these specialist organizations, a central research station is provided under the auspices of the Federal Government known as the *Federal Materials Testing Institute* (EMPA). This carries out research connected with materials and structures, and also carries out testing, offering a service for this purpose to local authorities, contractors, and manufacturers, many of whom have continuing arrangements with the Institute for the quality control of their products.

Holland

The Dutch standards (NEN) are prepared in much the same way as those in Scandinavian countries, and their use as an adjunct to the building control system is also similar. The municipalities have responsibilities for administering the control and co-ordinate their work through the Union of Netherlands Municipalities (VNG). This organization has a technical bureau know as KOMO, which carries out tests and issues certificates for product approvals. The VNG is responsible for a model building code, which concentrates largely on housing, and has been followed by the individual municipalities in preparing their own regulations. The model code makes reference to the Dutch standards, which are used to amplify the requirements and in this way serve as mandatory provisions where the code is applied.

France

In France a different system of control results in the adoption of the codes and standards being dependent rather upon the insurance companies than upon any direct legal expression of technical requirements. This tends to restrict the subject covered to the more primary physical hazards, because the starting-point of the influence guiding the system is the *constitutional* edict that the designers and contractors are liable for any defects in their buildings for prescribed periods. The liability extends to 10 years for defects of structure and foundations, weather proofing, and the like, and 2 years for minor failures. The law requires that designer and contractors should be insured, and, seemingly as a consequence, the insurers have the main involvement in the preparation of the criteria and in the inspection and control of the work. It is the construction industry's insurers who produce the model clauses in their standard policy which sets the levels of the technical standards. The policy requires that building work should comply with certain codes or standards (especially those issued as the DTU (*Documents Techniques Unifiés*)); that any component or particular technique used in building should have been covered by an Agrément or "Avis" certificate (that is to say, by an assessment carried out by an organization for testing which operates mainly under its own jurisdiction); and that the design and technical details should have been checked and the work supervised by one of a small number of approved central offices, who act for the insurance companies rather like inspecting consultants or assessors.

An effect of this arrangement is to give to the engineers in the offices a great deal of influence over the nature of standardization and the quality of work in the construction industry, which in turn is derived from the particular values that the insurers attach to the various aspects of the buildings' performance. These engineers make recommendations which govern what restrictions are appropriate to the insurance cover. Though their opinions are guided by the relevant DTU standards, they are concerned only with those aspects of building among the subjects covered by the *Documents Techniques Unifiés* that relate to the insurance cover. While they also use the Agrément evaluations, these, too, are drawn up with the 10-year or 2-year periods in mind. As a consequence, the official encouragement for industry to adopt standards tends to be limited to a narrow field of subjects and to be influenced by considerations of economics, to a greater degree that would seem to apply in countries where the aims of the authorities who exercise influence are directed by the wider public interests of health, safety, and amenity.

Austria

In Austria the influence on the use of standards is closer to the experience of the neighbouring Federation of West Germany. The Austrian Standards Committee, a national organization, prepares the Austrian standards (*Ö-Normen*). These are not mandatory, but can be adopted by the State government and given the status of obligatory codes.

An Austrian Building Research Institute is closely associated with this work, and together with various testing stations takes part in the general approval schemes which are related to the use of new or non-traditional materials and methods of construction. As in West Germany, the traditional pattern of the control system is established by the Federal constitution which requires that internal administrative matters, like building control, should be dealt with by State governments who prepare building codes. These prescribe procedures and in many cases require that any building must be carried out "in accordance with technological experience", for which the standards are adopted as guides. The scope of the codes is wide: dealing with planning matters, technical requirements for buildings, concerned with matters affecting health, safety, and amenity; and procedural rules which deal with how the codes themselves should be implemented. A draft model code, dating back to 1961, and subsequently amended from time to time, sets out guidance about the scope and content of regulations for building. It was drafted by a central committee on which were represented all the professional and administrative interests concerned with building and its control, and published by the Association for Housing Research.

Thus, a main influence on the direction of the construction industry in Austria comes from the members of the public expressing their consumer interests through their institutions rather as it does in the Nordic countries. The Standards, based on the general experience of the industry and guided by information from research, are absorbed into practice through their adoption as mandatory provisions by the building control system.

STANDARDS AND CODES IN THE UK

The BSI

The standards and codes of practice in the United Kingdom are produced by the British Standards Institution, which also has a hand in quality control through its activities of inspection, testing, and licensing. The Institution is independent, and operates separately from the central government's control of building through legislation. It owes its existence to a widely-based popular mandate from interests of many kinds, involving both industry and consumer. It is financed by subscriptions from industrial and manufacturing firms; trade associations; local authorities; professional institutions and other bodies; a grant-in-aid from the central government; and its own earnings derived from sales of its publications and charges made for various services.

Separate funding is obtained for its work of certification in connection with the use of its Kitemark; for testing and inspectorate facilities which are available to other organizations, private companies, and national standards institutes abroad; and for its services of "Technical Help to Exporters" (THE). Charges are made for testing, and fees are levied for licencing and for the services to exporters, which also benefit from subscriptions and a government grant.

Its terms of reference

The main aim of the Institution is to draw up voluntary standards by the joint efforts of representatives of all interests concerned and by their agreement, and to promote their adoption. To this end it has procedures to establish consensus views which are designed to give all interested parties an opportunity to be heard, and a method of resolving disputes among members of its technical committees without resorting to voting, but by action to find valid solutions to the technical problems encountered.

As mentioned previously, the BSI developed from an Engineering Standards Committee which was formed in 1901 by the Institution of Civil Engineers and other professional bodies, and which became the British Engineering Standards Association. It adopted its present name after the Supplementary Charter was granted in 1931 to the Royal Charter granted in 1929. The Royal Charter sets out its objectives as follows:

(a) to coordinate the efforts of producers and users for the improvement, standardization and simplification of engineering and industrial materials so as to simplify production and distribution, and to eliminate the national waste of time and material involved in the production of an unnecessary variety of patterns and sizes of articles for one and the same purpose.

(b) to set up standards of quality and dimensions, and prepare and promote the general adoption of British Standard specifications and schedules in connection therewith and from time to time to revise, alter and amend such specifications and schedules as experience and circumstances may require.

(c) to register, in the name of the Institution, marks of all descriptions, and to prove and affix or license the affixing of such marks or other proof, letter, name, description or device.

(d) to take such action as may appear desirable or necessary to protect the objects or interests of the Institution.

Its management

The work of the Institution is carried out under the aegis of an Executive Board which is ultimately based on the sanctions of its subscribing members and represents a range of national interests. Reporting to the Board are six Divisional Standards Councils, to whom the Standards Committees are responsible for initiating standards projects and deciding priorities in their fields. There are about eighty of these main Committees, but usually over a thousand technical committees are actively at work on standards. In addition, a Quality Assurance Council reports to the Board for the Institution's work of certification, and deals with a similar structure of working committees. The Board is also advised by a Consumer Standards Advisory Committee and a Coordinating Committee on Fire Tests.

The management structure comprises a Secretariat, concerned with policy development and coordination; a division dealing with standards; another with tests, quality assurance, and the service to exporters; and another taking care of the financial, personnel, property and managing services, and marketing activities.

The extent of the Institution's work is limited by its staff's ability to service the committees and governed by its annual budget, which runs at less than 0.01% of the UK's annual national product, though it claims to affect about half of that total output with its standards. The Institution places a high value on the importance of its work and expresses the view in its guidance to its committee's members that "well-conceived standards save the country money by reducing design effort, simplifying contracts, achieving interchangeability, reducing stocks, lowering component costs through quantity production, cutting down service failures and minimizing accidents. The work of BSI technical committees is thus *vital to national prosperity*".

Proposals for standards can be initiated by any responsible body, and in practice are derived from existing committees and by international standards organizations. Priorities are decided by the Standard Committees and the senior staff, and important consideration is given to the general demand for any particular standard and to its possible effect on national needs, in such matters as "the legislative fields of health, safety and environmental and consumer protection", though it is admitted in the BSI's notes for its chairmen that an adequate representation of users' or consumers' views may be difficult to obtain.

The work on a standard proceeds under the guidance of its technical secretary, beginning with an initial draft from a knowledgeable source on the subject, and accompanied by a published announcement of the proposal. The committee obtains different views and these are incorporated in subsequent drafting by the secretary. The draft standard is then given public circulation. The committee considers the comments received, and prepares the final draft for submission to the Standards Committee for approval. In carrying out this work the Committee may identify a need for research, and the Institution may then sponsor research, either through one of its member organizations or by obtaining funds from the government, or by seeking the cooperation of a government-financed research body, like the Building Research Establishment.

Its development

The development of the scope of the Institution's work has owed much to the growth of research activities; and conversely, the standards which it produces provide an important channel for the transmission of information from research to the practices of the manufacturing industries. This is particularly true of the *construction industry* which took up official research activities rather later than others. The government's building research station was created in 1926 and its work increased dramatically during the decades after the war, as similar work grew in the other countries of Europe. This research activity went hand in hand with the growth of work on standards and emerged as an important example of European and international collaboration.

The European Economic Community, founded in 1957, drew up a programme for legislation giving priority to the elimination of technical barriers to trade, and its council adopted the principle that *where possible the technical requirements needed in legislation should be described by reference to standards*.

The International Organization for Standardization (ISO) had been formed in 1947 with the BSI involved in a major role; and in 1961 the European Committee for Standardization (the CEN) was formed involving the BSI and other national standards bodies. The European Standards prepared by this body, if accepted by a "significant majority" of its members, are published as national standards by the countries approving them. Other bodies, like the IEC (International Electro-technical Commission), the ISCA (International

Standards Steering Committee for Consumer Affairs), the IFAN (International Federation for the Application of Standards), CENELEC (the Electrotechnical counterpart of the CEN) are examples of the growing number of international organizations concerned with standards, and the increasingly international emphasis that is being given to the whole idea of standardization.

All this has given a new dimension to the work of the British Standards Institution. Its procedures for preparing standards by the circulation of drafts for public comment have become the same for both national and international work, so that one standard is aligned for both purposes. This accords with a stated objective of the Institution: "to do the job once, do it right, and do it internationally".

Its involvement with international and European standards is now becoming of central importance to its work. In 1973 the UN Economic Commission for Europe, in underlining the ISO/IEC Code of Principles about the "reference to standards" in legislation and regulation, published a document claiming that if legal requirements were to be expressed as standards, the following advantages would accrue:

(a) the legislative work would be accelerated and simplified;
(b) the elimination of barriers to trade would be facilitated;
(c) the results of the work of international standards organizations could be more easily taken into account;
(d) technical regulations could be changed more easily to take account of technological account;
(e) technical requirements would be better observed as technical staff would be more accustomed to using standards in their daily work than laws;
(f) all technical regulations could be arranged within one unified systematic collection, if the method were to be applied consistently;
(g) the implementation of national technical regulations would be better secured and discordances between the national standards of different countries would be avoided if all interested parties participated in the preparation of the standards.

Along with this work, the Institution has extended its services to provide technical information to help industrial companies concerned with exporting their products or offering services abroad. The "THE" service provides information about the regulations and approval systems likely to be encountered, gives other information relevant to the countries receiving the exports, and helps by providing translations of specifications or arranging for tests and the provision of test certificates which are acceptable to the foreign authorities involved.

Testing and quality control

The business of testing and taking steps to confirm a manufacturer's compliance with a standard has been an important adjunct of the work of the

BSI since its inception, but it has been carried out with increasing emphasis and competence as the scientific facilities for research and testing have become more available. The Kitemark, which is BSI's certification trade mark, was registered as long ago as 1903. It enables manufacturers to certify their compliance with a standard by complying with a scheme of supervision and control in collaboration with the BSI Inspectorate, which includes regular inspections of the manufacturing process and random sample testing. Participation in such a scheme results in the manufacturers having permission to use the mark under licence. It is additional to the producer's own system of quality control, and the use of the Kitemark reduces any need for further testing or sampling by other purchasers, whether private companies or public bodies.

The system has been extended by the introduction of a *Safety Mark,* which is used to certify a product's compliance with standards, especially dealing with the matters of safety or legal safety requirements. This depends, too, upon very careful methods of checking.

The BSI's facilities for testing and inspecting are centred at Hemel Hempstead, near London, and among other facilities enable the Institution to act as an agent of overseas organizations, and to derive from its work of testing a range of research skills on which it has been able to base an increasing range of technical services.

The Agrément Board

Notwithstanding the potential of these services for making assessments of new products, a department of central government took steps in 1966 to create a British version of the French Agrément system to make "authoritative assessments of new building products", covering both materials and components. At the time, the construction industry was dealing with very large public building programmes, which created, among other things, a market for new and non-traditional products, especially of a kind that were intended to enable buildings to be erected quickly.

It was thought by the authorities involved, and supported by some sections of the building industry, that assessments were needed of various materials, products, components, and processes that would help such innovation in the industry; and that the need for this work had an urgency that would create difficulties for the BSI.

The Board was set up, accordingly, to make assessments based on scientific investigations of products, and to issue certificates of performance for the products for a fee charged to the manufacturer. A procedure was drawn up for this purpose and a certificate was designed which it was hoped would be used as an authoritative guide for the local authorities dealing with the enforcement of the building regulations. A theory was held that new materials and forms of structure were becoming available so quickly and in such numbers that the BSI's standards procedures would not be able to cope, and without the necessary standards the law-makers would not be able to confer the deemed-to-satisfy status in their regulations on new products in time to keep up with the demand. To avoid problems with the BSI, it was intended that the new Board would not deal with products already covered by a British Standard and would have a declared policy "to collaborate fully with the British Standards Institution...in furthering standards for new products".

As a consequence, the Board's premises were accommodated in Hemel Hempstead where it was convenient for communication with others "likely to have a close interest in its work". The government agreed that the Building Research Station should provide the services of a technical agency to the Board, and would make available for use its own laboratories and those of the Forest Products and the Fire Research Stations, with others situated nearby, which meant that the same facilities as were used by the British Standards Institution would be shared by the new Board.

The main excuse for creating an Agrément Board in the UK was to provide "an aid to local authorities in interpreting the Regulations in specific proposed designs" by carrying out "investigations which will secure the design data needed for application to the Regulations". Opponents of the idea were able to point out a problem: that although the system might be imported from the country of its origins, the same conditions that had brought about its development there could not be applied in the country of its adoption. Such French practices were unsuited to the situation in the UK, and contrary to the traditional methods employed there for building control.

In France, the designers and contractors of the building industry were legally obliged to have indemnity, so the insurers who provided it were able to insist on conditions for their policies, which included the requirement that products and methods must be assessed and certified by the system of Agréments operated by the Centre Scientifique et Technique du Batiment. This meant that in practice nothing could be used in building in France without such certification, so the compulsion for assessments being made was irresistible.

In the UK the same legal requirement for insurance did not exist, nor was there any *constitutional* provision to make designers and contractors liable, so there could be no such compelling force for the adoption of the Agrément system. If any comparable influence would be said to exist in the UK, it arose from the use of references to British Standards made in the regulations and by-laws. Although this did not make the BSI Standards mandatory, it had the effect of encouraging their use. To achieve even this degree of support for an Agrément Board's work to become part of the control system, it would be necessary for the certificates issued by the Board to be quoted in the building regulations as evidence that the product certified was "deemed-to-satisfy" the requirement. For the central government to incorporate such references to Agrément Certificates would have been for it to fly in the face of the international preference for "reference to standards", and to undermine the influence of the British Standards Institution, which enjoyed a high regard abroad and a formidable consensus of support at home.

At the level of local government there was another practical problem with the acceptance of the Board's appraisals in the work of enforcement. Its certificates were to be valid for three years, and this question of a limit of time did not fit into the customary philosophies of the British control system. In *France*, the Civil Code prescribed time-limits for liability of 2 and 10 years, so that the certificates issued there could deal quite properly with assessments of how long it was reasonable to expect a product to perform satisfactorily *as an acceptable insurance risk;* but there were no time-limits in British law, which was concerned with *health and safety,* for which it believed that the standards safeguarding the public must remain unconditionally through the life of a building.

Methods of testing

Notwithstanding these disadvantages, the work of the Board began, and manufacturers participated by applying for assessments and becoming associates in subscription schemes. The operation of the scheme had one particular effect that can be seen as a useful contribution to industrial practice in the long term: it gave an impetus to the application of scientific methods of *testing* and research in building.

As soon as its work began, the new Board had to work out the criteria against which any assessments of merit for a product's performance could be made, and to demonstrate how it would go about its tasks of checking and evaluation, in order to inspire confidence in its judgements. It soon inaugurated two series of publications for reference in the form of information sheets, and descriptions of the Agrément methods of assessment and testing. These latter became known as "MOATS". The information sheets described the requirements that had to be met for a product to gain acceptance, covering such matters as "safety, comfort, durability, maintenance, acoustical properties, lighting, ventilation, appearance, durability, and ease of operation". The "MOATS" gave information about the various tests used in the Building Research Station and other research departments in making the assessments. In terms of pure scientific theory much of this may have been very questionable, on the grounds that it used subjective processes under the guise of objectivity, but it helped to establish the idea that manufacturers should have foreknowledge of the performance required of their products by the users or customers. It also helped to promote an interest in how the inspection of a building was done to determine whether it complied with the legal requirements. This in turn led to the users gaining a keener awareness of the nature of the regulations and questioning whether their form contained descriptions that were precise enough.

Perhaps one outcome of all this was that the British Standards Institution began to produce more Standards that dealt specifically with methods of testing, based on the established experience of the leading research laboratories, and the advice of universities specializing in this type of work.

The emergence of this kind of standard had particular value to the legislators, who were able to make reference in the regulations to *standard tests as a measure of compliance.* In doing so they were conforming with the internationally agreed policy, and at the same time insisting on a form of evaluation that would improve industrial performance by increasing the information based on factual evidence.

THE USE OF STANDARDS AND CODES IN THE UK BUILDING CONTROL SYSTEM

Types of standard

By tradition, or the instinct of its legislators, it has been a principle of British building law that its instruments of control should be self-sufficient. It may be significant that in the UK, measures to control building came long before the making of standards in any organized form; and even after the formation of a Standards Institution, the two activities were seen as having quite separate purposes. The legal controls were concerned with the maintenance of public health and safety; while standards were to promote greater efficiency in industry. These distinctions were made clearer by the nature of the background influences in each case: the law-makers were prompted by the *public* in its role as the user of the built product; the standard-makers were the *industrialists* making things more convenient for themselves. It is no wonder that the law-makers have kept the standards at arms' length, and have made use of them only for ancillary or supportive reference, and then only when a great deal of experience has established their reliability.

These two worlds of the legislators and industrialists were linked by the interests of the architects, engineers, and surveyors, whose professional skills were increasingly at work on both sides. Under their influence the law-makers would be persuaded that the B.S.I. Standards should have a role to play in the legal control system; their influence too would lead to the development of different *types* of standards.

The two main types that have emerged from the B.S.I. have become known generally as *standards*, which deal primarily with materials and products, and *codes,* which are concerned with matters of design and method. Notwithstanding this distinction, both types, strictly speaking, are "standards", a fact borne out by the descriptive title used for any Code: that it is a *British Standard Code of Practice.*

The familiar British Standards (BS) prepared by the BSI and used by the construction industry are *standard specifications*, each being concerned with a material or product. These cover a wide range of subjects, dealing for example with aggregates for concrete, like gravel, crushed stone, blast furnace slag; sand for mortar, internal plastering, and floor-screeds; cement of various kinds; and more complex subjects like the structural work of steel. Such standards are supported by extensive experience, and are prepared by committees whose members consist of a majority of representatives of the industrial and commerce interests involved.

The BSI Codes of Practice (BSCP) are recommendations of good practice, dealing with subjects like the design of structural work in reinforced, prestressed, or plain concrete, and structural work in timber, aluminium, or bricks. A popular example is CP3 which is a "Code of basic data for the design of buildings", and comprises chapters which are published as separate books, dealing with lighting, thermal insulation, sound insulation and noise reductions, precautions against fire, loading of structures, and other aspects of performance. These are prepared by Code Drafting Committees made up mainly, if not exclusively, of professional advisers, representing departments of central government, research stations, and other specialist bodies.

A more recent development in the work of the BSI, which has emerged since the early fifties, has been the preparation of standards which describe *methods of testing*. These deal with material subjects like the testing for strength of concrete cubes; tests of fire resistance; or the moisture content of timber; and others concerned with more complex methodology, like "recommendations for field and laboratory measurement of airborne and impact sound transmission in building".

Their use as legal references

(1) As deemed-to-satisfy illustrations

The main use of both the Standards and Codes of Practice of the British Standards Institution in British building law has been their adoption as illustrations of provisions that are deemed-to-satisfy the requirements of a substantive regulation. This method of reference is used in the national building regulations and their Scottish equivalents; but not in the London by-laws, because, as we have seen in earlier chapters, these employ a particular technique of regulating that avoids the need for such references.

In the national building regulations, some examples of standards are quoted in relation to Part B (which requires that any materials used in building should be suitable for their purpose, and used so as to perform their functions adequately), as follows:

B2 Deemed-to-Satisfy provisions regarding the fitness of materials:
The use of any material or any method of mixing or preparing materials or of applying, using or fixing materials *which conforms with a British Standard or a British Standard Code of Practice* prescribing the quality of material or standards of workmanship shall be deemed to be a sufficient compliance with the requirements of regulation B1(1) if the use of that material or method is appropriate to the purpose for and conditions in which it is used.

and

B4 Deemed-to-satisfy provisions for the special treatment of softwood timber in certain areas:

The requirements of regulation B3(2) shall be deemed to be satisfied if—(a) the timber is treated *in accordance with the provisions of BS 4072: 1974;...*

Other examples of the use of Codes occur in relation to Part D8 (which requires that the structure of a building should be safe), as follows:

D11 Deemed-to-satisfy provisions for structural work of reinforced, prestressed or plain concrete:
(1) Subject to the provision of paragraph (2), the requirements of regulation D8 shall be deemed to be satisfied as to any structural work (whether cast in-situ or precast) of reinforced, prestressed or plain concrete if the work complies with –
  (a) CP110: Part 1: 1972 as read with CP110: Part 2: 1972 and CP110: Part 3: 1972; or
  (b) in the case of work of reinforced, prestressed or precast concrete, CP114: 1969, CP115: 1969 or CP116: 1969 as read with CP116: Addendum No 1: 1970 whichever is appropriate.
(2) The recommendations of the publications specified in paragraph (1)(a) shall not be used in conjunction with those of any publication specified in paragraph (1)(b).

D12 Deemed-to-satisfy provisions for structural work of timber:
  The requirements of regulation D8 shall be deemed to be satisfied as to any structural work of timber if –
  (a) the work complies with CP112: Part 2: 1971; or ...

D13 Deemed-to-satisfy provisions for structural work of bricks, blocks or plain concrete.
  The requirements of regulation D8 shall be deemed to be satisfied as to any structural work of bricks, blocks or plain concrete if—
  (a) the work complies with CP111: Part 2: 1970; or...

It should be noted that the deemed-to-satisfy provisions also contain other prescriptions than the Standards and Codes of the BSI. None of these provisions is exclusive. The inclusion of such illustrations is intended to present a choice of different ways of complying with the main regulation.

The deemed-to-satisfy references do *not* make the quoted Standards mandatory, but draw attention to them as having authoritative approval. An obligation is placed on the enforcing authority to accept what is done if it accords with the deemed-to-satisfy standard. It is a form of regulation that is popular with the industry, because it promotes the use of industrial standards without closing down any viable optional alternatives, and so does not impede the technological development of building.

Whether it is a truly practical method of regulating has always been questioned by the law-makers. A major problem is that neither Standards nor

Codes are drafted as "legal" documents. Any idea that they should be has always been rejected by the BSI drafting committees, who are faced with expressing technical information for use by others specializing in technical affairs. This may involve the use of diagrams, formulae, and the language of mathematics; or the statement of tentative propositions all of which are far from the precise, repetitive, and curiously disciplined language of the law. The preparation of a Standard may take a long time in the best of circumstances, even though it is designed to serve its own established purpose; to require it to be drafted as a legal document would be to frustrate its aims and perhaps make its drafting impossible.

Yet, since it is not drafted as a legal instrument, an inspector's task of deciding whether its recommendations have been complied with might be very difficult. A Code may leave so much to skilled judgement that a conclusion about whether its conditions have been met could be reached only after protracted debate. If this took place in a court of law, it would require a heavy expenditure of time and money.

An illustration of this problem may be best seen in the following quotation from the introduction to one of the chapters of CP3. The chapter opens with the following advice: "This chapter should be considered in conjunction with the other chapters, as certain recommendations in them may be incompatible, or may be reconciled only with difficulty, with recommendations in this chapter. The designer should, therefore, consider the functional requirements of a building as a whole, and *determine which recommendations should have precedence...*"

If such a statement of guidance is read together with the requirements of Part B, the difficulties are seen to be compounded. Part B1 requires, among other matters, that materials shall be "applied, used or fixed so as *adequately* to perform the functions for which they are designed", and B1(2) adds that these requirements "shall apply *only in so far as they are necessary* for ensuring public health and safety".

This latter provision is a curious one, because anything that was not necessary for health and safety would be *ultra vires* in any case, so that the statement hardly needs to be made. Since it has been included as a substantive regulation it adds to the whole cloudy collection of vague meanings that make up the law in this particular instance. The builder or designer must decide what is "adequate" for performance, and what is necessary for health and safety, and will be deemed to have done so if he follows a recommendation that he should consider the "building as a whole" and determine "which recommendations have precedence"! His conclusions must of course be agreed with the inspector if an enforcing authority is involved in any final sanction, and this implies another set of subjective judgements being brought to bear on the problems.

Such a regulation is workable only when everyone involved agrees to make it operate successfully. The underlying issue is whether the public wants to depend for its protection on *regulations*, or the *judgement of skilled designers*.

This kind of regulation purports to provide the safeguard, but it is a masquerade, because the onus rests on the designer, though the public's reliance on him is not made explicit. The real problems come to light in dazzling ways when there is a disastrous failure, and someone is required to find out what went wrong.

It can be argued that if the public made its dependence on the designer plain, it would get a more secure service, with none of the delays and arguments entailed in the regulatory process. But that is another question.

In both the national and the Scottish practice of making regulations, the basic use of BSI Standards and Codes has been in the role of deemed-to-satisfy provisions. This began in the days of the model by-laws, but has been consolidated and developed as a method since the sixties, when the making of regulations became the responsibility of central government. When used properly, it has served both the legislators and standards-makers well, without causing any real difficulties to the separate activities of making regulations or standards in either case. The law-makers have been able to "adopt" examples of what is needed in the knowledge that these have a wide consensus of support and acceptability in the national and international community, without being deflected in any way from their own task of prescribing for public health and safety. The standard-makers have had the benefit of an authoritative promotional sanction being given to their work, without their having had to make any additional rules about drafting, or to wrestle with any alien or unsuitable modes of expression.

(2) As substantive requirements

Another use of BSI Standards in British building law has been to incorporate them in regulations or by-laws as substantive provisions. In this form they embody the law and, for the purpose defined, become *mandatory*.

The most common examples of their usage are to be found in the London Constructional By-laws. Because these are instruments with somewhat narrower purposes than the national regulations (being directed more precisely to controls affecting structural safety and stability, and fire-resistance), the requirements relate to material and physical matters which have also featured from the beginning in the work of the BSI in drawing up standard specifications. Consequently, the by-laws have been able to make use of the standards for defining the requirements of the basic materials, in the typical ways described below.

Reference to the Standards is preceded by the definition in Part 1 of the by-laws, which states that "BS means British Standard" and "Appropriate Provisions, in relation to any BS, means such of the provisions of that BS as relate to dimensions, nature, materials, performance, strength and workmanship".

Examples include:

[3.01 Dead load]
(1) In calculating dead load, the unit weights of the materials shall be deemed to be those specified *in the appropriate provisions of BS 648: 1949 in the case of material therein mentioned* (unless ascertained to the satisfaction of the District Surveyor to be otherwise)...

[4.03 Aggregate for concrete]
Aggregate for concrete (a) shall consist of (i) sand, gravel, crushed or uncrushed natural stone in conformity with *the appropriate provisions of BS 882: 1954;* or (ii) foamed blast furnace slag in conformity with *the appropriate provisions or BS 877: 1939;* or (iii) air-cooled blast furnace slag in conformity with *the appropriate provisions of BS 1047: 1952;* or ... [etc.]

[4.05 Cement]
(1) Cement shall be (a) ordinary Portland cement in conformity with *the appropriate provisions of BS 12: 1958;* or (b) rapid-hardening Portland cement in conformity with *the appropriate provisions of BS 12: 1958;* or (c) Portland blast-furnace cement in conformity with *the appropriate provisions of BS 146: 1958;* or ... [etc.]

These examples represent a small selection from a large number of similar references, because most of the traditional materials covered in the by-laws are dealt with in this way.

In the national building regulations there are also some (rare) examples of the same use of BSI Standards, again relating to long-established materials.

For example, in Part L14, which deals with chimneys for Class II appliances, it is required that the chimneys must be lined with one of a number of specified alternatives, among which are "clay flue linings *which comply with BS 1181: 1971* and are jointed and pointed with high alumina cement mortar ...".

More specifically, and perhaps characteristically, the national regulations (together with the Scottish Building Standards Regulations in some cases) make use of some *Codes* of Practice as substantive requirements, as the following examples show.

In Part D2, dealing with the calculation of loading "... (a) dead loads shall be calculated *in accordance with CP 3: chapter V: Part 1: 1967;* (b) imposed loads shall be calculated (i) *in accordance with CP3: chapter V: Part 1: 1967...*, (c) wind loads shall be calculated *in accordance with CP 3: chapter V: Part 2: 1972...*".

In Part E4, dealing with the provision of compartment walls and floors for safety in fire, it is specified that certain buildings must be divided into compartments of given areas, but that these areas may, in effect, be doubled "if any building of purpose Group V is fitted throughout with an automatic sprinkler system *which complies with the relevant recommendations of CP 402: 201: 1952...*".

These illustrations are significant because they demonstrate that it is possible for the BSI Codes, which are no more than recommendations made by specialists, to be adopted as mandatory provisions and given the direct force of law, when they have become familiar or widely accepted enough for the purpose.

More recently the same "substantive" use has been made of BSI Standards of a different kind: namely, those which describe methods of testing. This type of Standard has become available largely as a result of the development of research being carried out in universities and government-sponsored laboratories. It has special significance for the future development of the control system and the regulations, as will be examined below.

Examples of the application of Standards describing tests occur in the London by-laws, dealing, as might be expected, with the more traditional matters, such as the following.

In Part 4.20, dealing with structural timber: 4.20(3) "the method of measuring gross features shall be in accordance with the *appropriate provisions of BS 1860: Part 1: 1959*" and (4) "structural timber shall be properly seasoned and *when tested by the method described in BS 1860: Part 1: 1959*, the moisture content shall not exceed 22 per cent".

In Part 6.03, dealing with the construction of enclosures to minimise the risk of the spread of fire: "A Class 11(A) enclosure shall ...(d) have its external face constructed of ...(iv) such other materials as the District Surveyor may approve as being durable and suitable for the purpose which... may include a combustible material...applied to a non-combustible backing which when *tested* in conjunction with its backing is graded not less than Class 1 for surface spread of flame *as prescribed by BS 476: Part 1: 1953.*"

In Part 4.07, dealing with concrete, it is specified that certain grades of mix must possesses resistances to crushing not less than those specified in a Table, which gives values for "resistance to crushing...when tested in accordance with Schedule III to these by-laws"; and Schedule III requires that "concrete cubes for work tests shall be made, cured and *tested in accordance with the appropriate provisions of BS 1881: 1952*".

And in Part 4.12, dealing with bricks and blocks, it is required that these "being of the descriptions specified in Table II, shall possess resistance to crushing not less than those respectively specified in that Table; provided that in lieu of the method specified in Schedule IV: (1) pre-cast light-weight aggregrate concrete blocks may be *tested by the transverse strength test specified in Appendix D of BS 2028: 1953* if such blocks are used only for internal non-load bearing purposes and their minimum transverse strength complies with Clause 12(b) of that BS; (ii) sand/lime (calcium silicate) bricks may be *tested in accordance with Appendix 'A' of BS 187: 1955...*".

In the national building regulations, and the Scottish Regulations, more use is made of BSI Standard tests, dealing with a wider range of subjects and performance. For example:

In Part E1, dealing with the interpretation of the provisions for safety in fire, the meaning of the phrase "fire resistance of a specified period" is described in relation to a part of the building, or a roof, or to plastic materials, in the following way: "any requirement in this section that an element of structure, door, or other part of a building shall have fire resistance of a specified period shall be construed as meaning that it shall be so constructed that a specimen *constructed to the same specification, if exposed to test by fire in accordance with BS 476: Part 8: 1972, would...satisfy the measurement of that test* as to stability, integrity and insulation for not less than the specified period ...". For roofs, the test referred to is BS 476: Part 3: 1958, and for "plastics material" BS 2782: 1970.

In part G6 dealing with the measurement of sound transmission, provision is made that "(2) measurements shall be *in accordance with sections Two A and Three A of BS 2750: 1956, and the method of normalising the results for both airborne and impact sound shall be that given in clause 3e(II) thereof*".

In part M5, dealing with special provisions for certain Class 1 oil-burning appliances, the first provision states "in this regulation any reference to hearth temperature, surface temperature or flue gas temperature is a reference to that temperature as determined respectively in accordance with *Test procedure No.11, Measurement method 8 or Measurement method 3 prescribed in BS 4876: 1972*". And in Part M8, dealing with Class II appliances, paragraph 4 describes measures for separating the appliance from any combustible material which nevertheless "shall not apply if the appliance satisfies the *test requirements specified in clause 14 or BS 1250: Part I; 1966*".

Such use of the British Standards and Codes of Practice as mandatory provisions in building legislation has a powerful influence on the development of practice in the construction industry. When reference is made to them as deemed-to-satisfy examples, it has the effect of encouraging their use, but without compulsion. When the provisions are mandatory, the adoption of the agreed standard process is obligatory. When the standard process is a test, the effects are even more far-reaching, because products cannot be used until they have been tested by an ordered method and assessed scientifically, so that the development of the industry is encouraged in an objective way.

The use of methods of test as criteria for compliance fits well with the growing practice of adopting performance specifications for the purposes of regulation. Indeed, performance specifications cannot be practical without the scientific knowledge which is needed to identify the essential levels of performance, or the skill being available to test their attainment.

Policies for developing the relationship of regulations and standards

Before the advent of formal research activities, when building regulations were by-laws made by innumerable local authorities, the development of regulating techniques was a somewhat random process, and its relationship with the work of the BSI was largely unco-ordinated. By the time when the central government took over the making of regulations as a national instrument of control, the influence of research had begun to affect the building industry, and this was emerging in the work of the BSI. It seemed no longer adequate that regulations and standards should be governed by separate policies having only arbitrary connections with each other. What seemed to be needed was a co-ordinated plan to link the (admittedly different) activities together in a coherent apparatus of control, so that each could play its own part, while contributing to the central harmony of the system.

The idea was expressed publicly in 1968 at the annual conference of one of the professional institutes concerned with enforcement, in a talk about possible future trends in the making of regulations, given by one of the government's advisers. In predicting an increasing use of the performance standard as a means to simpler and more self-contained regulations, the speaker described their relation to BSI Codes and Standards and the prospect of a "new apparatus for industrial management", pointing out that if performance standards were adopted as the main regulating technique a most important consequence would be the new lease of life for BSI Standards and Codes.

Relieved of being shackled to the instruments of law, these will be free to develop their true functions, and in *concert with regulations* will perform a vital role in the new apparatus of industrial management. Because the regulations will specify the performance required for the built environment, in all its aspects, national industrial standards will be able to define the consequential requirements of performance for each part, in terms of current industrial capabilities, accompanied by product specifications which will define what must be done to achieve that performance in each component *by methods based on confirmation by standard tests*.

The speaker went on to point out that:

The development is already augered by such changes as the extension of the terms of reference for one of the technical committees of BSI which has been introduced with the preface "that product standards and codes of practice will need to be supplemented by a new type of British Standard covering performance criteria over elements having similar functions in building. These new standards would form base standards against which industry could design new products, have them tested and prepare product standards very much more speedily than in the past". Together with the new building regulations, these new Codes and Standards will form a more consistent system to achieve the "attractive theoretical advantages" hinted at by BRAC. It could be an unsurpassed method of control, uniquely suited to consumer protection and industrial progress. The system would work like this: the regulations would define the minimum acceptable standards of performance for buildings; industrial standards would reflect a range above the minimum that could be achieved economically in normal practice; the codes, prepared mainly under the influence of theorists, would continue to recommend good practice aiming at higher levels of achievement. These would tend to set the pace to improve industrial standards, which in turn would play a positive part in raising the minimum standards defined in law.

According to this evidence, the notion of the national building regulations and BSI standards being guided by a concerted policy was being expressed within 3 years of the issue of the first set of national building regulations (in 1965). Within another 5 years it had emerged as a policy of the Councils for Building and Codes of Practice at the BSI, according to a spokesman of that Institution when speaking at the conference concerned with "Architects and the Building Bill".

By that time, in the early seventies, the BSI along with other standards institutions in Europe, had come to recognize how regulations had to protect society without stifling economic development in the building industry, and without having to depend upon an unpredictable enforcement system whose inspectors might exercise their individual judgement unequally. Its conclusion was that national regulations should state requirements broadly in terms of building functions, but not determine precisely how they should be met. The description of ways and means to achieve compliance should be left to the standards institutions.

Described in more detail, the theory was that ideally the building regulations should state the functional requirements and the minimum levels of performance required for health and safety in each case, dealing with structural stability, durability, fire resistance, space climate, lighting, sanitary provisions and so on as may be necessary, and making reference to standards and codes as examples of how these could be met. The standards institutions would demonstrate how the various levels of performance could be provided in terms of design systems, the production of materials and components, and the construction of buildings, by producing in a systematic progression the requisite product-specifications, design codes, and standard methods of test and assessment. The regulations could make specific reference to each as illustrating what was "deemed-to-satisfy". The whole process could be expected to accelerate innovation and development on a properly scientific basis, though it would depend heavily upon a parallel programme of research, and the adequate production of methods and equipment for tests and evaluations. It could also lead to more equitable schemes for insurance.

This theory, it was claimed, had gained acceptance by the International Standards Organization because in Europe, as in Britain, where in each country the regulations and standards had been produced separately, the advent of information gained from research had led to the recognition that building "problems" had not been identified and "coded" before the attempts had been made to standardize the "answers". The two activities had existed side by side and the links between questions and answers had not been co-ordinated in a way that now seemed both desirable and possible.

It was clear to those concerned with the making of regulations who might accept and advocate this policy, that any such attempt to refer to standards to support regulations would imply a progressive change in the amount and direction of research in the building industry. It would be needed at two levels and in parallel programmes: on the one hand in support of the regulations to identify hazards and the levels of performance needed for health and safety in the various aspects of a building's functions; and on the other in support of the standards institutions to examine the behavoural properties of materials, products, and assemblies, and to develop reliable ways of measuring and testing performance.

AN EVOLUTIONARY DOCTRINE

The need for an amendment policy

Discussions of theories like this were one outcome of the replacement of the local by-laws in Britain by the centrally-produced national building regulations. This had concentrated attention on all sides on the nature of the building control system. Its component parts came under increasingly critical scrutiny, and perhaps more than ever before were distinguished as separate functions comprising regulations, enforcement procedures, codes, and standards. All had grown from different backgrounds, so that each had faults that handicapped its efficient response to modern requirements; and the whole system of control to which each contributed had never been designed coherently, but rather "cobbled together" from what had happened to be available. It was recognized, too, that the system would not respond readily to pressures for change. Since Parliament itself was involved in creating the main instruments of the system, any radical changes would have to be regarded as hard-won reforms, requiring heavy commitments of time and effort.

While it is true that Parliament remains involved, the Acts and regulations that form the primary and subordinate legislation tend to follow different time-scales. The enabling Acts are usually made only after comparatively long intervals of time, because opportunities are rare and a great deal of support is needed; but regulations are made and amended by the process of negative resolution, which can take place more frequently. After the first national Building Regulations were made in 1965, amendments were made about once every year, and these were formally consolidated in new editions in 1972 and 1976. The pattern of amendments shows that there are already trends towards the adoption of the theories about the use of certain kinds of codes and standards that derive their information from research. Assuming that the ultimate aim of reforming the regulations should be to express them as "performance standards" (as BRAC have suggested), it can be shown how these can be brought into use by evolutionary methods applied through the normal process of amendment. Many of the changes introduced since 1965 by amendment show how the performance standard is evolving as a regulatory technique, but what is needed to ensure that positive progress is made is a conscious tactical plan for the complementary development of the statutory instruments (prepared by central government) *along with the codes and standards* (prepared by the Standards Institution).

This plan would be to use the deemed-to-satisfy illustrations in the building regulations as a means to the adoption of performance standards as the main regulatory technique.

It should be remembered that a "deemed-to-satisfy" provision is non-exclusive. It is made on the basis that any authority responsible for enforcement is legally bound to accept that the law has been satisfied if the deemed-to-satisfy specification has been carried out; but this does not exclude other specifications from being acceptable.

A series of planned amendments made over a period of time and following customary steps could lead to the full introduction of performance standards, provided that each step was taken only when it was practicable to do so in regard to the successful application and enforcement of the requirement. This timing would need to be judged by the regulating authority, the Standards Institution (representing all sides of industry), and their research advisers, making an assessment collaboratively.

The steps would accelerate the transformation of a specific requirement through the form of a functional requirement to its emergence as a performance standard, and would follow the process that has already been apparent in the development of some of the regulations, though not necessarily through any conscious effort to achieve long-term aims.

The start of the procedure

The sequence would start from the basic position of a regulation expressed as a specific requirement. As an example, it is possible to refer to a provision in the National Building Regulations which has already been partially subjected to the process, namely Part G, which began as a *specific requirement* made presumably in an attempt to control the transmission of sound between neighbouring dwellings, and which has since taken different forms, as the technical information about its subject has improved. In making this reference it has been necessary to modify the parts quoted, or to freely adapt their texts, in order to tell the story more clearly, and to distinguish the theme of development that the example is chosen to illustrate. The earliest form of the provision would have appeared in the days before metric values had been introduced, but these have been used here for consistency throughout. With these provisos and apologies, it is possible to conjecture that the original requirement would have begun much on the following lines:

Part G(x). Sound insulation of walls.
Any wall which separates any dwelling from another dwelling shall be constructed as a solid wall consisting of bricks or blocks not less than 200 mm thick with plaster not less than 12.5 mm thick on at least once face and having an average mass (calculated over any portion of the wall measuring 1 metre square and including the mass of any plaster) of not less than 415 kg/m^2....

The first change

The first step would be for an amendment to be made which would replace this substantive regulation with a *functional requirement* that identifies the aim of the provision. Along with this change the former specific requirement would be re-stated as a new deemed-to-satisfy specification, in order to illustrate how the new functional requirement could be met.

Following the example above, the new regulation and its supporting provision would take the following *functional* form:

Part G(x)[1]. Sound insulation of walls.
   Any wall which separates any dwelling from another dwelling or from another building shall in conjunction with its associated structure be so constructed as to provide *adequate resistance to the transmission of airborne sound*.

Deemed-to-satisfy provisions for the sound insulation of walls
The requirements of regulation G(x)[1] shall be deemed to be satisfied if the wall is constructed in accordance with any of the following specifications. A solid wall consisting of bricks or blocks not less than 200 mm thick with plaster not less than 12.5 mm thick on at least one face and having an average mass (calculated over any portion of the wall measuring 1 metre square and including the weight of the plaster) of not less than 415 kg/m^2...(Other specifications would be added as alternatives).

(It should be noted that the reference to the wall "with its associated structure" is necessary for technical reasons, and does not arise from any quirk of legislative style. In regard to sound insulation, a wall cannot be dissociated from the side walls, ceiling, and floor with which it is structurally connected, since these connections have a positive effect upon the reduction of sound by the barrier formed by the wall in position.)

The second change

The second step would be for a new deemed-to-satisfy provision to be added which refers to *an approved standard test* of the sound-reduction capabilities of structures. This would be a reference to a specification that, when subjected to a stated test and method of assessment, has been found to achieve a stated value. Such a provision could be added only when a reliable method of testing has been developed and used for a long enough period to be acceptable as a standard.

For example, the functional requirement quoted above as Part G(x)[1] would remain and the following specification would be added to those also quoted above as a first alternative [the description is an amalgam of the provisions of Parts G2 and G6 of the Building Regulations 1976, but slightly abbreviated for the purpose of this illustration].

The requirements of regulation $G(x)^1$ shall be deemed to be satisfied if—

the wall and its associated structure are identical with, or are similar to and unlikely to provide less resistance to the transmission of sound than, a wall and its associated structure which, when tested in accordance with regulation (y) at all frequencies set out in the Table to this regulation, limit the transmission of airborne sound so that the reduction at each frequency given in column (1) of that Table does not fall short of the appropriate value given in column (2) of that Table by an amount which causes the aggregate of such deviations to exceed 23 dB; or...

Regulation (y)

(1) Measurements shall be in accordance with Sections 2A and 3A of BS 2750: 1956, and the method of normalising the results for both air-borne and impact sound shall be that given in clause 3e(ii) thereof.

(2) The value of the sound transmission of a particular construction shall be taken to be the average of measurements made between not less than four pairs of rooms each pair having a separating wall...of an area of not less than 7 m² and each room having a volume of not less than 25 m².

Notes: 1. The Table to the regulation would give the sound reduction for walls in two related columns; Column 1 defining values of Frequency (in Hz), and Column 2 values of sound reduction (in dB) showing a recommended value for each Frequency.

2. Regulation $G(x)^1$ is the functional requirement for sound insulation outlined above.

3. Regulation (y) would contain more provisions. Those given above are the references to test procedures for which dependence is placed on BSI documents.

This provision may seem unusually complicated for a reference to a test, but its principles are straightforward. *It is designed to obviate the need for every wall built under the regulation to be tested in situ.* It means in effect that any wall construction that has already been built and tested under prescribed conditions (in the standard test), and has been found to achieve the required performance, can be used, provided that it is reproduced in accordance with an identical specification. In this way, any form of construction that has been subjected to the standard test, and can provide satisfactory evidence of this (like, for example, an Agrément Certificate) has a passport to acceptance as being in compliance with the regulations. The convenience of this method can best be illustrated by reference to a large housing estate, where the method would qualify for acceptance all those separating walls that followed the tested specification, without each individual wall having to be tested on site by a repeated and time-consuming operation.

Once this reference to a standard test has been adopted as a deemed-to-satisfy measure, it will encourage manufacturers and others to subject their constructions of different materials and designs to the standard test in order to prove compliance. As this action develops into a normal practice, there will be a flow of information about the way different structures perform under the same test procedures for sound reduction. In turn, this should lead to the emergence of rules for designing for sound insulation which, when applied, could be relied upon to achieve predicted performance values in the complete structure. (The process would be similar to that which has already taken place in the development of structural design for the different materials used in structure, where the growth of information about the way structures perform under measured conditions of stress has led to the adoption of theories for calculating structures, and formulae that, once applied, will lead to a structure of predictable strength and safety under specific conditions of load.) When an adequate body of experience has been built up through such testing, it would be possible to proceed to the next move in this evolutionary development of the regulations.

The final change

The final step would be a further amendment to the substantive part of the regulation. The functional requirement would now be removed and replaced by a regulation expressed as a performance standard. There would be two ways open for doing this.

The first and most obvious would be for the reference to the standard test, as previously used in the deemed-to-satisfy provision quoted above, to be re-stated as the substantive requirement. This would seem a convenient solution for the legislative purpose alone, because it would achieve the same practical advantages for enforcement as described previously. The regulation itself would not make the *attainment* of the actual performance a *mandatory* obligation, so that tests on the finished construction on site in each individual case would not be necessary. All that would be necessary for compliance would be evidence that the construction had been done in accordance with a specification that was identical to one that had already been tested and approved. This type of regulation has already been adopted as the basis of provisions dealing with structural fire precautions, which are among the more recent of the measures included in the national building regulations.

Following the example used previously, the final regulation designed in this form would be a mandatory requirement on these lines:

Part $G(x)^2$ Sound insulation of walls
Any wall which separates any dwelling from another dwelling or from another building *shall* in conjunction with its associated structure *be identical with a wall and its associated structure* which, when tested in accordance with BS xyz (date) …at all frequencies set out in the Table to this regulation, limit the transmission of airborne sound so that …etc.

The second way open to the legislators would be for the actual performance to be made the substantive requirement, which would mean that every wall constructed under the regulation would need to perform, if tested, in the degree required. It would not necessarily be accepted for compliance if it had been built as a copy of an approved, tested construction.

This would not be as radical a change as may at first seem, because the provision would be following a path already pioneered by the structural regulations. In those regulations, of course, the final transition from the deemed-to-satisfy provision to the substantive performance standard has not yet been made, as the requirements are for the structural work to function in its tasks with "adequate" safety. But the official guidance given is for it to comply with the Codes of Practice which are named for each of the structural materials in use; and these contain the factors of safety which, in effect, identify the *standards* of safety required, and are descriptions of the various ways of designing structures in accordance with the accepted theories of structure. In practice, it is enough for the designer to demonstrate that calculations have conformed with those principles for the design to be accepted as complying with the Code, and consequently with the mandatory regulation. The arrangement does not necessitate each structure being tested to the full limit of the designed load before it is accepted. In the same way, when methods of calculating for sound reduction have led to acceptable systems of design, it should also be enough for those calculations which are shown to follow the established theories to be accepted as evidence that the wall will perform as it is required to do in respect of sound insulation. This ultimate type of regulation, using the same example in respect of sound insulation as referred to previously, would take the simplified form of:

Part G(x)³ Sound insulation of walls
Any wall which separates any dwelling from another dwelling or from another building *shall* in conjunction with its associated structure when tested in accordance with BS xyz (date)...at all frequencies set out in the Table to this regulation, *limit the transmission of airborne sound* so that...etc.

Of course, to ease the final adoption of such a provision, it would be possible to quote as a deemed-to-satisfy provision a Code of Practice that sets out, on the information gained from testing, how walls should be designed and built to ensure that the required performance is achieved. This would enable compliance to be demonstrated by reference to the calculations and the design theories employed.

Prerequisites

This planned progression towards the adoption of performance standards as the main legislative technique in regulations would work only to convert existing specific provisions into the new mandatory form. It would not of itself result in the whole set of regulations matching up with what an enlightened public may require of its legislative instrument for building control.

It would be preferable first to review the contents of the regulations in relation to the purposes defined in the enabling Acts and, if necessary, rearrange the subjects and add any that are missing to complete the coverage. The present layout of the subject-matter tends to follow the traditional arrangement of a bill of quantities. That is to say, it reflects the sequence of building operations, dealing first with the preparation of the site, foundations and structure, and then proceeding to superstructure, plumbing services, fittings, finishes and so on. It would be more suitable to consider what aspects of the performance of buildings are affected by the need to provide for health and safety, and to identify what standard of performance is required in each case.

For example, two main sections could deal with setting the standards for health and safety. The standards of health would provide for environmental conditions, covering standards of space, thermal, atmospherical, lighting, and acoustical performance; and sanitary conditions, covering standards for the provision of accommodation and equipment, waste disposal, water supply, and so on. The standards of safety would provide for the standards of safety in regard to fire, structure, installations, and hazards of use.

Other measures for securing "welfare and convenience", or the conservation of energy, could then be collected into separate sections where provision for them was not possible under the treatment of the subjects in the two main parts.

Most, if not all, of the existing subjects in the regulations could be fitted into this kind of classification, so that once rearranged they could be allowed to follow the evolutionary process of development until the array of performance standards was complete.

The guiding principle behind this concept of rearrangement is, of course, that the regulations should be concerned only with setting the standards, not with detailing how these should be embodied in the building. Information of this kind would be for others to provide, and the most likely source would be the Standards Institution.

The evolutionary doctrine and the role of BSI Codes and Standards

If the Building Regulations were to be developed in this systematic way, they would emerge eventually as statements of the basic standards of performance required by law. They would give no further information, but contain only a comprehensive account of these legal prescriptions, so that everyone affected by the building controls would be able to discover what the law required by making reference to one self-contained statutory instrument. The regulations would be relieved of any implied need for them to function as manuals describing *ways of complying*, which is what they have tended to be in the past, though unintentionally, as long as they took the form of "specific requirements". They were never designed as manuals, so they could not have been expected to function in such a role with any real efficiency, anyway; and for them to have attempted to do so would have been to usurp a central purpose of the Standards and Codes of Practice. In relation to this change to a singleness of purpose for the regulations, the BSI would have an important complementary function in the streamlined control system, and its work would reinforce that of the law-makers in the following way.

We have seen how, in their new form, the regulations would specify the *performance* required of buildings, and in each aspect of it would define the *minimum standard* acceptable in law. In support of these controls, the BSI Codes of Practice would continue to be *advisory* documents, functioning as design manuals and as practice manuals to describe methods of achieving the various aspects of performance. Existing series of publications, like those providing a "code of basic data for the design of buildings" would be developed in parallel with the legal instruments. In general, the Codes would recommend what may be regarded as *good practice,* and in this respect would be describing higher levels or norms of achievement than would be strictly necessary for legal purposes, but they would contain in "appropriate provisions" the rules of design or practice that could be relied upon to embody the minimum standards.

The BSI Standards would be required to play a supportive role in a similar way, without changing their character. Ideally, there would need to be three kinds of Standard, each taking its cue from the definitions of performance in the regulations, as follows: there would be (a) Standards which would specify the levels of performance for various *materials* and *components,* as would be consequential to the requirements of performance laid down in the regulations; (b) Standards which would be product specifications defining what must be done for the required level of performance to be achieved in each material, product or component; and finally (c) Standards specifying methods of testing products and assessing results which could be used to ensure that each of the required aspects of performance is being attained.

Of these three types of Standard the second and third are already in production for some of the subjects of the regulations, although their presence does not result from any particular guidance about a concerted policy for directing the development of the controls by the law-makers. Neither do the existing product standards necessarily aim at any particular level of performance with a view to its being relevant to the regulations. The less familiar type of Standard referred to in (a) above would be that which interpolates from general requirements of performance, the specific qualities needed of each type of product. The preparation of Standards of this kind would depend very much on the progress made in developing adequate methods of testing, for which a systematic programme of research would be needed.

If arrangements like this were to be put into effect, there would be a combination of regulations, BSI Standards and Codes which would function as a coherent apparatus of building control. An advantageous outcome of this might be that the combination could act in a positive way to promote a gradual improvement in the standards achieved in buildings.

These promotional influences might work because of the polarity that would come to exist between *the regulations*, whose general influence would be to set the minimum levels of performance, and *Codes* concerned with recommending higher standards.

The Codes would advocate the optimum standards within the normal scope of practice at any one time; and by so doing would be encouraging a better general level of practice. As the provision of this optimum performance became standard practice for the industry, it would enable the levels of performance laid down as "standard" in the BSI Standards and product specifications to be raised, reflecting the attainment of these improved "norms" of practice. As such higher standards became economical through their wider application, it would be possible for the legislators to improve the minimum standards described in the *regulations* to equate with the new norm.

Research and training

To describe all this as an evolutionary doctrine is not wholly appropriate, because it would need to be helped along by a consciously planned strategy in order to ensure its success within an acceptable time. Despite its practical basis, there are a number of ways in which it would be breaking new ground, and in these areas there would be a pressing need for research. Indeed, the demand would be not only for research, but for "development" work to bring the results of research into practice, and all this would need to be integrated with the general strategy. The main tasks for research have already been described, but should perhaps now be examined in greater detail.

The first priority would be the identification of the various aspects of the *performance* of buildings that need to be controlled in the interests of the health and safety of persons using them. Much work on this topic has already been done, so that the task would include the collation of existing information prior to the exploration of further facts. The knowledge gained from these activities would set the pattern not only for the definitive clauses of the regulations, but also for the supportive Codes and Standards, so there is a need for close liaison between the authorities involved. For the law-makers concerned with formulating the statutory controls it is not simply a matter of identifying the requisite aspects of performance and the qualitative standards required to safeguard the public's interests, but of knowing what can be achieved by the building industry within its normal levels of cost; and what, in consequence, may be regarded as practicable for the law to demand.

The other tasks for research are more familiar, and have been featured in other contexts. One is to do with *design* systems. Legislation that uses performance as its criterion would not be possible unless there are in common use such well-understood practices of design and production that can with predictable success embody the stated standards in the completed product. In some aspects of performance, like those relating to structures and environmental conditions, the designers are already equipped with tested theories and modes of calculation. These are constantly being improved; but other procedures like them are needed for all the other relevant functions of the building which are to be the subjects of the regulations. A concerted effort is needed to develop these methods of design and production, whether they are for materials, or components, or for the building as a whole. All this information would need to be selected and arranged in relation to the new requirements.

To complete the control system, it would be necessary to have *testing* facilities readily available that can be relied upon to check the results of the provision. Research is needed in this connection for the introduction of tests and methods of measurement and evaluation. Such facilities are also essential to the practicability of adopting standards of performance as mandatory requirements.

Although priorities may be suggested by the general logic of the needs, these three research tasks would be likely to proceed in parallel, because some aspects of performance are already more familiar than others and ways of dealing with them have developed along the evolutionary paths to different degrees. Consequently, the research activities in the three categories would overlap. Also, the types of research would be serving different purposes and responding to diverse promoters. The first and third types can be seen as "user" responsibilities, because they serve the public needing the protection of the law; the second lies squarely in the sphere of the construction industry, and properly comes under the aegis of the Standards Institution where the technological consensus is available to guide the action.

It is important within the context of the country employing a system like this that the sponsorship of the research should properly reflect the need for it. For example, in the UK it would seem wrong in principle for the construction industry to finance the work which would set the standards and provide the means for checking compliance. Unlike other industries more guided by their own market research, it is concerned with end-products that are too complex to be readily sensitive to the "market", and therefore which are more in need of long-term planning. In these circumstances, it is apt that the public, being in need of the protection and making the demand, should express its user requirements clearly. This means that public-sector finance should be the main contributor to the funds for the research aimed at identifying the standards, and at developing the test facilities; while the private sector (or construction industry in this case) should be the main source of finance for research aimed at design systems and technological ways-and-means.

Of course, in addition to these preoccupations, the problem of *safety* requires continuing exploration. It would be desirable in the interests of the efficiency of the control system for the public to be able to identify the numerous hazards to safety, and to quantify the risks involved in each case, so that it can ensure that the safety measures are adequate and also are provided at a cost which is proportionate to the risk. Problems like this apply not only to parts of buildings and individual buildings, but to the environment as a whole. Applied research of a statistical nature is needed and facilities should be available (like police and fire-brigade reports, and information collected by insurers of property for guiding premiums) to enable a constant watch to be kept on the incidence of accidents of all kinds, so that the control system is able to react sensitively to increasing threats to public safety. This type of research, too, should be sponsored by the public sector, though perhaps with the granting of facilities for private-sector participation in certain aspects.

The concept of employing regulations, national codes, and standards in a combination for the purpose of building control also implies that an ordered approach to the provision of education and training is essential, to ensure that all who may be involved in the enforcement of the regulations—however arranged—may be adequately qualified.

It is already accepted and widely understood that the BSI Codes of Practice which recommend methods of design are produced by experts for the guidance of specialists, and can be put to proper use only by persons with the requisite skill and knowledge. The same principle will apply to anyone involved in the interpretation of the new range of reference codes, whether for the purpose of design or enforcement.

In the final count, the control system depends for its efficiency and success on the persons creating the buildings being competent to meet the requirements of the regulatory criteria, and on all involved in the control system to have a proper understanding of how it functions so that procedural problems and bureaucratic delays can be avoided. Accordingly, it would be for the public to decide what special qualifications would be appropriate, and to take advice to this end from its industry, institutions, legislators, consumers, and others to see that the means are properly matched to the ends.

CHAPTER SIX

User requirements for a system of building control

THE CHANGING ATTITUDE TO BUILDING CONTROL

In the United Kingdom since the war many events have combined to influence the public's attitude to building control. These have shown the need for the controls to be improved, or provided the opportunities for changes to be made in the system; and in one way and another have focused the attention of the community on the way the control process works, and how its design might be made more suitable.

These influential events have been widely variant, creating a whole climate of change. They include: the large post-war building programmes, which caused huge demands to be made on the building industry at a time when it was losing its resources of manpower to newer industries; the reorganization of local government which followed the Redcliff–Mand Report, and brought opportunities for the reconstruction of the enforcement system; the increase in the pace of technological change, due largely to the response of the building industry to the demands being made on it, which helped to expose the inadequacies of the existing legislation; the entry of the UK into the European Economic Community, which revealed the need for technical standards and building controls to be brought into harmony on an international basis; the legal changes resulting from judgements in court that favoured building owners (reflecting the consumer-oriented values), which made the enforcement authorities liable to claims for damages arising from any mistakes they might make in not rejecting faulty buildings; the mounting costs of building failures, which were given dramatic prominence in the Ronan Point disaster, and later in the demolition of high-density urban housing schemes because of the inadequacies of some of the industrialized-building systems; and generally the growing power of the public's reaction against bureaucratic authority which, rightly or wrongly, led to its insistence on simpler procedures, and less expenditure on administration.

Affected by this background of change, the community became more conscious of the conceptual ideas behind its existing system. The notion emerged, for example, that the Building Regulations—which were seen as the core of the controls—should be designed primarily to suit the needs of their two main types of user, namely the public as "consumer" of the built environment, and as "customer" of the construction industry, who needed some safeguards; and the industry itself, as supplier and producer of the buildings to meet the "market" demands. In this context it was widely acknowledged that the contents of the building regulations should cover all aspects of the performance of the built environment that might affect the health, safety, and convenience of its users; and at the same time, as a matter of equal importance, should be expressed in a way that allowed for ready compliance and efficient enforcement. The form of control, it was held, should be designed in each case to enable the public to improve its standards without too much disruption; and to allow industry to introduce new materials and techniques, or generally to innovate in the interests of better productivity, without too much procedural frustration.

It can be seen now, in reflecting on these developments, that if the national community (forming the public-at-large) is to be regarded as the prime-mover in creating the controls for building, it should not be encouraged to consider the making of a control system in isolation from its other public interests.

The public, seen in this synoptic sense, is not only the law-giver, but also the owner of the building stock, which is a fixed national asset. It is also, in consequence, interested in the development of the skills and technology of its building industry, because it relies on these for the improvement of the stock and for the speedier output of more stock for less effort.

So, while it is important that regulations should be designed as effective legal instruments, no community can afford to give these aspects of control any absolute priority over other interests essential to its long-term well-being, like the need for industrial development, and the need to have options available for choosing between types of product and methods of manufacture.

It is useful to consider the design of a control system on the UK model with these generalities in mind, and since it is a fundamental rule of good design that any instrument should be properly suited to its purpose, the first steps involve an analysis of what its users require of it.

THE PUBLIC'S NEEDS

A reminder is needed at this point that in the United Kingdom the control of building is exercised through the medium of the common law. Building legislation forms part of the penal code, and any failure to comply with its requirements would entail for the transgressor, upon conviction, the heavy penalties associated with a criminal offence.

Reliance on the processes of law may be fitting enough for the purpose of control, but it carries with it some inherent disadvantages. In the first case, the requirements grow by accretion, until the machinery of regulation is encrusted with all manner of stipulations and standards, so that it may be difficult for anyone to discern its essential parts, or get them to work properly. In the second case, reforms become difficult, because changing the law is a slow and somewhat complex process, even when the objectives of reform can be seen clearly enough by a sufficient majority to carry them through. Finally, and not the least of problems affecting the basic efficiency of a control system, the very apparatus of control becomes fascinating to its operators and administrators, and their interest in its complexities can finally obscure their understanding of what it is intended to do. The existence of this attitude can be detected in the public statements made by the public servants involved; and different views expressed by others involved in the give-and-take of the system in action. For example, a statement issued by a representative of the RIBA, which may be taken to reflect the views of the "consumer" on the receiving side of the law, and which was released at the time of public debate about a new "building bill" during the seventies, proclaimed that: "the public, as 'consumer' is primarily concerned to know that *buildings,* when complete, *will satisfy its needs for health, safety and welfare.* It wants its requirements to be described and checked in a way that does not result in any unnecessary or bureacratic waste of time. In the public's view of priorities, it is the *END PRODUCT that counts";* while another pronouncement made by a member of a department of the central government's administration held that "the object of building control is the *regulation,* in the public interest, of the construction of buildings".

Although the latter statement refers to the "public interest", those words are almost in parentheses, and the main thrust of the logic is the sylleptical argument that the object of control is regulation. An unwary listener to this gospel of the administrators can be led into a bureaucratic labyrinth and be expected to accept further statements which promise more puzzling diversions, like "the present law is complex partly because it reflects the complexity of modern life, and the variety of situations requiring some form of statutory control". Statements like this reveal a willingness, among dedicated public servants, to adopt legislative remedies as a normal way of dealing with problems affecting the community.

If the control system is to avoid being overwhelmed by such disadvantages, a periodic reassessment of its usefulness needs to be made, and the public must from time to time re-assert what it wants to achieve by its constraints.

The public as beneficiary of the national fixed assets.

The primary role of the public in controlling building relates to its custodianship of the national building stock. Its interests as beneficiary and user of the built environment determine what it requires the controls to do.

Since it employs the common law as a mode of control, it is fitting that only the most essential needs should be dealt with in this way. Whenever possible its objectives should be achieved by the provision of incentives rather than by the threat of legal constraints.

The public's essential needs are already familiar. It wants above all to have buildings that conform with acceptable standards of safety and health. That is to say, it wants to be as safe as possible in its built environment: safe from fire, from structural collapse, and from risk of injury; and in regard to health, safe from disease or contamination.

It wants these qualities to be embodied in the buildings which are the end-product of its construction industry. It is this that it has in mind in expressing its requirements: the provision of buildings that are not hazardous. In making the law, the public is expressing the same theme as when it asks for safe aeroplanes and ships and road-vehicles. It also wants to achieve this aim with the least amount of bother, so it gives reluctant and secondary attention to what means are appropriate.

It requires, too, that these qualities should be present throughout the life of the buildings, but this, in itself, is an additional requirement, resting on the presupposition that the maintenance of buildings should also be an enforceable duty.

In regard to motor-cars, the public requires periodic inspections as a means of ensuring that they remain safe enough for use, but it does not make the same provision for buildings, and this implies that it expects buildings to be so constructed as to remain secure through the predicted period of their life, or rather, that they should retain the same degree of security as was found to be acceptable when they were built.

Traditionally the corporate body of the public, as patron of the construction industry, has expected these standards, which it sets for its members to follow, to be provided with the least possible cost to itself. That is to say, it expects its experts to perform, and the necessary checks to be made to ensure that the building stock is safely up to standards, in ways that do not add greatly to the normal costs of the provision. It has always appeared to accept the principle that the enforcement of its own laws should be funded by itself, but there has been nothing absolute about this, and fees have been charged to defray some of the costs involved. It has perhaps become ensnared in difficulties arising from this principle, which are due to the separation of the two activities of enforcement and production, leading to higher costs in each case, though these might be hidden, or difficult to attribute to specific causes.

In recent times, other less fundamentally essential needs have been added to what the public wants its legislation to cover, namely welfare, convenience, and conservation. The last named represents a change from the time-honoured purpose of building regulations to deal with a different kind of national demand, that is, the need to conserve the supply of fuel, power, and water, by avoiding their wasteful use in buildings. The subjects of "welfare" and "convenience" are less readily distinguished from health and safety, and seem to indicate more of a wish by the legislators to give themselves extra headings to cover items of secondary detail than any positive demand by the public justifying legal controls.

As regards the basic needs for acceptable standards of safety and health, there are two major difficulties which the public must take into account in establishing its requirements and creating its controls.

The first is to do with the problems of setting and achieving the desired standards. It is not possible to attain a condition of absolute safety, whether it be in regard to the stability of the structure or the spread of disease. Precautions can be taken that are extensive, elaborate, and costly, but no matter how much money might be spent, absolute freedom from risk is impracticable. The standard of safety that can reasonable be made a require-ment of the law is a matter of judgement, and its degree must be supported by an adequate consensus. A balance must be struck between what can be regarded as socially acceptable; what the costs of attaining the standard might be; and what might be the consequences of any failure. In many ways the choice is like that of selecting a speed-limit for the purposes of safety on the road. Few members of the public would support a maximum limit being set at an unreasonably low speed with a view to greater safety; while in any case it is impossible to justify the choice of any particular speed as representing an optimum for safety. In regard to buildings, the designers are having to make assessments of this kind throughout the development of their work. In preparing a structure, for example, the designer makes two successsive assessments in estimating its strength; the first being to do with the strength of each element, and the second with the strength of the structure as a whole. In doing so he uses highly developed techniques of analysis, based on mathema-tical or experimental premises, but still requiring an exercise of judgement. In practice, this may mean adopting varied factors of safety for different purposes, guided by established estimates of the dangers. In attempting to set the *legal* standards of safety, the *public* is concerned with the *probability* of different circumstances that might affect safety, and the *gravity* of the effect of any failure or inadequacy. If it can collect the statistical evidence of the incidence of various hazards, as an insurance company does in order to evaluate the risks in setting its premiums, it can go some way towards establishing what standards of safety it needs; but it will have to depend on the skill-levels of the industry to get the standards embodied in the buildings.

The second difficulty affecting the creation of suitable controls is to do with the prospect of change. It is inevitable that the standards will have to be changed from time to time as knowledge expands and provides a better understanding of the nature of the dangers. Recent experience can be quoted to illustrate this point. The Ronan Point disaster laid emphasis on the dangers inherent in faulty gas installations in high-rise buildings; on the consequences of internal pressures being applied to structural panels in addition to normal design-loads; and on the need to make provision to localize structural collapse in order to arrest its progression through a tall building. Other, less dramatic, structural failures showed up the inadequacies of high alimuna cement; and, following storm damage to buildings, scientific studies at the building research establishment led to revisions being made in the provisions for the calculation of wind-loading on buildings, to improve their safety in bad weather conditions. These are examples of the expansion of knowledge about structural problems, where the new information can be incorporated into the provisions without too much difficulty because the subject is a familiar one. There are other examples where the physical problems are less traditional, like evidence of lead pollution of the atmosphere in towns, due to exhaust fumes from petrol-driven vehicles; and the air-pollution in enclosed spaces caused by cigarette-smoking, where the new information reveals a physical danger of a kind not previously covered by the system of building control. All this implies the need for a flexible approach to the art of law-making, and indicates that, while a clear expression of the need for safety is to be desired, there should be room for standards to be altered and for new subjects to be covered, as the occasion demands.

Of course, the public does not want to have disasters as a means to the improvement of its building control system (as the last paragraph may seem to suggest); but rather it wants a control system as a means to the prevention of disasters. Unfortunately, the evidence of history supports the view that disasters have always come first, the controls being introduced subsequently in an effort to prevent the same thing happening again. Even in recent times, most substantive amendments to the regulations have been prompted by accidents. This practice of "regulating by disaster" is likely to remain as long as the public chooses not to spend the money needed to monitor hazards, assess probabilities in a scientific way based on statistical information, and generally predict what safeguards might be necessary to avoid accidents.

Expenditure of this kind needs to be seen as a premium paid by the public as an insurance against unreasonable risks in the use of its building stock. At present, without such organized expenditure on any adequate scale, the public pays its premium in the form of the death and injury to persons, or the damage to the environment, resulting from the occasional disaster.

This illustrates the remaining item in the catalogue of the needs of the public as custodian of the national building stock: the need for some form of security in the event of any failure in its system of safeguards. There are two problems likely to arise, one relates to the malfunctioning of the control system itself in regard to a particular case, when a building fault has "slipped through" undetected and the building has been wrongly accepted as complying; the other relates to the occurrence of some new kind of danger, against which there are no existing measures in the regulations. In theory, this second problem, too, can be construed as a malfunctioning of the control system, on the grounds that its "forward scanning" process should have been able to predict the event. At present, the public compensates in an *ad hoc* way by finding the money from public expenditure for remedial measures whenever necessary, as was the case, for example, after the Ronan Point disaster, when a great deal was expended from the public purse in reinforcing other high-rise blocks which had been built or were being built using similar techniques that had proved to be susceptible to progressive collapse when damaged locally.

For dealing with these problems, the public requires two kinds of indemnity. The first is the central and major kind for dealing with the disasters against which the control system itself should function as an insurance. If there is an adequate surveillance of the probability of danger, the system itself should function as an efficient protection, and a judgement could be made of the residue-risk of any random calamity. The measures for dealing with that risk could then be decided: whether to accept it as an unsecured liability, or to insure against it. The decision would depend on a balance being struck between the level of ongoing expenditure on risk-probability studies, which should have the effect of reducing the probability of *unforeseen* dangers; and the cost of indemnification for the remaining risk of a "disaster".

The second kind of indemnity has a more familiar form and a more modest scale. It is the kind that would cover any claims on the public for damages arising from a malfunctioning of the control system. There seems little doubt that in a consumer-dominated community, the public institutions will be liable to claims for compensation for damage due to any "negligence" in the administration or enforcement of the laws governing building. The public must, therefore, secure itself against such liability, or else take steps to divest itself of any too burdensome responsibility for the management of its system of control.

It is doubtful whether these basic needs could ever be established with sufficient authority for the public to take action, excepting by some commission or inquiry (like the Robens Committee), but they can be summed up very briefly in general terms. The public needs buildings to be safe; to conform to adequate standards of safety and health through their predictable life; and to enable their users to secure a reasonable conservation of energy and water. It wants measures to ensure that these requirements are provided with the least trouble and cost, but with optimum surety; and it would like to be shielded from the worst consequences of failure.

The public as the owner of property

While the public-at-large has its own interests in the national building stock, and needs controls to protect them, the owners of the property on whom the constraints are placed are themselves members of the public, and together form a property-owning community of sufficient size to lend importance to *their* requirements of the building control system.

This community is made up of individuals owning buildings; authorities of central and local government, and other public bodies and agencies; private firms, and companies of varying size representing their shareholders; and investors in property or "real estate", among whom are those who represent the universal interest of life assurance and superannuation.

This property-owning section of the public has a similar basic interest in its buildings having adequate standards of safety and health, and efficiency in regard to conservation. It needs these standards to be properly related to the use it wants to make of the buildings, and it wants to avoid failures or inadequacies in the construction that would *reduce the value of the property*, or turn assets into liabilities. A key requirement of the building owner in this respect is that the conformity of the building with acceptable standards should be widely and firmly acknowledged. It is simply a question of its owner *believing* it to be safe, but of all members of the public accepting that it *is* safe, so that its "market value" is unimpaired. Justice must not only be done, but must be seen to be done as a matter of course, for this purpose.

A prime interest here, then, is not only for the owner to have a building of adequate standards, but also for that owner to know precisely what standards are regarded as acceptable by the public. For this purpose, there is a need for the legal criteria to be stated for all to see in plain terms and for the relevant information to be readily available.

A building owner, too, needs to be able to plan for his property to conform with the public's standards at minimum cost and within predictable budgets; and to be able to get confirmation, with the least delay or procedural difficulty, that it has complied.

A further and ultimate requirement of the building owner is the need for security against risks of inadequacy. Like anyone else buying a product, he needs to be assured that it is not flawed and, being responsible for its compliance with public standards, he needs to cover his liability by having access to compensation in the event of damage from failure.

For this purpose the owner needs conventional insurance; but, curiously, it is in this area that he is very poorly served. At present, if he suffers loss due to failure in a building, he can seek recovery by civil action against the suppliers for negligence. But what is needed, in plain terms, is not this recourse to legal remedy, but direct access to recompense when things go wrong.

It is strange that this should seem difficult, because owners are able to make satisfactory arrangements to deal with damage to their property once it is in use. The normal property insurance gives cover for damage due to fire or storm and other hazards in return for the regular payment of an insurance premium. But in the event of damage being due to an inherent fault in the original construction of the building, the recompense lies in some supplier's or designer's indemnity beyond the reach of the owner except through some civil-court action, which can be protracted and expensive.

There would seem to be no easy solution to this problem, but it is one that should be remedied as a matter of priority so that owners, designers, suppliers, and inspectors involved in the process of creating buildings and bringing them into use can revert to normal relationships. At present, in regard to dwellings, the Defective Premises Act which came into force in 1974 places special obligations on anyone involved in the provision of a house, and a practical remedy for defective properties is given to house purchasers through a scheme operated jointly by an association of house builders, though the benefits are available only if its members have been employed in providing the dwelling. In general, however, the insurance cover is provided by the builders and designers for their own protection, and the building owner cannot receive any recompense from it for defects in the building until these have been shown to be due to the fault of the builder or the negligence of the designer. Yet the cost of the insurance, being part of the overhead costs of producing the building, is reflected in its cost to the building owner. Though there are many pros and cons with regard to this matter, and though reliable firms will often take careful steps to remedy defects to protect their own good name, the underlying principle is unsatisfactory. It is that the building owner is meeting the burden of cost for the insurance, but has no direct access to its benefits in the event of remedial action being necessary. Of course, the cost is only being met indirectly, and there is indirect access to remedies, but the owner has no security without initiating legal action, which can involve special procedures and protracted delays. It may produce briefs for the lawyers, but it would not seem to be an operation that is beneficial to building owners and those concerned with them in the business of supplying their buildings.

Some more direct form of security ought to be devised in which insurance cover is made available to the owner as part of the contract, direct options being offered for different types of cover and for various periods of time. Subtle refinements may be possible, such as reductions of premium for the employment of accredited builders, manufacturers, or designers, on the basis of favourable "no claims" records, but the insurance cover would be by direct contract between the owner and the insurers, and would offer the possibilities of the prompt settlement of claims when things go wrong.

Of course, complications can arise for these arrangements according to the degree in which the enforcement of building law is provided as a "policing" service by public authorities. The greater the separation of this service from the business of providing the buildings, the greater is the likelihood of complication, because the "police force" or inspectorate becomes a third party in the network of responsibility, and accordingly can attract blame for faults and give grounds for further civil action.

It is of particular importance to the public, in both its roles (as general beneficiary and particular property owner), that these questions of liability are cleared up, and that the system of building control is designed so that all its users can be satisfied with the measures open to them for their security against risks.

In its role of property owner, the public's requirements of the building control system can be summed up as being similar to those of its more general role, but with different emphasis. It wants its buildings to have acceptable standards of safety and health and other aspects of performance. Therefore, it wants these "norms" to be properly established for clear reference, and its compliance with them to be formally acknowledged and widely known. It needs to be able to acquire confirmation of this acceptance with the least dificulty, delay, or extra cost when the building is being provided, and needs to be able to make secure arrangements for compensation if things go wrong.

The public as employer of the construction industry

The construction of buildings and their infrastructure is an industry of national concern. While the public has its interests in the stock produced, and the effect of the built environment on the health and safety of the people involved, it has other interests as an employer in the nature and efficiency of the industry on which it relies for that production. The activity of building is one of the most historic occupations of mankind. The industry has long-established traditions and supplies basic necessities at both popular and elite levels of demand. It is large in comparison with other industries, is traditionally labour-intensive, and has been accustomed to using a larger proportion of unskilled operatives in its work-force than more modern industries. It has always played an important part in the economic life of the community.

In managing the national economy, the public uses the construction industry, rightly or wrongly, as a regulator of its stop–go policies. This implies an expectancy that the industry is capable of performing in different ways in prompt response to changing demands. In times of "reflation", or when the management of demand calls for high levels of output, the industry is expected to expand rapidly and increase its production, and in times of full employment this means developing capital-intensive methods for fast build-ing. In times of "recession", the demand can be reduced dramatically, and the industry is expected to be able to discard its high-energy techniques in favour of more labour-intensive and traditional ways of building, while maintaining its efficiency at the appropriate scale of activity. It is also expected to be able to switch its production from one type of building to another, as the public may inaugurate programmes of building for different purposes: schools, hospitals, houses, factories, leisure-facilities, and so on. Of course, within each type it has to be able to produce schemes which are greatly different in scale and complexity. Since in production-engineering terms, a building is a "unique-production" project, rather than one created by "mass-production" or "pro-cess-poduction" techniques, these varied requirements call for great flexibility on the part of the producers.

The industry must at all times be able to maintain the standards required of its products, and is expected, along with other industries, to pursue well-established goals, such as: to improve standards; to increase productivity; to retain competitiveness; to use less energy per unit of output and to avoid waste and contamination; to reduce costs; and to achieve greater predictability and reliability with budget forecasts and completion times. In consequence, apart from its problems of management and technical competence, the industry needs all the scope it can get for research, development, and innovation, together with its retention of traditional skills.

Because it is the public that places these demands on the construction industry, the public has a fundamental interest in its ability to respond. The key-word to express this interest is *options*. The public needs its industry to provide it with many options, and to keep them open: options on types of project; options on methods of production; and options of scale in product and output.

Consequently, the public needs to ensure that whatever constraints are imposed on the industry to control building in its other interests, these controls must be designed in such a way as to *avoid reducing the options,* or preventing the industry from attaining whatever flexibility or innovation it requires to meet the demands made on it.

THE NEEDS OF INDUSTRY

Apart from the interests that the public has in its role as the "consumer" of the built product, the other interests involved in the processes of building control are those of the various sections of the construction industry. If the public is seen as the law-maker, or controller, the industry must be cast as the receiver of the law, or the productive-force to be controlled. Of course, these categories cannot be rigid, because the legal responsibility for compliance is laid on the *owner*, who is not a part of the industry; and conversely, the main source of information for the law's criteria is the *industry*, whose members also provide a consensus of support for what might be regarded as the *norms of practice*, and which therefore represent standards that are economically feasible for imposition as legal standing orders. But in broad terms, the industry submits to building control, and as a user of the system has needs that must also be taken into account.

Broadly speaking too, the main sections of the industry can be distinguished as the designers and the producers. The designers are the professional advisers, that is to say the architects, planners, building economists; civil, structural, environmental, and services engineers; quantity surveyors; management specialists and others that function mainly as agents of the clients, but who form the designing and managing contingent of the construction industry. The producers include the builders; civil engineering and other contractors; manufacturers of materials, components, equipment, and plant; suppliers and others making up the main body of the national construction industry.

Designer's needs

Although most design work is now a multi-professional activity (involving, among other disciplines, a constant assessment of costs and practical options) the prime inventors or generators are the architects, engineers, and planners. It is upon their work that the constraints fall in the first place and, consequently, they are users of the control system whose needs must be considered for its design.

The process of design has been the subject of much descriptive literature. A popular, and often debated academic and theoretical topic, it has also been expanded for practical purposes in authoritative reports by the main professional institutions of the industry. Each of the institutions of civil, structural, mechanical, and electrical engineers has produced its official manual, and much of this work is reflected in the Codes of Practice of the BSI dealing with the design of buildings and various forms of structure.

The Royal Institute of British Architects (RIBA) has produced its *Handbook of Practice and Management* in which are set out the procedures followed by architects in their development of a design, and these are summarized in the booklet describing the *Conditions of Engagement*. Members are obliged by their charter and code of conduct to uphold these practices "for the mutual benefit of clients and architects". Nevertheless, there remains a surprising lack of awareness in the public-at-large about how the process works, and what procedures are likely to encourage the best results. It is a sign of such philistinism that the national building regulations (which may be regarded justifiably as the public's *design criteria* for building) are arranged in a way that reflects more of the step-by-step practices of building on site, than of the stages of the designer's work, although these processes are where the constraints apply.

Yet the constraints can work efficiently and economically only if they are framed to fit without disruption into the design process. A successful design is the result of skilled judgement. It is the assessment of much information and the evaluation of possible solutions, and the synthesis of the elements of the problem into an optimum congruity. If information is not ready at the appropriate time, nor agreement reached during the significant stages, the formulation cannot be balanced and the judgements cannot be made efficiently. The design will be flawed, or unsuited to its requirements, and lacking in cost effectiveness.

At the inception stage a designer begins with a brief as an initial statement of requirements, and then makes a preliminary technical appraisal and forecasts an "outline timetable" and a way of proceeding. The problem then is to collect, in closest collaboration with the client, and with other relevant users and designers, all the information available of the client's requirements, and all of the facts and factors that will affect the form, space, and content of the building. This information is analysed and assimilated, and preliminary solutions are explored; outline proposals are presented to the client with approximate costs; further instructions are sought when necessary; and briefing instructions are amended if desirable in the light of the fuller understanding of the scheme.

The next stages of the process are the preparation of the scheme design involved, and an outline specification, an estimate of the cost, and a timetable for remainder of the work on the project. When these have received the client's approval, the work on the final detailed design is able to begin.

Once the design has been settled, changes cannot be introduced without the cost being affected. The design team must now concentrate on completing the details and preparing all the information and instructions needed for production, comprising working drawings, specifications, and bills of quantity. Subsequently, the tenders are invited, the contractor chosen, and the contract signed, and the work on site proceeds under the surveillance of the designer in whatever way is required by the conditions of the contract. When the work is completed under this form of management, the designer inspects the finished building and, depending upon a satisfactory result, will issue the certificate of completion.

In this cycle of production the process of design is of critical importance, and engages many talents. Everything that is used to form the fabric, structure, and mechanism of the building must be covered by it, if the building is to be created in an ordered and economical way. The execution of the design—that is, the making of the building—involves plant, a labour force of many skills, and large commitments of time and money; and depends upon the many responsibilities being accepted and discharged.

The aim of designers is to produce a building that fits the purpose of the owners and users, and properly fulfils its function. To do this they must acquire at the outset a thorough knowledge of what the client needs; but they must have, too, all the information necessary to determine how the building should perform in all its aspects to meet these requirements. This covers subjects like loading (in itself a complex subject dealing with many types, combinations, and frequencies of loading); fire resistance; water-tightness; thermal and sound insulation; internal climatic conditions of lighting, ventilation, heating, and humidity; drainage; sanitary provisions; and so on. The final design, which is a synthesis of these elements, must provide all the qualities of strength, durability, and reliability that are appropriate, and do so within the limits of cost and time available. The prevailing discipline governing all design decisions is the question of what produces the best value for money. The designers, therefore, in balancing all the factors to find the optimum level of performance, must measure all choices against the yardstick of economy.

In making these analyses and evaluations, the designers are not working in a void. They are supported by, and have reference to, a body of expert knowledge and experience. Their guiding philosophies of design have been postulated, discussed, elaborated, checked, developed, confirmed, and practised. They work in a forum of recommended design procedures, employing either the familiar rules whose value has been firmly established from experience; or more experimental methods recommended by specialists. Among the published documents giving guidance available to them are the Codes of Practice, drawn up by the British Standards Institution, and therefore based upon expert opinions, widely acknowledged.

The end-product of all this activity should be a well-designed building, which, to merit such recognition, should have—in accordance with the time-honoured epigrams—the qualities of "commodity, firmness, and delight"; "simplicity, unity, and necessity"; and satisfy the conditions of "function, safety, and economy".

It is important that this process should be recognized in the context of building control, because the aims of the design cannot be achieved if either the information is not available at the appropriate time to be taken properly into account, or the process of the design work is disrupted by requirements being added or changed after the stage of synthesis when the factors have been evaluated and balanced.

The law-makers who fashion the building controls should take account of what the designers need of the system if they are to contend with these problems successfully. The mandatory provisions should be clear statements of the standards of performance required, and set within the scope of normal practice; the information should be complete and available at the outset of the work, and expressed in a form that provides room for optional solutions. There should be unequivocal clarity about where the responsibility lies. Enforcement should be by a process that is integral with the design procedures: flexible, efficient, speedy, giving decisions at the right time, and involving experts of equal professional competence well able to interpret the published guidance and evaluate the particular proposals.

The needs of producers

The traditional method of producing buildings in the UK is for the responsibility for the management and execution of the operations on the site to rest with the building contractor. This is no longer as straightforward or customary as it used to be, but the essential pattern is still recognizable. The classic method is for tenders to be invited in competition by the owner or the owner's agent, and a general contractor to be selected. A contract is then signed representing an agreement between the contractor and the owner, by which the contractor undertakes to construct the building within a given period of time, in return for payments to be made to him by the owner at intervals during the period, based on valuations of the work done. The contracts are usually expressed on well-established pro-formas, which contain many conditions of engagement, including a requirement that the contractor must not contravene the building legislation in any way during the progress of the work. Whatever else may have been done before the start of the work to ensure that the design does not contravene regulations, this civil contract entered into by the general contractor places a further obligation upon him to ensure that all is in order.

This "classic" form of procedure also includes the participation of professional advisers, namely architects, and engineers where required, who are responsible for the technical surveillance of the work, according to their own contractural arrangements; and quantity surveyors, who carry out valuations to enable the architect to certify payments due for the work completed. Under these provisions, the architect is responsible for carrying out a final inspection, and if everything is in order, for issuing a certificate of completion, by which the finished building is formally handed over to its owner, either on the basis that it *is* satisfactorily in accordance with the contract, or that it is acceptable but for some identified shortcomings which must be remedied before the payment due under the contract is completed.

In the past, the general contractor carried out most of the work using his own staff and equipment. Supplies of materials and components were obtained from special merchants, and some sub-contractors were used for the supply and fixing of elements requiring different technical expertise, like the structural steel framework, or the heating and electrical services. A central function of this type of general contractor was the management of the work of the contract. The complex business of getting all the different supplies to the site at the right time, and ensuring that each phase of the work was executed without delay, so that none of the work-force was kept idle, was in the hands of the general contractor. This meant his keeping a special staff on the site to programme the operations, order materials, and generally see that the work progressed as smoothly and efficiently as possible.

As buildings became more complex, and the equipment and skills needed for their construction became more costly, so the proportion of directly employed staff and of directly owned equipment has grown less. It is now not uncommon for sub-contractors to be used for all parts of the work, each specializing in the supply and erection of a particular element; or in the provision of skills, or equipment. Since it is not unusual for the installation of the services to account for more than 50 per cent of the total cost, this section of the work is sometimes done by a separate contract.

Notwithstanding these developments, the predominant practice has remained that the general contractor provides the contract management and co-ordination. Yet the growth of specialism is likely to change this too. Already a process known as "direct professional control" has come into use, whereby the management role of the former "general contractor" has been taken over by the consultants, so that the suppliers and sub-contractors are providing their services directly to the owner, under the supervision of the management team. It might be predicted that this kind of direct co-ordination of experts may become the standard practice if it results in greater efficiency and economy, but it is also clear that at present, all these methods of operation are currently in use by the industry.

Essentially, however, whether there is contractual separation or not, the activities fall within the same framework of management. The owner's instructions are received from the professional designer in the form of drawings, specifications, and bills of quantities making up the contract documents; the work is pre-planned to conform with the timetable of the agreement; materials, components, labour, and equipment are brought together on the site for the creation of the built product which, when completed, is handed over to the client. This, then, is the essential function of the producer: to embody the design in the finished building; to receive instructions which comprise the details of an established design and to put them into effect to create a building. In principle, this remains the same whether or not the design work is done by consultants under separate contracts. Some large firms of contractors offer an "all-in service", which includes design; others may offer direct building contracts, apparently dispensing with any formal design input, but the procedures they use are fundamentally similar, because nothing can be built unless it is first designed and conceived as a plan of action, no matter how crudely.

Other determinants of how the industry works have been touched upon in the earlier section dealing with the public's expectations of its construction industry. These other influences are mainly economical, deriving from the normal pressures of the "market economy", and can be recapitulated in summary as follows.

Contractors deal with all kinds of production methods, called for by a variety of types of project, from building adaptations where the design and techniques are unique to the job, to large repetitive schemes where techniques of mass-production may be appropriate. They must respond to changing demands, sometimes massive to the point of overload during periods of economic buoyancy, sometimes minimal, during the times of recession. At all times they are in competition with each other; and with other industries competing for the use of the national resources of finance and labour. As a consequence, they are involved in a continuing quest for better productivity, better materials or better ways of using familiar ones, and better control over operations. The imposition of other constraints of a legal kind are additional impositions on this survival business of building, and give cause to the industry to keep its objectives firmly in mind.

In this respect, the contractors' short-term priorities are to do first with their need to receive their instruction about what has to be built; secondly with their tasks of organizing and carrying out the work; and finally with their responsibilities for handing over a satisfactory product at the end of the day. Their long-term priorities are to do with their need for flexibility about how best to get things done, and their need to preserve their freedom to develop technology and method.

Translated into requirements affecting the design of a system of building control, these priorities produce guide-rules as follows. The producers need the legal requirements to be stated clearly as *design criteria*, so that these can be incorporated in the designers' instructions at the outset of their work and can also be available for the guidance of the manufacturers of particular materials and components. Contractors want to know that the details they receive as instructions defining what they must build already incorporate all that is needed to meet the law's requirements. If the compliance of these details has been properly acknowledged by the law-makers, all that remains for the builder to do is to carry out the instructions, and to give them faithful expression in the finished product. They need authoritative inspections to be carried out at the crucial work-stages to give them confirmation that they are doing this successfully, if they are to avoid abortive effort and wasted time. They would of course prefer to rely on one inspecting authority for the surveillance of their work to discharge all of their obligations under their contract and under the common law, so that they can carry out their work efficiently without having to contend with many inspections by different people. At the end of their contribution to the project, they need someone with appropriate authority to agree and certify that they have properly discharged their duties, so that the finished building can be handed over to its purchaser with a formal guarantee that it is satisfactorily in accord with the stated requirements.

Beyond these needs affecting their efficiency in performing individual contracts, the producers have wider interests in work of the law-makers in formulating the national constraints to be imposed by law. Their participation in the creation of *standards* or "norms" is already an essential ingredient to the success of such specifications being acceptable to a suitable majority of users. With regard to *legal* criteria, they should be party to agreements about what measures are reasonable and within the compass of common practice, so that the law-makers are able to set their constraints with confidence that they will be practicable and enforceable without the nation having to face undue penalties of cost. They should also be satisfied that the legal criteria are expressed in a way that makes apparent what the aims are, while leaving open the means that may be adopted to achieve them; and they should be assured that the systems for checking results are scientifically reliable; and can produce, as readily as possible, information that is acceptable to the law-makers and law-receivers alike.

The do-it-yourself tendency

The art of building (like that of music-making, painting, sculpture, and other erstwhile activities of an elite) has entered a period of popularization, which has come to exist as though in counteraction to the high technology based on the specialism and scientific developments needed to serve modern social and industrial aspirations. Indications are that this inclination to "do-it-yourself" is likely to continue and to grow. It does not require any far-fetched space-age or micro-chip-era forecasting to predict that the time available for leisure in wealth-producing communities will increase with the development of auto-mative techniques. In these circumstances there will be more time for people to apply themselves to creative work of their own choice, like repairing buildings, gardening, and other occupations being represented as part of the "good life". Large commercial undertakings are already devoted to the supply of equipment for everyman: handtools; gadgets; workshop aids; pre-cut components; modularized parts; ready-mix materials; and all the paraphernalia of the "towards-2000" handyman. Apart from the stimulating effect of these techniques, and the spread of information about them, this tendency seems the natural extension of the trends that have always been present in the building industry. Although the greater part of building in terms of the *value* of the end-products has been attributable to the major firms, much of the small housing work and most of the repair and maintenance of buildings has been done by a multitude of small firms. A high proportion of this work has been carried out without the benefit of professional advice, although this, too, is showing signs of becoming "packaged" and available for use at the popular level. Owner-occupiers wishing to improve their properties are increasingly able to discard the jobbing builder in favour of carrying out the work themselves, and this includes plumbing and service installations, as well as painting and decorating.

This tendency has been reflected in the growing demand that the building control system should make special provisions for the small-scale operations. The proposals in the Government's Command Paper on the *Future of Building Control in England and Wales* in 1981 *that there should be one form of regulation for domestic buildings, and exemption for minor works involving small risks to health and safety,* follow in the train of recommendations made originally in the Guest Report (1957) and developed by subsequent committees.

The Guest Report stated (para. 218) that "for the benefit of the *practical builder* and those administering the law, we would hope that it may be found possible to draft the regulations in a somewhat more readily comprehensible form..." and in referring to this in a discussion paper issued during the early seventies, the Joint Committee on Building Legislation at the RIBA pointed out that "the needs of the public vary *from those of the designers*, including those with new concepts, who need requirements clearly and simply expressed and allowing the maximum flexibility for advances in design and technical improvement; *to the jobbing builder, who needs the simplest requirements...*". The Joint Committee also referred to a particular recommendation of the Guest Report that "we believe it might help in the smooth operation of building control if the simple and smaller projects (which form the vast majority) could be dealt with by a separate set of relatively simple regulations (or at least particular regulations separately distinguished) leaving the more complex regulations for application to larger buildings, where more difficult criteria are involved...".

In considering these different and apparently irreconcilable needs, the Government reflected in its 1981 Command Paper that "for *domestic buildings* the Inner London Byelaws might provide a good model...", and this reference to by-laws cast in a particular mould gives a clue to what the real needs of the "Do-it-yourself tendency" are, in respect of the building control system.

First, it must be said that the principle *that minor works* which represent limited risks to health and safety *should be exempt from control* has been widely accepted, and there is no doubt that the first wish of all "jobbing builders" and practical amateurs in the art would be that they should be free of all legal building constraints. Nevertheless, this principle may be difficult to achieve in practice. For example, it was the simple connection between a gas–cooker and its supply pipe that had been badly fitted that leaked the gas that caused the explosion that led to the disaster of progressive collapse at Ronan Point. Small problems lead to bigger ones, and the line of exemption may be difficult to draw.

This said, it seems basically untrue or misleading to claim that the public's requirements for safeguarding its health and safety should be less demanding or more simply expressed for domestic buildings than for any other type of structure. Nothing could be more simple to express than that a building should be safe (whether it is a house or an office block); that its structure should avoid wasteful heat-loss in the winter; or that its elements should have adequate resistance to fire. In basis terms this is to say that any shelter should be safe, warm, and not burn readily. The expert practitioner will understand the complications of meeting these requirements and will know what to do; the amateur will, at the worst, be ignorant of the implications, and at best will understand the aims but *not* know how exactly they can be achieved.

Taking this theme one step further, it is no good telling the amateur that *"the structure of a building...shall safely sustain and transmit to the foundations the combined dead load, imposed load and wind load"*; or that any *"element of structure, door or other part of a building"* should *"if exposed to a test by fire in accordance with BS 476: Part 8: 1972...satisfy the requirements of that test..."*; or that *"the calculated average U value of perimeter walling...shall not exceed 1.8"*. These statements are expressed simply, and are readily comprehended, but it would take an expert to understand what must be done in terms of building in order to produce a construction that complies; and this is as true of the structure, components, and insulation of a *small* building as it is of a *large* one.

The do-it-yourself practitioner who turns his or her attention to repairing the engine of a car is well provided for, because the manufacturer of the car will provide a manual giving a step-by-step description of what has to be done, and what tools and parts are required. The design criteria which determine the engine's performance, and ensure its safety, are not necessarily given, but if the instructions are followed the repaired engine should provide those standards of performance and safety.

REGULATIONS OR BUILDING MANUALS?

The real difference between the requirements for complex and for simple buildings is not so much due to the buildings themselves as to the skill of their creators, upon whom the law-makers must place their reliance for getting things right, whether they like it or not. The legal requirements for buildings can be expressed most clearly and simply *if the public is prepared to rely upon experts to design and construct them*. If reliance is placed instead on untrained practitioners, like the small "practical builder" or the do-it-yourself amateur, then the regulations would need to be in the form of *manuals* of good practice, aimed specifically at ensuring that the minimum standards for securing safety and safeguarding health are achieved in the small–scale buildings and their service installations. Like the popular guide-books to good cooking, such manuals would contain recipes or *specifications for good building*, illustrated as need be in a way not possible for legal instruments; but they would be lengthy and expensive to produce, and only practicable for small or uncomplicated buildings.

It can be agreed that the London by-laws resemble this kind of descriptive document. They read rather like manuals, being written as specific requirements and giving prescriptions of what must be done, so that they could be used as useful models for the preparation of regulations for the jobbing builder, or the do-it-yourself enthusiast.

CONCLUSIONS

It is of course for the public to decide how best it can go about achieving its objectives of having a built stock of good quality, which also meets its standards of safety, health, and energy conservation. In order to do so, it must choose how far it should depend upon the skill of experts (having regard for its ability to ensure that it has these in appropriate degree), and how much scope it should allow for amateur or untrained practitioners. Its traditional equivocation about this choice has produced the present form of its building control, as regards the statutory instruments and the methods of enforcement. The more it allows the participation of untrained or unqualified persons, the greater will be the bulk of the documentary expression of the law, and the greater will be the cost of law-enforcement.

Future possibilities and options

In order to consider what further developments may affect building control in the United Kingdom, it would be useful to have a brief reminder of the nature of the present system. It is one of a type which places reliance upon the legal procedures of the common law for its function and enforcement. It receives its authority from Parliament, and depends wholly upon the departments of central government and the local authorities for its administration and performance. In this sense, it conforms with the view which has become popular among economists that it is one of the tasks that should be left to government, because it is a function the government does well, and which the private sector cannot do, like taking care of the external and internal security of the nation. Seen in this light, building control is like an extension of the task of policing, or internal security, and is rightly left to the public sector. There can be no doubt that, hitherto, this is where the duty has lain in the UK.

It is equally plain that the building control system has never been static. Although changes have been slow, or have occurred only at widely spaced intervals, the control system has developed over the decades in a background response to the social, technological, and economic influences on the life of the national community. Changes are likely to continue, not least because it is comparatively recently that the control was more directly centralized under government auspices; and with the creation of a Building Regulations Advisory Committee by the responsible Secretary of State, and the issue of national building regulations, more attention has been concentrated on the controls and how well the system works.

It would be useful, in consequence, to see what the present trends of change may be expected to bring in the immediate future. The changes now envisaged as a result of some 17 years of reform, since the replacement of local by-laws, are likely to contain the first fruits of that experience, and to represent the first conscious attempt to re-design the system as a whole.

What can be predicted in the short term are empirical developments which have the value of being practical, in terms of how they will work and how they will be supported by the community and industry alike. They are, however, projections from an existing state of affairs where many imperfections have become ingrained in a control system which might have been very different and more in keeping with existing demands had it been started afresh.

Together with this view of the future, therefore, it would be useful to project a theoretically ideal version of a system of the UK type, having regard for all that can be seen to have happened in its development so far. Of course, this can only be a theoretical view of perfection, visible from the present vantage point in the time-scale of the system's development. Nevertheless, it would provide an interesting model against which to compare the system that now seems likely to emerge, shaped by past experience and present convenience.

THE EMERGING SYSTEM: A VIEW OF THE IMMEDIATE FUTURE

The clearest indication of how the building control system will develop in the immediate future is contained in the Government's Command Paper on the *Future of Building Control in England and Wales* which was presented to Parliament in 1981 and upon which consultation and action has since been proceeding. Many of its proposals have been referred to previously, but taken together they show significant changes in the way the building control might be exercised.

The proposals represented a somewhat radical change of policy, revealed as a withdrawal by the Government from the former total dependence on public controls, to a preference for placing reliance on the private sector wherever possible for the operation of the system. Significantly, it was intended that the legal framework of control should remain in official hands, but as much of the work as could be relinquished without this structural change should devolve to the private sector.

This meant in practice that the central government would retain the responsibility for making national building regulations, even strengthening its position by renewing its efforts to align the London by-laws with them technically; the local authorities would remain basically responsible for enforcement; and both central and local authorities would retain their functions in relation to relaxation, appeals and determinations. However, provisions for others to be involved in certification and arbitration could result beneficially in a considerable transfer of the work-load of enforcement.

The Government had introduced these policies earlier, using slogans like "maximum self-regulation", "minimum Government interference", "total self-financing", and "simplicity of operation", to describe what was needed of any new arrangements for building control. In aiming to give effect to the proposals, it was responding to the widely-held view that there should be a halt to the growing use of legal constraints to achieve desirable ends, a reduction of the complexity of statutory requirements, and a curbing of bureaucratic control.

The Command Paper spelled out the possibilities for this withdrawal of officialdom from the regions of control that had hitherto been exclusive to central and local government Departments. In the first place, the scope of the control should be reviewed to make sure that it covered no more than was absolutely necessary. The preservation of public health and safety was still essential, and should remain as the primary purpose of building legislation. To this could be added the aim of conserving energy, but no more; and with these objectives in view the building regulations should be examined to see that they contained no requirements other than were absolutely necessary to these ends.

In the interests of simplicity, the building regulations should be re-cast in two forms for two kinds of use. For simple domestic buildings the regulations should be issued giving detailed standards in a direct way, perhaps like the specific requirements of the London constructional by-laws; for other buildings of great complexity, of the type for which professional advisers might usually be engaged, the national regulations should be expressed as functional requirements, stating their purposes clearly, and referring to a "wide range of approved guidance" which would not be restrictive and which might include the Standards and Codes of the BSI and the Certificates of the Agrément Board.

The remaining proposals for reform were aimed at reducing governmental interference and excluding bureaucratic involvement as far as possible from the operation of the system. These proposals are best summed up as being intended to promote *self-regulation*, either by exempting certain building owners or types of work from the normal methods of enforcement, or by granting others the right of obtaining private "certification" as an alternative to having their work checked by the local authorities' inspectorates. Broadly speaking, the method of exemption was proposed for the buildings in public ownership; and the recourse to private certification was for the private owners.

The proposals for exemptions were far-reaching and would lead to about half of the total national output of buildings being removed from the procedures of enforcement as operated by the local authorities. Exemptions would apply in the following way. The operational buildings of the statutory undertakers, which include schools and colleges, and to which the building regulations do not apply, would continue to have complete exemption. All other buildings in public ownership, namely those owned by the Crown bodies (such as governmental Departments, the Property Services Agency, the Health Authorities, and so on); the local authorities; governmental agencies and other statutory authorities, (like the Welsh Development Agency, the

Passenger Transport Undertakings, the Regional Water Authorities, British Airways, etc.), would be required to comply with the *technical requirements* of the regulations, but *would not need to follow the enforcement procedures* for obtaining the local authority's consent. Those public bodies that were accountable as local authorities or through Ministers to Parliament would be entirely exempt from the procedural requirements, which meant that they would not need to give notice to the building control authorities of an intention to build, submit details and plans, or have the work inspected by the enforcement officers, in the normal process of building control. The other public bodies, not directly accountable, would not have this complete exemption, but nevertheless would be free of the need to submit to detailed supervision. They would be able to certify to the local enforcement authority that their work had been checked and was in compliance with the regulations, in a process of self-certification, instead of depositing plans and submitting to inspection by the local authority.

Notwithstanding these concessions, all these public bodies, whether exempt or self-certifying, would need to have consultations with the fire authorities as required under Section 16 of the Fire Precautions Act 1971; and would be required to notify local authorities by depositing plans or other information before starting work, to enable those authorities to carry out their duties under various other sections of Acts providing for public health and safety, like the Public Health Act 1936, the Water Act 1945, the Fire Precautions Act 1971, and others. (These provisions dealt generally with drains and sewers; the removal of refuse; means of access and exit from public buildings; domestic water supply; food storage; and such other precautions as it was hoped would, so far as practicable, be eventually swept up into the main body of the central building regulations.) A further concession was proposed for the public bodies with full exemption in connection with arrangements for the relaxation of the building regulations. They would be given the power to relax or dispense with the requirements of the building regulations for their own building projects, instead of having to go through the procedure of applying to the responsible department of the central government. The "self-regulating" Authorities, on the other hand, would be required to proceed on these matters in the normal way.

Proposals were also made for exemptions being granted to certain minor works, and other categories of building, like those for agriculture or industry, which were *not used by persons* excepting occasionally for maintenance, on the grounds that these types of building involved only a limited risk to health and safety. Some would be fully exempt from building control, others would have options that would enable them to avoid some of the procedures, like depositing full plans with the local authorities, while ensuring that the authorities could carry out their other health functions and be able to inspect if necessary.

The other proposals for "self-regulation" were aimed at introducing a system of private certification in place of an exclusive dependence on the public enforcement authorities employing their building inspectors. It was acknowledged that the statutory functions of local authorities for building control should not be usurped in any way.

They were at present empowered to "enforce building regulations in their district", and so were able to prosecute offenders who contravened the building regulations, and to take steps to make good or remove altogether any works that were not in compliance. *Such duties* under the general law were appropriate to local authorities, and, it was thought, *should remain firmly within their province.* The proposal was that, without disturbing these legal responsibilities, certain prescribed certifiers should be able to carry out the work of checking plans, and inspecting the work on the site, as a private service on a fee basis. Under the existing legislation, the Secretary of State would have the responsibility for deciding who should be able to certify, and what kind of projects should come within their scope of this new service.

In making the national arrangements for the approval of certifiers, the Secretary of State would be guided by professional qualifications, practical experience, and the possession of indemnity insurance. There might be two classes of certifiers, one for the smaller, less complex buildings, and the other having a special competence for dealing with the larger projects. Approval would normally be by naming persons, but professional practices might be able to qualify, depending upon their technical and administrative resources, and membership of a prescribed professional institution might be one form of qualification for approval to certify. While the central government recognized that certifiers should have sufficient indemnity insurance against claims for damage in the event of negligence in certifying, in order to protect building owners and developers it had no proposals for deciding how this should be done, but asked the community of insurers to work out how this need might be met.

The certifiers' duties would be confined to the checking of designs and the inspection of work on the site. They would issue two certificates: one to confirm that the design had been checked and shown to be in compliance, the other to confirm that the work on the building had been inspected and that the construction had been completed in conformity with the building regulations. The first would be issued before any site work began, and the second before the building was taken into use. The certificates would be issued to the building owner, who would be required to lodge them with the building control Authority for the area.

It would be a legal offence for the owner to allow work to start before the first certificate was deposited, and to occupy the building before the second had been accepted by the enforcement authority. The certifier would not be able to issue relaxations but would have to negotiate for them with the local authority; and would also be required to consult fire authorities and to provide evidence to the enforcement authority that this had been done. The onus of legal enforcement would remain with the local authorities. They would have to be notified by the certifier if work was not being done in accordance with the regulations, and would use their powers in the normal way prescribed by the Acts to ensure that it was corrected, or the unsatisfactory work removed. Local authorities would also check the certifier's credentials when certificates were lodged, taking care especially with the evidence of proper indemnity insurance; and would also be responsible for checking the certificates to make sure that they dealt properly with the types of work in question.

Certifiers would not be able to deal with the approval of their own projects or of work in which they might otherwise have been involved in a supervisory role, excepting for certain kinds of minor works, or works in categories of "self-certification" as would be defined in the regulations. Neither would certifiers be able to approve any work for which they did not have the requisite expertise, but for this purpose would be able to obtain certificates from "sub-certifiers". Thus, on a complex project where different kinds of engineering skills might be required, there would be a "head certifier", whose responsibility would be to check and submit the sets of certificates covering the whole scope of the work, making sure that all was in order, and that each sub-certifier was properly competent and insured to cover the requisite portion of the work being certified in each case.

In addition to these proposals for private certification, a further and equally radical change was proposed for dealing with appeals and determinations.

The reason for this was that the existing procedures tended to cause delays that were expensive to the owners and the public authorities alike. The building owners or developers were able to appeal to a magistrates' court to dispute a local authority's rejection of plans and details deposited with them; or to the Secretary of State against a refusal by an enforcing authority to grant a relaxation of the regulations, or to dispense with a regulation in a particular case; or to refer a dispute about the application of regulations to the Secretary of State for settlement by determination, *provided that the reference was made jointly* with the building control Authority concerned. These arrangements had been devised, among other aims, to achieve a consistency about answers to questions arising about regulations, but experience had shown that such appeals or references were usually called for at a time in the progress of the design or construction work on a project when delay could be especially disruptive and expensive.

It was thought likely that with the new building regulations making greater use of functional requirements, the type of dispute might well change from *questions* about relaxations to *arguments* about what particular technical solutions might be accepted as satisfying the regulations. In short, there would be more controversy about the interpretation of the legal requirements. The points at issue would be mainly technical, rather than legal, and it was felt that such questions should be dealt with quickly by some method of local arbitration that could be flexible, readily worked, but authoritative.

The solution preferred by the central government was that owners should be able to take their disputes to local independent professional consultants for a third view, by way of a new process of informed arbitration. The national government would have to approve a range of experts to cover the whole country, but beyond this the method would require the least amount of central supervision. It would mean that all types of experts could be available and accessible locally, so that reference could be made to them quickly. They would be expected to keep up-to-date with the information and ideas affecting their particular specialism in each case, and this would help to ensure a reasonable degree of consistency in the judgements made by them affecting the interpretation of the regulations.

These arbitrators would be paid by the building owners and local authorities who referred problems to them, so that the arrangement would be financially self-supporting. Their decisions could not be legally binding, so the opportunity for further reference to the magistrates' courts would need to remain as available; but this, it was hoped, would only be called for in a small number of cases. The expert views of arbitrators would be made available as evidence for such legal proceedings. On other cases, where the issues in a dispute might be legal rather than technical, such as when an authority might refuse to accept a certificate, the disputants would also be able to refer to a magistrates' court.

The aims of the proposed system in summary

The government's aims in making these proposals were clear enough, and to many of the reformers in the industrial community that had borne the brunt of the bureaucratic constraints, they seemed almost too good to be true. The changes proposed seemed to be both comprehensive and far-reaching, because they would affect the legal instruments forming the criteria of the control on the one hand, and the system of enforcement on the other.

The first reform was directed at the requirements which lay at the very core of the control system: the building regulations, which would be reduced in their scope to deal with no more than the absolute essentials, and changed in their format and mode of expression to be more readily comprehensible to their users.

This done, their enforcement would be changed by a few simple but very effective measures. In the first place there would be exemptions for as many as possible, either from the procedural requirements of obtaining the consent of the enforcement authorities—as would be a privilege granted to public bodies; or from the application of the regulations altogether—as would apply to some minor works; or from parts of them dealing with the submission of details for approval—as would apply to certain other types of building.

These exemptions would probably remove more than half of the total annual construction programme of the country from the direct surveillance of the enforcement system. For the rest, originating from private sector clients, reference for consent could be made to nominated private certifiers instead of to the local authorities' inspectorates. These latter long-established executors of the building control system would remain with largely unaltered terms of reference, but their operations curtailed by circumvention. In short, the legal framework of control would be called upon, in the main, only when formal and drastic measures of compulsion were needed.

By these means the central government proposed to "reduce the commitment of public resources, both locally and nationally, to this function" of building control, while preserving "the high standards of safety in buildings" and enabling "control standards more easily to keep abreast of new developments in building techniques and materials".

THE SHAPE OF THE NEW SYSTEM

The new form of the building control system would ostensibly centre on two sets of regulations, one provided for the qualified expert, and the other for the small builder or self-appointed amateur. These would contain such design criteria as were thought to be essential for the preservation of public health and safety and the conservation of energy. They would apply to all buildings (excepting only those specifically exempted) throughout the land. As to their enforcement, this would be done by the public bodies in respect of their own building programmes, while the system of certifiers would operate for the private sector's building, so that in principle, both public and private sectors would be governed by a form of self-regulation.

The public enforcing authorities would preside over all these measures for compliance, rather like referees, to ensure that the rules were taken properly into account: trying to maintain fair play and to see that in general the system worked as an adequate public safeguard.

The underlying force of compulsion in the system would continue to be its sanction by Parliament and its encompassment in the penal code, providing public bodies with the power to take offenders against the system to court by legal prosecutions; and allowing the building owners to sue for damages if their interests were damaged by the mistakes of guardians or suppliers.

Its prospect of success

Other proposals for reform have been made by enthusiastic advocates in the past, and have been put into effect, but have not entirely achieved their desired objectives. For example, the proposal to replace local by-laws with one centrally-produced set of national building regulations had had the objective of replacing the diversity of over a thousand local authorities' by-laws with the unity of one set of requirements having wide support. In practice, and with the benefit of hindsight, the by-laws were seen to have been simple documents with no great variations, and the national regulations which replaced them soon became complex statements purveying specialist technical concepts in a difficult legal language; so the result of the reform seemed to many to be of doubtful benefit. Equally, the proposed reform of the framework of local government had been thought likely to provide an opportunity to improve the system of enforcement by making it a duty of the larger authorities; but in practice it became one of the many tools of the district authorities, who attempted large-scale recruitment on low-scale budgets, again (in the view of many critics in the construction industry) with detrimental effects.

In the light of this experience, and the wide support for the idea that reform is necessary, it is worth questioning whether a new system based on proposals of the kind put forward by the Government is likely to achieve the practical benefits at which it has been so hopefully aimed.

The building regulations form the central feature of the control system. They are the factor common to all its aspects: whether of administration, legislation, or enforcement. The public bodies and private developers; the inspectors and private certifiers; all are affected by their requirements. It is important, then, that the changes proposed for the regulations should achieve their purposes, as a prerequisite to the success of any other reforms to the system.

The objectives for changing the regulations are concerned with reduction and simplicity. They have been described in much the same way as a politician talks about policies for which he needs public support—by referring to general principles with which it is dificult for anyone to disagree, but without showing in any detail how those principles are connected with the practical course of action he is proposing. Rather in this vein, the government's proposals projected the view that there should be a *simplification* of the regulations; and consequently that there should be a simple set for plain men doing simple jobs, like domestic buildings, and a complex set for the experts doing complicated technical projects. In short, *there should be two sets of building regulations*. It followed from this proposition that the "plain man's" edition should be modelled on the London by-laws, these being authoritative specifications of how work should be done; and the experts' set should be expressed as "function requirements", which could be backed by the full range and variety of official documents—like the BSI's Standards and Codes, and Agrément Certificates—used by designers for guidance.

A closer examination of these proposals, taking account of the theories emerging from past practice, must cast doubt on their adequacy. In the first place it seems a contradiction in terms that the legal criteria should be made less cumbersome and more simple by replacing *one set* of regulations with *two sets*. All past experience shows that by-laws and regulations continue to grow at all times. Their accretion by amendment seems impossible to resist. The central set of building regulations, produced for the first time in 1965, has increased constantly in size and complexity. To allow it to divide into two forms in less than two decades after its birth, is like submitting to the notion that it is a living cell governed by irresistible laws. Two sets will now be able to grow separately, and this will increase the body of building law and add to its complexity, if history is to be a guide. In the second place, according to the conclusions drawn in the previous chapter, it is a false premise that experts need complicated rules, while the plain man can be guided by simple ones. Rather is the converse true, that the expert is competent to accept a simple statement of aim as a rule to follow, and design a structure to comply with it, whether the building is small or large. The plain man does not necessarily know how this can be done, but will need a detailed descriptive guide.

The first problem, then, is that the simple rules for simple buildings are likely not to be simple at all in practice, but bulky and complicated manuals laying down what must be done, rather than what the public wants to achieve. This, in turn means that a type of regulation technique will have to be used which has already been criticized and rejected as a too rigid method of control. The "specific requirement" has the acknowledged disadvantage of denying flexibility and preventing technical development. If this is used to control domestic building, then houses will become stereotyped, because neither plain man nor expert will be able to depart from the strict norm of the manual, unless special provision is made for departures from the rules, and this is likely to cause difficulties. Of course, it cannot be intended that housing should be deprived of the opportunity for technical development, so these problems would have to be solved. But they seem to be created by the proposals, and could be avoided if other practical steps to improve the building regulations were taken.

The next problem at issue is the method which it is proposed to adopt for the second set of regulations for "more complex types of buildings where professional advisers are likely to be involved". The disadvantages of the technique of the functional requirement have already been described, and were identified by the advisory groups who studied the practice of building control two decades ago. These disadvantages have not been resolved, and would still be encountered if functional requirements were used. A particular problem is that regulations made in this way are not self-contained, so that their apparent simplicity can be misleading. A law that requires some aspect of a building's peformance to be "adequate" or "suitable" is too vague to be effective, and in consequence needs further supporting documents. The result can be that the meaning of the law has to be interpreted from a collection of documents, many having a different legal status and not used in any mandatory function excepting perhaps in the context of the regulations. The result produces confusion, not only about what regulations really mean, but also about the standing of the reference documents when used for their own basic purposes.

Ideally, the legal requirements should never be ambiguous or indeterminate, and the need for clarity cannot be waived on the pretext that the regulations will be used only by experts. If it is intended that reliance should be placed on the experts, then the law should be explicit and require that only experts should be used. This would achieve an ultimate simplification in the documentation.

All this points to the conclusion that so far as the building regulations are concerned the proposed changes are not likely to achieve the better level of efficiency as hoped for in the building control system. The control of domestic building will not be improved by the contrivance of a separate set of old-fashioned constraints; neither will the management of complex buildings be made more efficient by the issue of vague regulations cross-referenced to guidance contained in many other documents. It is a truism that bad regulations remain bad whether directed at amateurs or experts. Equally, the qualities that make regulations good and efficient remain constant regardless of the competence of those who might be expected to interpret them, as a violin made by Stradivarius remains a work of art in itself, no matter what skill is possessed by its player.

With regard to enforcement, the proposed reforms seem to follow more closely the acknowledged theories of good practice. It seems reasonable for the public to place its reliance on self-regulation as a principle, because it depends wholly on its construction industry for the production of buildings, and much effort and financial investment goes into the training of the designers and managers who control the work, and who must do their tasks well or involve their employers in unacceptable financial and legal penalties.

It can be argued that it is wrong in principle, however, for the building owner to have to pay for the control that is exercised over his activities in the interests of the public. In general it has been the practice of the community to foot the bill for its own guardians of safety in other matters, and to regard any payment made by a private member to those guardians as warranting grave suspicions. The aim of the reforms in this case is that the building control system, with its methods of enforcement, should be "totally self-financing".

By this it is meant that its costs should be met in full *by those who are subjected to its control*, rather than by those on whose behalf the controls are exercised. It would be useful to consider whether this might be achieved in practice.

At present, the responsibility for enforcement lies with the local authorities, at the level of district councils, and this conforms with the traditional practice of building inspectors being employed by local councils to inspect and approve plans, and generally to have whatever surveillance is required by the regulations over the building work in the council's area. The new proposals would mean that public bodies, when building, would not be subject to the enforcement procedures of these authorities (except in some cases only in minor ways). The private sector building owners would be able to employ private certifiers instead of using the publicly-employed inspectors, and would be required to pay for this service, whichever alternative they might choose. Furthermore, if they had a dispute about the meaning of the regulations as interpreted by the controlling authorities and wished to take this for determination to arbitration, they would be required to pay for that too.

This seems to imply that the public bodies are able to escape from the enforcement part of the control system, together with its costs, while the private-sector clients remain involved on both counts. Of course, there is no real change envisaged for the public bodies, because in the past these have been largely exempt from the control of the local enforcement authorities. In practice this has meant that the public clients ensure that their buildings comply by carrying out their own checks. For this purpose one method commonly used has been that the designer obtains a second opinion, by having checks made by a suitably qualified colleague within the same organization. Since schemes like this have worked well enough in the past, there seems no reason to doubt that they would work in the future. The anomoly seems to arise in the treatment of the private sector, especially if major firms are involved as clients who employ their own designers "in house", in departments comparable in size to many loal government organizations, or who employ competent firms of consultants. The system of obtaining a second opinion from an appropriately qualified colleague could work as well as it might do in a public office, and this could obviate the need for a payment to be made by the same client, unless for reasons of insurance some kind of separate accountability was necessary. If the public paid the fee for certification, the awkwardness would not arise; and there have been precedents for this, as some enforcement authorities have made a practice of consulting experts to reinforce their own inspectorates when dealing with buildings which have represented special problems in one way or another.

Certain disadvantages may be identified at the level of the smaller scale of building. It is here that the clients or building owners are obliged to operate on low budgets, yet it is a level where a great deal of "customerized" building takes place, at the position where (to use the management jargon) there is the interface between the industry and the individual members of the public as its customers. These individual clients may seek (for reasons of false economy as may be) to avoid using consultants, so it will appear to them to be an imposition if, having taken the step of appointing a qualified agent, they find that they also will have to obtain separate certification by paying an additional fee either to another consultant or to a building inspector. Faced with these expenses, such a client may well be prompted to undertake only the inescapable expense—namely that of paying for the approval of the building inspector. Since the taks of enforcement has been allocated to the smaller local authorities (at district council level), who are also forced to discharge their duties on low budgets, the quality of the design "input" may well suffer. The unfortunate effect of these arrangements would seem to be that all of the incentives operating at the small-building level are to depress the quality of the buildings, and, as these modest buildings form a large part of the built stock, to depress the quality of the environment for the individual members of the public. Of course, it would be desirable if all the pressures worked in the other direction: to encourage the participation of skilled and qualified designers at the local level. There would be some practical prospect of this if a separate reference and additional payment to a certifier was not required, as would be the case either if the public paid the certification fee, or if suitably qualified designers could be self-certifying.

Of course, returning to the general levels of scale in building it can be conjectured that if the thorny questions of liability and insurance are not resolved, there would be incentives for qualified designers *not* to beome involved with certification. This is because their open-ended liability for any latent damages arising from their own designs is already too onerous a burden, and their participation in certifying would add similar liabilities for the projects of other designers, giving clients the opportunity to sue two consultants where previously action was possible against only one! Seen in this light, there would be good reasons for qualified consultants to leave the tasks of certifying to the public building inspectors, who would be equally liable for the buildings they inspected and approved.

These questions of indemnity lie at the heart of the problem of improving the building control system. Liability is seen as a crucial problem by the industry and the enforcement authorities alike; and any advantages that the proposals for reforming the system may promise will never be realized if the present issues of negligence and latent damage are not properly resolved.

In regard to these, the interests of the public and the individual building owner can be seen as becoming coincidental. If a new building has faults, *the owner wants the mistakes put right as quickly as possible with the least cost to himself.* The paramount need is for remedy, rather than the attribution of blame. At present, an owner is in the worst position possible in such an event, because the question of blame must be resolved before any remedy can be obtained. This means that a great deal of time and money must be placed in hazard, even though the question may never be resolved, in which case the owner is doubly the loser.

In the same situation, that is, when a new building proves faulty, *the public wants to find out what went wrong so that steps can be taken to avoid the same thing happening again.* The paramount need here is to establish the cause and who, or what, is to blame, so that the regulations can be amended, the standards re-assessed, or licences (if any exist) revoked, as may be necessary to improve practice and reduce the risk of any re-occurrence of the trouble. The public (unless it is also the owner) does not have any prima-facie interest in the cost of repairing the fault in the particular building, but is concerned only to see that the danger is removed.

Perhaps the solution to the problem of indemnity lies in taking a proper account of these priorities. The argument would then appear as follows. If the regulations were to be kept up-to-date as a protection against hazards, a building that proved to be faulty would almost always be one that did not comply with them. If the owner could obtain insurance cover against faults occurring during a period of acceptable duration after completion, *so that the problems could be remedied without delay* and without substantial extraneous expenditure on legalities, his needs would be met. At the end of the period covered, the normal building insurance would take over. Of course, the cost of the initial insurance would probably have to be related to the reliability of the producers of the building, and this would have the useful side-effect of providing an incentive for better practice. With this kind of indemnity available for the owner, as an identifiable part of the initial cost of building, the problem of remedying the faults promptly would be resolved. It would remain for the public to take action under the building legislation to identify whether there had been any non-conformity with the *legal* standards and if so where the blame might lie, so that steps could be taken to improve the safeguards or take action against the culprit as may be appropriate.

Such a system would probably work best if the control was exercised entirely by "licensed" certifiers or by some process or self-regulation, so that the public enforcement authority could concentrate on the surveillance and co-ordination of those involved, and take action more judicially in the event of any failure.

THE BEST OF BUILDING CONTROL: A MODEL SYSTEM

Notwithstanding these criticisms, the 1981 political proposals for reforming the system of building control may be seen as well-directed in principle. They echoed the many voices that had been raised in complaint against various aspects of the existing arrangements, though these objections had often been made without any really accurate perception of what the system was intended to do and how best its faults might be remedied.

The problem of producing a better system in present times remains not so much in identifying what improvements are needed since these are well established, as it is in deciding precisely what changes are necessary to achieve the hoped-for benefits *in practice*.

The two crucial factors in the making of a truly efficient system, the master-keys of building control are the *regulations*—which must be apposite and simply expressed; and the *arrangements for liability* in respect of latent damage or faults in building, or (put another way) the methods for dealing with building faults that have slipped through the system. Of course, there is a third factor of major importance, namely the surveillance of construction work to ensure compliance with the law. This process of enforcement needs to be superimposed on the normal methods of managing projects and inspecting work with the least disruption or unnecessary duplication of effort.

The building regulations must come first in this hierarchy of importance. Those who create the regulations as instruments of control must recognize the underlying principles that govern their form, if they are to produce well-designed legislative provisions. *This means deciding to whom they are to be addressed,* and how they are to be enforced. If regulations are to achieve their ends in practice, and yet be expressed in simple and direct terms, these factors are of particular importance. Simplicity is a refinement of skill that is difficult to acquire.

In the first place it must be recognized that what the public wants from its environment to safeguard its own interests is the same for all types and sizes of buildings. The construction must be safe, resist fire, offer its users the means of escape in times of danger, and provide an environment well suited to the physical well-being of its occupants which offers no threat (within reason) to their health.

These desired standards of safety and comfort can now be identified accurately enough using up-to-date scientific knowledge, and it should now be possible to agree what level of standards should reasonable be expected for buildings. With such requirements given as the criteria for design, there are experts that can be relied upon to design the buildings to embody the standards. Others who do not have the expertise are not so reliable, and would need to be given a step-by-step description of exactly what must be done.

In short, what governs how simple the building regulations can be in practice is determined not so much by the complexities of their own content, *but by the level of expertise in those to whom the provisions are addressed.* To refer to a previous example, a skilled designer knows how to create a structure that has stability. If the public is content to rely upon that skill, it remains for its law-givers to state that the stability of structures is a requirement of the common law, so that the designer understands the importance of the matter in the eyes of the public. Others who do not have the engineer's design-skill would not know how to create a structure with stability, though they may know as technicians how to connect its parts together. If reliance is to be placed on them, they must be told *first* that the law requires the structure to be stable, and *secondly* what processes of construction are considered necessary to achieve the required result. In such a case, the law-giver would have had to carry out the design and would be specifying a particular solution to the problem in sufficient detail to enable it to be built. This would result in lengthy and complicated regulations, producing a narrow range of solutions.

The design of the regulations, therefore, must be powerfully influenced by the public's decision about where it intends to place reliance for its buildings: whether wholly upon the experts, or otherwise to allow anyone to build. An example of this cause and effect is to be seen in the regulations for school buildings which were issued by the former Ministry of Education as a department of central government responsible for the extensive school building programme of the fifties and sixties. These regulations were made to control the standards of the school buildings being provided by the local authorities (mostly County Councils and County Boroughs), and produced under the direction of professional designers: the architects and engineers available at that time. The designs of the prospective buildings were inspected by similar experts in the Ministry, to whom all plans were submitted for approval before the finance could be provided for the work to begin. *The regulations were brief documents,* setting out the environmental standards as heating, lighting, ventilation, thermal and sound insulation, together with standards for fire resistance and means of escape, and for the provision of sanitary accommodation, in ways that had already been made familiar by the chapters of the British Standard Code of Practice CP3 giving "basic data for the design of buildings". By comparison with the by-laws, and later, with the national building regulations, these instruments of school building control were models of brevity, and were applied effectively without any outstanding difficulties of interpretation or delay.

In countries like the UK, where a great deal of public money, skill and time goes into the education and training of the designers and managers of the construction industry, there exists a large body of such specialist advisers who are backed by their professional institutions, which have well-founded reputations for good practice. Their intake of members should be commensurate with "market needs", and their numbers adequate to deal with the nation's construction programmes.

The regulations

In order to design building regulations of model simplicity, it is necessary to assume that buildings will be designed and built under such expert control. That is to say, that buildings will either be designed and built by people of appropriate and credited skills, or the plans and finished products will be inspected and approved by them acting as agents to the building control Authority.

With this decision taken, the national regulations can be designed as brief documents, describing in scientific terms the standards of performance required by law. Since the requirements for securing the health, safety, welfare, and convenience of the persons using the buildings are the same for all building types, there will be only one national instrument of control, and this will be succinctly expressed.

If there are to be types of building whose production can be expected to remain in the hands of others than the professional advisers, then the national regulations could be supplemented by official manuals which would explain in specific steps what must be done to ensure that the building should comply with the law. Such manuals, if required at all in practice, would have the status of "deemed-to-satisfy" provisions.

The building regulations themselves would be confined to the purpose of identifying what standards are required by law to safeguard health and safety. These would be set at the minimum levels commensurate with their purpose. The cost of achieving them would be the nation's premium to ensure an acceptable degree of safety, and this cost must be within the country's means.

The regulations would be comprehensive, in that they would contain all that the law requires for the control of building. They would include, for example, such provisions for the conservation of energy and water as affect buildings, and provisions for the amount of space about buildings as appropriate for the purpose of health, access, and so on; so that from the point of view of the planning laws, the regulations would be relied upon to provide, as it were, the "building-bricks" for planning, each brick being an amalgam of building and the space essential to it.

These aims could be met by regulations having five main sections. The first would deal with the administration provisions, similar to those required in all existing control instruments; the second with provisions for health; the third with provisions for safety; and the fourth and fifth, respectively, with the provisions for the conservation of energy and water. Some proposals on similar lines were set out during the seventies by the Royal Institute of British

Architects, in a paper produced to outline its policy in relation to building controls in the UK, and in which it also listed the relevance of existing national regulations, codes, and standards to the various new sections. This preoccupation with fitting-in the bits and pieces of existing regulatory provisions was later shown to be a somewhat limiting factor in preventing the kind of radical change that was in fact necessary.

The five sections would be drawn up on the following basic pattern:

1. ADMINISTRATIVE PROVISIONS
   (Dealing with the legal issues of title, commencement, and revocations; interpretation; application; and various procedural matters.)

2. PROVISIONS FOR HEALTH
   (Dealing with the standards required for environmental conditions, sanitary accommodation, and the installations for sanitation and drainage and the disposal of refuse. The provisions would include for "welfare".)

   2.1 Environmental Standards:
(a) Special standards	(i)	about buildings,
	(ii)	in buildings;
(b) Thermal standards	(i)	heating,
	(ii)	heat transmission;
(c) Atmospheric standards	(i)	ventilation,
	(ii)	air cleanliness
	(iii)	humidity;
(d) Lighting standards	(i)	natural,
	(ii)	artificial;
(e) Acoustic standards	(i)	insulation against external noise sources,
	(ii)	isolation of internal noise sources,
	(iii)	other provisions.

   2.2 Sanitary Standards:
(a) Standards of sanitary accommodation per building use;		
(b) Protection from damp and infestation;		
(c) Sanitary appliances;		
(d) Drainage	(i)	surface water drainage,
	(ii)	soil and waste drainage:
		(a) above ground
		(b) below ground;
(e) Disposal of refuse.		

3. PROVISIONS FOR SAFETY

   3.1 Standards of safety in fire:
   - (a) Identification of risk;
   - (b) Constructional precautions;
   - (c) Installational precautions;
   - (d) Warning devices, smoke, and heat detectors;
   - (e) Fire extinguishing and fire fighting installations;
   - (f) Access and means of escape.

   3.2 Standards of safety of structures:
   - (a) Suitability of site;
   - (b) Standards of loading [dead, imposed, wind loads];
   - (c) Foundations;
   - (d) Structure above foundations;

   3.3 Standards of safety for the building fabric:
   - (a) Suitability, durability, and use of materials and components;
   - (b) Elements of building construction.

   3.4 Standards of safety of installations, equipment, and building services:
   - (a) Heat-producing appliances;
   - (b) Mechanical ventilation systems;
   - (c) Electrical installations;
   - (d) Gas installations;
   - (e) Oil installations;
   - (f) Water installations;
   - (g) Lift, escalator, mechanical walkway, and conveyor installations;
   - (h) Air handling installations;
   - (i) Telecommunication installations.

   3.5 Standards of safety in use:
   - (a) Stairs and circulation areas;
   - (b) Floor surfaces;
   - (c) Wall surfaces;
   - (d) Lift shafts, other shafts, galleries, and open wells;
   - (e) Fumes and noxious products;
   - (f) Detection of pollution;
   - (g) Prevention of pollution of water;
   - (h) Security of occupational user;
   - (i) Vehicular traffic.

4. CONSERVATION OF ENERGY
   (Measures dealing with the conservation of fuels, insulation, etc.)

5. CONSERVATION OF WATER
   (Measures providing for the prevention of waste, undue consumption or the misuse of water.)

Enforcement

The new apparatus for enforcement would consist as now of a central government Department acting as the national focus of building control, dealing with the making and amending of regulations and certain kinds of disputes and appeals, and carrying out liaison with the local authorities responsible for enforcing the regulations in their own areas. The difference would be that the local authorities would be the County Councils, not the District Councils, who would each appoint a chief officer with delegated powers, who would in turn appoint a qualified staff of appropriate skills and competence, taking account of the need for the department to have the respect of the professional cadre of the construction industry, and others.

A further difference would be that the functions of checking the plans of proposed works, inspecting the constructional work on site, and issuing certificates, would be carried out by private certifiers having the approval of the Secretary of State of the appropriate department of central government.

These certifiers would work largely on the lines set out previously and described in the Command Paper of 1981; that is, they would provide certificates to the local building control Authority, and that Council would discharge its general duty under the public law to enforce the building regulations in a "reasonable and responsible way", using the power to bring prosecutions for contraventions, or to require offending works to be removed, as may be appropriate. However, developers—or prospective building owners—would not have the option of relying on the local authority building control officers for inspections, but would in every case apply to an approved certifier to deal with their project.

The accredited certifiers would be able to certify the projects which they had themselves designed or supervised, provided that these projects were included in the "self-certifiable" categories; and for projects not within such categories they would be able to certify provided that they obtained a second opinion from another appropriate specialist.

The function of the County authority, while enforcing the national building regulations, would be to deploy its small staff of high-calibre officers to co-ordinate the work of the certifiers in its area; to liaise with other authorities; and generally to promote the work of building control and to ensure that it is carried out with adequate skill and care. County Councils might maintain their teams in central places, or have regional officers operating in districts rather on the lines of those allocated to the District Surveyors in London, but the aim would be to provide a focal point and a leadership to preserve a high quality of control.

The officers concerned, therefore, would liaise with certifiers; provide information about new amendments, appeals, and determinations; hold seminars; and generally ensure that the system is operating satisfactorily. Each County would have the same *type* of services as has applied in London, where a County Architect has been at the head of a staff of district surveyors, but the duties allocated to this *elite* would be different in the way described.

The concept of this form of enforcement is that the industry which is the subject of the control would be relied upon for self-regulation, and it would perform this task through its existing network of qualified professional designers and managers, under the surveillance of the public authorities. This surveillance would consist of the central government granting approval to certifiers, and thereby maintaining an influence over the quality and competence of inspectors; while the local authority would keep the control system in its own area up-to-date and effective.

Such a system would be more cost-effective than the present form of control. In theory, the certifiers should be paid by the public authorities, since the service they would provide as certifiers would be a service to the public-at-large, rather than the particular service they would be providing to their own clients. On the principle of "who pays the piper calls the tune", such a method of payment would reinforce the ability of the public authorities to ensure that the necessary standards of competence were maintained. But the system would not be made invalid if this method of financing it were not to be adopted. If the certifiers were paid by the developers, as proposed in the Government's Command Paper, the control to maintain standards could still be exercised through the method of "approving" or "licensing" the certifiers to perform their service.

Insurance

The building control system places constraints on the building owners, developers, and the construction industry, which are made effective by the use either of penalties or incentives.

In the UK, the dependence is upon penalties, and traditionally these have been of the legal kind. As the building firms have grown bigger, and the habit of using professional consultants has grown, so there has developed an increasingly important role for the insurers to indemnify builders and designers against damages resulting from negligence.

It can be argued that this involvement with insurance, which appears to have begun as a blessing, has become a curse for the industry. The knowledge that a large-scale indemnity cover exists can provide an incentive for a building owner to sue for negligence even on slender pretexts, on the grounds that there is money available to pay for the damages. As has been shown previously, the open-ended liability that now exists has led to a situation that appears to favour nobody. The prospective costs of damages due to failure have become too great to be covered adequately by any reasonable expenditure on normal indemnification; the industry's insurance costs have grown to enormous proportions; while for the normal building owner the delays to be faced in taking action to achieve remedies have become too great to be acceptable.

It is not possible to arrive at a solution to these problems in isolation from the insurance industry, but it is perhaps worth while to conjecture what could help to bring the system back to normality.

The influences that might produce a solution seem to lie on the one hand with the "consumers" of the built products—that is, the owners as developers of buildings; and on the other with the public as prime-movers of the legal building control system.

Originally, as we have seen, the public saw fit to rely upon the processes of the common law to protect itself from building faults that might endanger its basic interests. The penalties applied to transgressors of the penal code are the punishments applied to criminals, and are clearly very different in kind from the financial penalties of remedying damage. Yet the financial consequences of making mistakes have grown until they outweigh all other penalties and divert attention from the task of simplifying the legal controls, by obscuring any clear recognition of its ineptitudes.

It can be said of this situation that the public is not entitled to depend for its own protection upon the private arrangements for indemnity of designers and builders, nor upon the civil-court actions taken by private building owners to recover damages due to negligence; but rather it must protect its own interests and enforce its own requirements through the strength of the common law and must see that the penalties or incentives of that system are sufficient to ensure that it works well as a safeguard. *In short, so far as the public is concerned a builder or designer should be sufficiently deterred from being negligent by the threat of the retributions of the common law of building control regardless of the existence of any other threat imposed privately.*

If the public, as law-giver, relies upon the construction industry to regulate itself through a system of approved or licensed certifiers, it has two kinds of safeguards. It can prosecute the owner of the building that is in default, using the processes of the common law; and it can take separate action against the certifier (if the building was wrongly approved) by endorsing or removing the certifier's licence. The second of these constraints is new, and its effect would be to reinforce the public's ability to make building control in practice work as a self-contained influence.

The reverse side of this coin from these penalties would be the existence of *incentives* for the certifier who made no mistakes. Good practice of this kind could have an effect on the cost of certifier's own professional indemnity, rather like the no-claims bonus on a car insurance premium, and provide a reward for competence.

Turning to the influence of the "consumer", or the individual building owner, it can be said that the legal judgements, that appeared to favour the consumer-cause, may well be acting against such interests in the long term. The open-ended liability has meant that action could be taken to recover damages for a latent fault long after the completion of a building—perhaps even a lifetime later—when great sums have accrued for compensation. But the greater the passage of time, the more difficult it may be to attribute blame and prove negligence; and the greater the sum at stake, the more redoubtable is the defence, so that the owner must face extensive costs in taking action, without any guarantee of success, *as an addition to the burden of having to live with the fault in the building.*

The consumer's interest, as mentioned previously, is to get the fault put right as quickly and inexpensively as possible. His interest would be better served by some form of insurance that would provide cover against inherent building faults, under which reimbursement would be accessible without the need to establish blame.

If a building proves faulty when built, it must also have contravened the building regulations, assuming that the regulations themselves were satisfactory. (This issue has not been as clear in the past as it would be in the future, because in the past the regulations have required only that their *plans* should be examined and accepted or rejected (excepting in London) and nobody has been required under the common law *to inspect and certify the completed building on the public's behalf.* The new arrangements for certification would change this, and any fault which became apparent in a building *after* its completion would give rise to questions about the inspectors final report and certification.) If the building regulations had been contravened, it would be for the public to find where the blame lies, and accordingly to take some action under the powers given by the building legislation. Once the public had discovered the cause, separate actions may follow against the culprit as might be either appropriate or worthwhile.

What seems clearly needed in all this is at least agreement about a period of time after the completion of a building when action can be taken over negligence involving latent defects, so that building owners can make satisfactory arrangements for insuring their building after that period; *and so that more manageable arrangements can be made by all concerned with the hazards affecting the initial (but now definitive) period.*

The arrangements that might be evolved from an assessment of all these influences, might be summed up as follows.

All certifiers, designers, and builders would be insured against actions for damages due to negligence during an agreed period (say of not less than 6 or more than 10 years), after the completion of a building. Since the period would be limited in duration, the costs of insurance would be kept within reasonable bounds, and if possible, benefits might be allowed to accrue from good practice resulting in "no claims".

All building owners would be able to insure, as a part of the cost of the initial contract for building, for defects occurring during the same initial period. Their readiness to sue for negligence would be tempered by their access to reasonable compensation, and would probably be confined to cases where negligence had been clearly evident.

The local authorities responsible for the enforcement of the national building regulations would take action to establish if the building had been at fault in respect of the same contravention of the regulations, and what the cause of the problem might be. This action might be taken by some local tribunal, or by reference to a local specialist in some form of informal arbitration, or as a function of the highly qualified team of enforcement officers of the County Councils. This activity would provide valuable feedback about the aptness of the regulations and the effectiveness of enforcement. Decisions and assessments would be available promptly, and would be taken without those involved being influenced by the pressures of legal claims and counter-claims; and would be arrived at in a way that would ensure that the technical knowledge gained would be added to a public accumulation of experience, which would help to promote better practice.

CONCLUSIONS

With the installation of such a system of building control—comprising new regulations more suited to the public's needs and the needs of the construction industry; radical changes in enforcement achieved by upgrading the role of the responsible local authorities and the status of the staff engaged, and placing reliance upon the qualified professionals of the industry for inspection and certification; and improvements in the arrangements for insurance and the methods of tracing and remedying faults—many benefits would be gained by the public.

In the first place, the public would acquire safer and better buildings, because the new clarity of the roles of enforcement and the new simplicity and directness of stated requirements would promote better practice in building.

Secondly, the public would gain from a removal of the delays that have affected building, due to the bureaucratic procedures of control. For example, the control of work on the nation's building programmes would not be delayed by the limitations of the staffing complements in local authorities. Qualified and responsible designers would not need to back-track over their work in order to get conditional approvals from persons not constantly in touch with the progress of the design.

Thirdly, there should be an increase in the efficiency of the building industry, in terms of higher productivity, especially at the level of management and design, because the professional sector of the industry would be more effectively involved in and committed to the direct action of enforcement.

Fourthly, economies would arise from the better use of skilled resources. The professions would help in effective "policing" and the building-control officers in the local enforcement authorities would be able to concentrate their efforts on monitoring standards of risk to keep regulations up to date, supervising the general effectiveness of inspection; obtaining feed-back from its peformance; and generally improving the control system by attending to areas of difficulty and disseminating information.

Finally, better regulations would be likely to emerge because the management section of the construction industry would have a more lively interest in and influence upon the legal provisions made and their effectiveness in practice.

The wider context

THE INTERNATIONAL OUTLOOK

It has been shown in previous chapters how, during the second half of the century, there has been a dramatic growth of awareness among the national communities of the wider context of the world in which their own country is but a part. The process has been promoted by factors of cause and effect which have operated in every sphere of human activity, and the influences are too numerous to describe here, except in briefest summary. There has been a steady growth of output of industrial and agricultural products, increasing the wealth available to the international communities; and with it a growth of world trade. This in turn has led to a great realization of the importance of monetary supplies and the relationship between national currency values, and a sharper knowledge of the common dependency of everyone on the supply of such vital commodities as energy. At the level of governmental activity there has been an emergence of co-operative groupings like the European Economic Community for the mutual benefit of powerful trading partners; and the propagation of United Nations development programmes through the World Bank, attempting to promote decade by decade the creation of the infrastructure, housing, and industries of the Third World. At the level of public participation, the improvement of communications, with the development of satellite broadcasting, television, and other electronic methods of disseminating news, the new facilities for travel, leisure activities, sport, and educational exchange have all brought the people of the world to a closer view of each other. The knowledge that nations are interdependent has become generally accepted, and, in European countries especially, most of the major administrative undertakings are carried out with due recognition of their place in this broader dimension.

Changes affecting building control

Through the same half-century, students of building legislation have been aware of similar remarkable changes affecting the development of building control systems. In the case of such legislative matters, it is perhaps truer to say that the change has been in the climate of thought about the systems, rather than in the systems themselves, which in practice change more slowly. *Theory*, in systems of administration, tends to jump well ahead of *practice*, and in affairs where Parliament itself must be the prime mover, developments can be frustratingly slow.

PROPHETS OF CHANGE

As long ago as the sixties there were advocates of the change then seen as necessary in the building control system in the UK and prophecies that have since been shown to have been remarkably accurate. At a meeting of the Muncipal Building Surveyors in 1968, the broad trends affecting the building regulations were seen to auger an adjustment of the regulating techniques to the context of social and technical development by the continuing adoption of performance standards. It was prophecied that this would depend on the proper use of knowledge from research, and the deployment of the appropriate levels of professional and technical skills in operating the building control system. The changes that were likely to affect the system were reviewed as applying to all of its aspects.

The regulations, it was thought, should be thoroughly rearranged, beginning with a re-classification of the subjects covered. These should be classifications of aspects of performance, and of the hazards to safety; and should deal with environmental conditions and take account of all manner of services installations. The technique of the "specific requirement" should be eliminated in favour of the "functional requirement" and ultimately the performance standard. The regulations should be seen as a national "tool of management", and must, therefore, take account of what language would be most effective for that purpose—verbal, graphic, or mathematical, or a combination of all three—so that efficient methods of design and production could be fully realized. The whole process should be guided by an extensive programme of "consumer research" to establish appropriate standards for each aspect of performance, supported by a parallel programme of industrial research to develop reliable design methods for attaining the performance, and standard test procedures for enabling its provision in the finished product to be properly checked.

The hazards to safety should be re-defined (it was thought) so that the degree of risk could be computed, and some kind of scientific evaluation given to the precautionary measures, to ensure that the levels of cost were kept at commensurate levels. These would need to be related to the life expectancy required of buildings.

To ensure that the new criteria would be made to work successfully, it was proposed that the enforcing authorities should be reorganized and restructured to larger regional groupings, and should make use of the skilled personel of the construction industry deployed in appropriate numbers for the task, and firmly linked with a central authority responsible for creating and administering the new national building regulations. It was advocated that a new relationship should be developed between these groups and their activities and those authorities engaged in the processes of education and research. Also, the creation of the national Standards and Codes of Practice would have to be orchestrated to a state of harmony with the new-style regulations. There would have to emerge some established methods for assessing the performance of buildings, and perhaps (it was thought), two main types of testing facilities: one working under government sponsorships and offering a service to the legislative and enforcement authorities for identifying standards and for testing or assessing the building; the other working in conjunction with industry to provide for the testing of materials and components against the prescribed requirements.

THE BACKGROUND OF HEAVY DEMANDS FOR BUILDING

All this prophecying can be seen from the standpoint of later decades as arising from the pressures of great activity in the construction industry. The massive programmes of social and commercial building were generating all kinds of change: in techniques, with the experimentation in "light-and-dry" prefabrication and in "heavy" industrialized processes; and in administration, with the development of the client-consortia with the cost-controlled design methodology and systematic use of ranges of components. Everything seemed to be happening at once, and among all the complexities it was difficult to see clearly enough how to give effect to the essential reforms, which could be achieved only by wide support from both industry and administration, acting in unison. In the UK, everyone was too busy building to worry too much about how it was controlled (except where controls could be seen as serious impediments), or where the real responsibilities lay. Indeed, *everyone assumed that they knew*, until disasters intervened to prove otherwise.

The demand for building was not confined to the UK, but affected other European countries, who dealt with their building programmes in different ways. There was, inevitably, an exchange of knowledge and experience, and many technical ideas crossed frontiers and were used or developed in practice in different environments. The British "CLASP" system won a prize in an international exhibition in Milan, and was exported in modified form; the heavy repetitive concrete systems of the USSR were developed in France, modified, and humanized in Scandinavia and exported to Britain for the housing schemes so much in demand, which were later to become so unpopular. These exchanges led, in very practical ways, to a wider understanding of the problems of international trading in ideas as well as products, but also to a common will to surmount shared difficulties.

STANDARDS IN THE INTERNATIONAL CONTEXT

Much of this was reflected in the work at the British Standards Institution on Standards and Codes of Practice, where the same whirl of activity, on an international stage, was producing extensive change and enforced development, through the same decades.

The British Standards Institution had for a long time conducted its affairs not only in the service of its own country, but also within the environment of the Commonwealth, where it held an acknowledged authority gained from long practice. Consequently, it was accustomed to the difficulties and complexities of operating in the extra-national dimension.

Nevertheless, the main problems of producing national Standards, by seeking a wide consensus of support from voluntary participators representing different industrial and commercial interests, are encountered within the national confines of an Institute's own purlieu, and the BSI has never been a stranger to these. It has always been a complicated matter to work out the formula for a Standard for publication with sufficient support from all the parties involved.

The notes which are published by the BSI for the guidance of the chairman and members of the committees working on its Standards give an indication of the obstacles to be overcome. These point out that the "Standards must have a reasonable consensus of view behind them, but agreement should not be bought at an excessive price in watered-down content or delay in publication...". Problems may arise, according to these notes, between committee members engaged in international markets, who might favour a bolder, progressive standard; and others operating in a "protected home market", who would be more intent on maintaining the status quo. The chairman has the "authority to overrule trivial objections, but the minority voice on a committee must receive his careful attention, especially if it 'reflects user or consumer views'", but if it becomes "clear that the views are irreconcilable" on matters of major importance, then "action must be taken outside the committee". The notes remind the committee members that the Institution is striving "to get standards quickly to those who need them"; that "this inevitably imposes some disciplines"; and that while "decisions can rarely be unanimous: some give-and-take is usually essential". Among the rules devised to help progress is the edict "that matters which have been decided at an earlier meeting may not be re-opened", and many others deal with procedural customs that have been developed empirically during the arduous life of the Institution.

For committees dealing with international and European standards, the rules become more explicit, and more closely bound by protocol. For every international standards committee there has to be an equivalent BSI committee, which "appoints and briefs the UK delegation", and that delegation has a "principal spokesman", and is furnished with working documents and agendas for study at a prescribed period in advance of the meeting of the international committee. For those meetings a number of advisory "ground rules" apply, concerned with how the "UK view" is "at all times" represented, and how any "unforeseen development" at an international meeting should be dealt with.

The complexities of this work of creating Standards at national and international level are formidable, and are reflected in the received wisdom of the Institution. In issuing guideline notes for UK delegates, the Institution expresses the view among its "points to remember" that "the existence of a sound British Standard (or draft) is a positive contribution at international meetings towards the production of an international standard...a national standard should...be flexible enough to allow for compromise, *thus increasing the likelihood of its acceptance as the basis of the international standard"*, presumably the problem being that "some entrenched national attitudes do not create a suitable climate for international standardization". This implies an acknowledgement of the belief that a direct and simple proposal for discussion is a most valuable contribution to successful leadership: that among all the conflicting voices and the confusion of interests, a straightforward proposal is most likely to concentrate everyone's attention and to survive at least as a basic framework for the accepted solution.

The need for this attitude of "keeping your head when all about you are losing theirs", becomes very apparent when the Institution's position is seen against the proliferation of international activities that has taken place through the same decades of the second half of the century as those to which we have referred. Apart from the Commonwealth Standards Conference bodies, the UK Institution is concerned with the work of an impresssive array of organizations preparing European and International Standards, each with their implied "mutual recognition", directives, procedures, technical criteria, and formulae of reference. In Europe there is the European Committee for Standardization (CEN), with about 46 technical committees"; the European Committee for Electrotechnical Standardization (CENELEC), comprising 28 technical committees; and CENCER, the CEN's certification body; leaving aside other bodies dealing with more specializing electrical and electronic equipment. In the wider international context, there is the International Organization for Standardization (ISO), which has published 3,000 ISO Standards since January 1972, through the participation of 150 technical committees, more than 550 subcommittees, and over 750 working groups.

CONCLUSIONS

The purpose of making this brief review of the now familiar recent history of national building regulations and international Standards in the post-war period is to demonstrate two points as conclusions that can be drawn.

The first is that it would seem to be inevitable that building control systems in a shrinking world or a community of increasingly interdependent nations will be influenced towards a common form. Differences are likely to be eliminated as unnecessary barriers to trade, and as unacceptable anachronisms of social inequalities. Certainly the communities would be well-served if the technical regulations could be arranged in parity, because if the design criteria were unified there would be better opportunities for a general technological advance.

The second is that any such standardization of legislation would be practicable only if there are factors that are universally accepted as common to all the members of a particular group of countries wishing to co-operate. In the light of the local and sometimes entrenched complexities, and the traditional international diversities of the law, the strategy for unification can succeed only if it is simple and is developed from these common essentials.

These aims that can be seen to be indisputably shared have been identified in previous studies carried out in the UK, and by international bodies in Europe in the late sixties and early seventies; that is to say, at a time when building output was high and industries were struggling to meet an unprecendented demand. They may be inferred anew from the information given here in previous chapters. *In all countries, the motives that are undeniably common to all systems of building control are those of health and safety.* Other subjects are dealt with in different ways in different countries, and there are other functions common to many, but the universal consensus confirms those two interests as of paramount importance.

Another important conclusion is that, whether or not it is the result of a conscious aim, a major role of building legislation everywhere is to make explicit where the main responsibilities lie for the production of buildings that are safe and sound.

These indications of the priorities of international requirements should influence any attempts at national level to change or improve the building control system of any country in the modern context. They provide an incentive for the law-makers to concentrate on the essential issues among all of the numerous demands of local and narrower interests. *The attention of governmental authorities involved in building legislation should be directed above all else to the need for the building regulations to be expressed in the simple terms appropriate to determine the standards of performance that would safeguard the interests of public health and safety.* Other functions might also be served, but if these primary aims can be related and grouped in a unified section, the design criteria can be made to serve the wider demands for controlling the environment. *Such measures can be stated in the most elegant form if they are directed to the experts on the assumption that the design, construction, and management of building is a province of the skilled professional technologist.* The law can concern itself with that level of competence in the first place: there can be many ways of interpreting the requirements for more limited use by less-qualified builders.

The content of the regulations and the form they might take can be grouped together as one aspect of reform; the other linked and inseparable aspect is that of *responsibility. It is necessary for the public in each country to clarify upon whom it should rely for the provision of safe buildings that are good value for money.* The question can be resolved more readily once the decision is taken to insist that it should be the buildings themselves, as end-products of the construction industry, that have to be checked for compliance with the required standards. If owners and developers were debarred by law from using a building until it had been certified as suitable for occupation, there would soon be clarity about responsibilities. The ultimate reform is the one which makes clear to everyone, in a way that is acceptable to all participants, who is responsible for what.

Bibliography

Acts of Parliament

Building (Scotland) Act 1959 (7 & 8 Eliz 2 Ch 24) HMSO. Reprinted 1977 (ISBN 0 10 850 303 8).

Building (Scotland) Act 1970, Chap. 38, HMSO (SBN 10 543870 7). (An Act to amend the Building (Scotland) Act 1959 and for purposes connected therewith).

Energy Conservation Act 1981, Chap. 17, 21 May 1981, HMSO (ISBN 0 10 541781 5).

Health & Safety at Work etc. Act 1974, Chap. 37, HMSO. Reprinted 1975 (ISBN 0 10 543774 3).

Limitation Act 1980, Chap. 58 (An Act to consolidate the Limitation Acts 1939 to 1980). 13 November 1980 HMSO (ISBN 0 10 545880 5).

London Building Act 1930 (20 & 21 Geo 5) (Chap clviii) (An Act to consolidate the enactments relating to streets and buildings in London) 1 August 1930 HMSO (ISBN 0 10 850160 4).

London Building Act (Amendment) Act 1935 (25 & 26 Geo 5) (Chap xcii) (An Act to amend The London Building Act 1930) 2 August 1935, HMSO (ISBN 0 10 850203 1).

London Building Acts (Amendment) Act 1939 (2 & 3 Geo 6) (Chap xcvii) (An Act and to amend the enactments relating to streets, building and structures in London) 4 August 1939, HMSO (ISBN 0 10 850080 2).

Public Health Act 1936 (26 Geo 5 & 1 Edw 8 Ch 49) (An Act to consolidate with amendments certain enactments relating to public health) 31 July 1936 HMSO.

Public Health Act 1961 (9 & 10 Eliz 2 lu 64) 3 August 1961 HMSO.

Unfair Contract Terms Act 1977, Chap 50 (26 October 1977) HMSO. Reprinted 1980 (ISBN 0 10 545077 4).

Agrément Board, *The Agrément Board and its work.* (Sfb Aa 2) (UDC 061.6)

Ashley, Stephen, *Professional Indemnity: Building Services,* The Journal of the Institution of Building Services, **3**, 9, Sept. 1981.

Associate Committee of the National Building Code, National Research Council, Canada, *NBC News* (Quarterly).

Atkinson, George and Miriam Gray, *Building legislation in Scandinavia*, BRS Library Bibliography **230**, Nov. 1969.

Atkinson, George, *Building Law in Western Europe: How Responsibility for Safety and Good Performance is Shared*, BRS/UPBW CP 6/71.

Atkinson, George, *The Performance Concept in Building: The International Theme*, BRE CP 11/71.

Atkinson, George, *Building Regulations—The International Theme*, BRE CP 16/74.

Atkinson, George, *Technical Building Control in France*, BRE CP 46/74.

Atkinson, George, *Building Regulations: Can We Learn from the Scandinavians?* BRS News, **9**, 0000.

Atkinson, George, *Product Liability*, The Journal of the Institution of Building Services, **3**, 9, Sept. 1981.

Atkinson, George, *Standards, Codes and Approvals: Their Role in Building Regulation in Europe*, BRS News, **13**, 0000

British Standards Institution, *BSI—Its Activities and Organisation*, PD 4845:1977.

British Standards Institution: Council for Codes of Practice: *British Standard Code of Practice CP3: Chap. III (1960)* (UDC 699.844:534:83) *Code of Basic data for the design of Buildings (formerly Code of Functional Requirements of Buildings): Sound Insulation and Noise Reduction* BSI, Oct. 1960.

Building Regulations Advisory Committee, *First Report 1964*, HMSO, Feb. 1964.

Cibula, Evelyn, *Building Control in Switzerland*, BRS Current Paper CP 21/70.

Cibula, Evelyn, *Building Control in West Germany*, BRS Current Paper CP 10/70.

Cibula, Evelyn, *International Comparison of Building Regulations: Loading Requirements*, BRS Current Paper CP 38/70.

Cibula, Evelyn, *International Comparison of Building Regulations: Thermal Insulation*. BRS Current Paper CP 33/70.

Cibula, Evelyn, *Systems of Building Control*, BRS Current Paper 31/70, BRS/MPBW.

Cibula, Evelyn, *Systems of Building Control*, Building International, May 1970.

Cibula, Evelyn, *The Structure of Building Control: An International Comparison*, BRE CP 28/71.

Clarke, Michael, *The Building Regulations, Codes and Standards*, Paper delivered at a conference at the RIBA entitled "Architects and the Building Bill", 23 January, 1972, Royal Institution of British Architects.

Daldy, A.F., *The Scope of Building Legislation*, BRS Current Paper 20/69, BRS/MPBW 69.

Department of the Environment, *Proposals for a Building Bill: Consultative Document*, Aug. 1972.

Department of the Environment and the Welsh Office, Joint Circular: 23 November 1981: 1. *Building Regulations, 20 November 1981* (DoE Circular 34/81; WO Circular 53/81). 2. *Clean Air Acts 1956 and 1968: Chimney*

241

heights (DoE Circular 25/81; WO Circular 13/81).

Department of Scientific and Industrial Research, *Report of the Building Research Board for the year 1936,* HMSO, 1937.

Dobson, D.E., *Building Regulations: A Review of the Position in Some Western Countries,* S.A. NBRI Bulletin, **54**, Pretoria 1968.

Ennals, K.F.J., (Department of the Environment), *Background to the Building Bill,* Paper delivered at a conference at the RIBA entitled "Architects and the Building Bill", 23 January 1972, Royal Institution of British Architects.

Garland, Patrick, Q.C., *Limitations of Actions in Respect of Defects in Buildings,* Blundell Memorial Lectures 1978, Current Problems in Property Law. Given under the auspices of the Senate of the Inns of Court and the Bar and the Royal Institute of Chartered Surveyors.

Garnham Wright, J.H., *An Occasion for Reform,* RIBA paper, January 1976, The Royal Institute of British Architects.

Garnham Wright, J.H., *Enforcement and Control,* In S.S. Chisslik and R. Derricott, eds., Occupational Health and Safety Management, John Wiley & Sons Ltd, 1981

Garnham Wright, J.H., *Fighting Your Way Through: The Complexities of National Regulations and the Methods at Present Adopted for their Enforcement,* Paper delivered at RIBA Eastern Region conference, Royal Institute of British Architects.

Garnham Wright, J.H., *Future Trends in Regulations: Possibilities and Difficulties,* Seventh Annual Conference of Municipal Building Surveyors, September 1968, Incorporated Association of Architects and Surveyors.

Garnham Wright, J.H., *Patron, Designer and Public in Twentieth Century Wonderland,* Paper delivered at Twelfth Weekend School of the Institution of Building Control Officers. Lancaster University, April 1978; published in *Building Control Through the Eyes of Others,* IBCO.

Garnham Wright, J.H., *Performance Standards: How to Introduce Regulations Expressed as Performance Standards by Evolutionary Methods,* RIBA Policy Paper 1972, Royal Institute of British Architects.

Greater London Council, London Building Acts 1930–1939: *Constructional By-laws with Explanatory Memorandum,* Publication 156, GLC, 1968.

Guest Report, *The Report of the Committee on Building Legislation in Scotland,* HMSO, 1957.

Honey, C.R., *International Comparison of Building Regulations: The Control and Arrangement of Regulating Documents,* BRS Current Paper CP 37/30.

House of Commons, *Health and Safety at Work etc. Act 1974: Explanatory and Financial Memorandum,* HMSO, 1974 (ISBN 0 10 30 7474 0).

Institution of Municipal Engineers, *Anns (and others) v. London Borough of Merton or the Saidee Dutton Principal,* Submission by the IME to the Joint Committee on Building Legislation, Published in the *Chartered Municipal Engineer,* April 1978.

Institution of Structural Engineers; *Aims of Structural Design, A Report of the*

ISE, August 1969, ISE publications.

Joint Committee on Building Legislation, *The Form and Content of the Building Regulations, A paper for discussion,* Royal Institute of British Architects.

Jones, Glyn, C., Q.C., *Limitations of Actions in Respect of Defects in Buildings.* Blundell Memorial Lectures 1978 (Joint paper with Patrick Garland), Current Problems in Property Law, given under the auspices of the Senate of the Inns of Court and the Bar and the Royal Institution of Chartered Surveyors.

Kelly, T.J., *The London Building Acts 1930 and 1935, and other legislation relating to buildings in London with Byelaws and Regulations and an introduction and annotation of the Acts,* Kelly's Directories Ltd, 1938.

Ministry of Public Building and Works, *The Building Regulations 1965: Technical Memoranda—Fire—Stairs—Space: General Index,* HMSO, 1966.

Royal Commission on Local Government in England (Chairman: Rt. Hon. Lord Redcliffe-Maud), *Local Government Reform: Short Version of the Report 4039,* HMSO, 1969.

Royal Institute of British Architects, Building Control Committee, *The RIBA and Building Legislation: The Outline of a Policy in Relation to Building Control in the UK 1972,* BCP 72/57 RIBA.

Royal Institute of British Architects, Building Control Committee, *Proposals for the Form and Content of the Regulations,* July 1977, RIBA.

Royal Institute of British Architects, *Building Control, An Updated Version of the 1972 Policy Paper on Building Control,* February 1978, RIBA.

Royal Institute of British Architects, *The Future of Building Control in England and Wales,* Submission to the Department of the Environment in Response to a Consultation Paper, June 1980, RIBA.

Royal Institute of British Architects, *The Future of the Building Regulations,* Seminar Papers, March 1979, RIBA.

Royal Institute of British Architects, Professional Services Board, *Building Control,* A paper prepared as a basis for discussion with the Department of the Environment published in the *RIBA Journal,* 1971.

Royal Institute of British Architects, *Towards a Building Act, Comments on the DoE Consultation Document, Proposals for a Building Bill,* RIBA Journal, Jan. 1973.

Scottish Development Department, Building (Scotland) Act 1959, Building Standards (Scotland) Regulations 1963, *Explanatory Memorandum: Administrative and General, including Parts 1, 2, 7, 13, 14 & 16,* HMSO, 1964, SO Code No. 49.531.1.

Scottish Development Department, Building Standards (Scotland) Regulations, Consultation Document: *New Form of the Regulations,* HMSO, 1977.

Secretary of State for the Environment and Secretary of State for Wales, *The Future of Building Control in England and Wales,* (Cmnd 8174) Feb. 1981, HMSO.

Segal, Walter, *A Time for Change,* Architects Journal, 1 Sept. 1976.

Statutory Instruments
1965 No. 1373: Building & Buildings:
   The Building Regulations 1965 HMSO 1965.
1966 No. 1144: Building & Buildings:
   The Building (Second Amendment) Regs 1966 HMS0.
1967 No. 1645: Building & Buildings:
   The Building (Third Amendment) Regs 1967 HMSO.
1973 No. 1276: Building & Buildings:
   The Building (First Amendment) Regs 1973 HMSO.
1974 No. 1944: Building & Buildings:
   The Building (Second Amendment) Regs 1974 HMSO.
1975 No. 1370: Building & Buildings:
   The Building (Third Amendment) Regs 1975 HMSO.
1976 No. 1676: Building & Buildings:
   The Building Regulations 1976 HMSO 1976 (ISBN 0 11 061676 6).
1981 No. 1338: Building & Buildings:
   The Building (Second Amendment) Regulations 1981 HMSO.
Thompson, D., *Europe Since Napoleon,* Penguin Books, Harmondsworth, 1966.
Ventrella, Tony, *Contract or Not?,* The Journal of the Institution of Building Services, **3**, 8, Sept. 1981.
Wilson, Angus, Socotec-Bullen & Co. *Decennial Insurance of Works,* The Consulting Engineers' Journal, Mar. 1978.
Wood, Prof. J.C., C.B.E., *Buildings—The Continuing Control of Safety:* Paper delivered at a conference at the RIBA entitled 'Architects and the Building Bill', 23 Jan. 1972, RIBA.